In His Loving Service

In His Loving Service

by Henry Hildebrand

BRIERCREST BIBLE COLLEGE
CARONPORT, SASKATCHEWAN, CANADA S0H 0S0 • 306/756-2321

ISBN 0-942684-08-7

Published for Briercrest Bible College by Camping Guideposts, 5118 Glendale St., Duluth, MN 55804, Lloyd Mattson, Editor.

Scripture references from the *Living Bible* and the *New King James Bible* are used with permission from the publishers. Unless otherwise identified, other Bible quotations come from the King James Version.

Printed in the United States of America

Contents

To my darling Inger, who blends her life completely with mine.

Thank you to President Budd and Dean Magnus who encouraged me to write the Memoirs; to Betty Schultz, typist; to Joy Johnson, editorial assistant and proofreader; to Shirley Wiebe, secretary; and to Lloyd Mattson, editor.

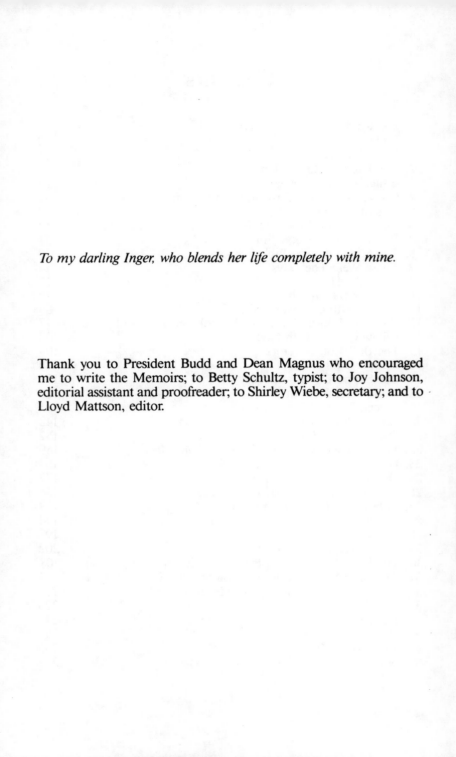

Foreword

In perusing these memoirs, the reader will be captivated by the unfolding, amazing story of an institution that is manifestly the work of God and of the life of the man God called to found and lead it.

The author relates the events of his humble beginning in Russia. He reviews God's providential guidance in his family's immigration to Canada. In fascinating detail he traces the leading of the Lord to the climactic events of his conversion, Bible school education, call to the ministry, and the invitation that opened the door to Briercrest, the tiny village that was destined to be the birthplace of Briercrest Bible College.

It was there that I was introduced to the author of these memoirs and to the institution in which our life-long association was to unfold. I have known Henry Hildebrand as teacher, counsellor, esteemed co-worker, and friend. His example of godly living has been an inspiration to me over these fifty years. I believe that a careful reading of this story will prove to be a blessing to every reader as, through these pages, each becomes more intimately acquainted with this servant of the Lord.

These personal reminiscences reveal the measure of this God-called man and his lovely wife who has so loyally shared his remarkable career. The measure of which we speak is to be evaluated, not merely by length of years, though they have been many; nor yet in heights of attainment, although well-deserved honors have been accorded in recognition of his successful leadership. The measure of Henry Hildebrand is seen in depth of character and breadth of influence upon so very many lives. His real stature can be measured only by the powerful moral and spiritual impact on others that through the years has spread in ever-widening circles and continues to this day.

These modest memoirs point up the distinguishing marks of this servant of Christ that so consistently characterize his life—qualities of humility, integrity, and untiring devotion to duty; enhanced by genuine lovingkindness and congeniality toward everyone with whom he comes in contact.

The rehearsal of the author's recollections speaks eloquently of a divinely blessed ministry, a ministry with many facets. As husband and father in his home, as administrator in his office, as counsellor in his study, as instructor in the classroom, as expositor in the pulpit, and now as a writer recording what God has wrought during one life span, God's blessing is evident.

Generously endowed with gifts of leadership, and consistently displaying the fruit of the Spirit in his daily walk with God, Henry Hildebrand has left an imprint for good and for God on his family, students, and associates, as well as upon multitudes of loyal friends to whom he has endeared himself.

As one such colleague who owes so much to Dr. Hildebrand's godly example, I take pleasure in commending to all the thoughtful reading of these memoirs that comprise the sacred memories of this God-called man who, while being first of all God's servant, has also been ours—as expressed in his oft-repeated words, epitomized in this book, "yours in His loving service."

Orville Swenson

Preface

God purposed to bless the Canadian "Great Wheatlands."

That is the origin of the story of the Bible school movement on the Prairies. Let me share with you this great story, and let me focus these memoirs on the school I know best.

I had to be pressed to write this account, because I am more interested in what remains to be done than in the past. I am still more interested in making history than recording it! Driving with one's eye on the rear-view mirror is not safe.

In the years when I rode the trains, I preferred a front-facing seat near a window so I could view what was coming. Occasionally, some scene proved so captivating that I was compelled to turn for a longer look. That was my experience as the Briercrest story passed before my mind's eye. I have selected highlights from that longer look for purposeful, profitable reflection.

Reflecting on God's goodness is healthy for soul and mind. Moses wrote, "And thou shalt remember all the way which the Lord thy God led thee these forty (fifty!) years" (Deut. 8:2). David wrote, "Because thou hast been my help, therefore in the shadow of thy wings will I rejoice" (Psalm 63:7).

As Inger and I contemplated God's goodness these fifty years, we saw many events from a higher perspective, some in a new way. At times we laughed. At other times we cried. At all times we rejoiced to remember God's faithfulness through the half-century I now share with you. Truly I say, "What God hath wrought!"

This is a human story—a very human story—how God overruled infirmities and weaknesses. Since love covers a multitude of sins, I saw little value in playing upon weaknesses of saints, except to show how God's "strength is made perfect in weakness."

This is a success story, with God at the centre of the stage (Prov. 3:5-6). At first I hesitated to write these memoirs because of my limited perspective. Perhaps I was too close to the events to see the broad outline. Yet this same closeness taught me that, had it not been for God, there would have been no memoirs to write! This is not the story of a private life but of a public ministry that God has owned and blessed.

As I led the work described in this book, my associates worked hard too, and, oh so often, they made me look good! "Each gave his strength" and his life. I discovered early that whatever I could do others could do better. So it became my duty to seek the best available talent for the task and to enlist that talent for a life-time ministry.

In these memoirs I will endeavor to show how God prepared a servant to become His instrument in founding a college, and how God prepared a nucleus of believers living in a scarcely-known place (Briercrest) to begin a Bible college. This story of providence tells how these believers were led to the Saviour, how I was introduced to them, and how the saints in a small village left their mark on the college that remains to this day.

God placed a burden on the hearts of these saints to provide Bible training for prairie young people. At the same time, I was ministering in rural Saskatchewan as a missionary of the Canadian Sunday School Mission, gripped increasingly by the dearth of Bible knowledge in Western Canada.

My memoirs will describe how these burdens were joined, resulting in the founding of Briercrest Bible College. The experiences of those early days present many examples of faith and sacrifice. While immediate growth was evident, no one could foresee the school's size and influence today. Loyal associates, supporters, and—most of all—students had a large share in bringing Briercrest to its present strength. Today we have third-generation students, young people whose parents and grandparents too were students at Briercrest.

Over the years, Briercrest has been blessed by a healthy supporting constituency. Through prayer and giving, the early supporters remained, to stand by the work for life. How their interest was developed and sustained will be of great interest to all who are engaged in a work of faith. The financial policies of the school will be fully discussed.

A chapter will be given to the Bible college movement in Canada, particularly on the Prairies, where three-quarters of the Bible colleges make their home, though the Prairies claim hardly one-fifth of Canada's population.

The preparation and selection of Briercrest's second president will also be of great interest. After leading the school for forty-two years, I saw transition accomplished without a ripple. The school continues to grow increasingly under the new leadership.

I will discuss how the college endeavored to reach its original goals, and how it has refined and enlarged those goals to serve world evangelism and the Christian church. We shall consider the future of Briercrest under President Budd, and learn of steps now being taken to enlarge its great ministry.

There is no natural explanation for the unique birth and phenomenal growth of Briercrest Bible College. It is with this in mind that I present this fascinating story.

Editor's note: *For the sake of clarity, Briercrest Bible College has been used uniformly through the book, even though for the first decades the school was known as Briercrest Bible Institute. The original name was retained in certain quoted passages where it seemed appropriate.*

1

Early Childhood

**And that from a child thou hast known the holy scriptures . . .
2 Timothy 3:15**

I was born in the village of Steinfeld in southern Russia, about 100 kilometers north of the Black Sea. It was beautiful, nestled across a quiet valley with either end anchored to the upward slope of the hills. The Sansaghan River meandered through the valley toward the sea. How often we romped in the wooded ravine and flats. And swim! Hours at a time.

Steinfeld was a typical Russian Mennonite village. The *Kulaks,* estate owners, occupied either side of the main street with its sidewalks. The living houses were near the street graced with beautiful flowers and trees. Back of the houses were the stables, threshing floor, and grain containers. Each farmyard covered about ten acres, with fruit trees, flowers, and vegetable gardens. Grazing lands stretched west and north toward the river flats, while the grain lands reached out for miles, part of the Ukrainian Steppes.

Steinfeld was one of four Mennonite villages which were settled toward the latter part of the nineteenth century. The residents had purchased the Schlachting and Baratov Estates, with their many, many acres. Steinfeld was located east of the Krivoyrog Iron Mines, with railroad connections to the south and west. The frequent passenger trains made my young eyes dance!

Steinfeld's school and the two churches were located near the centre of the village, while at both ends lived the new settlers, *An-*

siedler, newly weds about to begin their farming pilgrimage. In time, as they prospered, they would buy or build a home on main street. Steinfeld boasted two typical Dutch windmills and a steam mill with a swimming pool off to the north of the main street.

The village churches held regular Sunday services, Sunday schools, and mid-week Bible study and prayer meetings. They sponsored youth meetings, *Yugendvereins,* with plenty of music and even drama, especially at Christmas time. Adult and youth choirs were very active and shared in annual music festivals, *Saengerfests,* with choirs from neighbouring villages.

The school offered regular grades with the three R's predominant. It organized its own music, drama, and sports program: ball, soccer, skating, sledding, etc. A junior high school in a nearby village gave opportunity to those who wished to further their sons' and daughters' education.

In 1910, my parents managed to purchase an estate on the eastern slope of the village facing north toward the main street. So they moved from the end of the village to their newly-acquired estate *(Bauerhof).* This was my little "Bethlehem" where I was first introduced to my Savior, the Prince of Peace, "whose goings forth have been from old, from everlasting." I was born into this new home on November 16, 1911 (Julian Calendar), the youngest of thirteen children: six brothers and six sisters. I was the second son of my father's third marriage, and I was named after my grandfather on Mother's side. This was not particularly to maintain the honour of the family, nor to lead the next generation, so much as it was the custom to name children after relatives. Actually, I would rather be a descendant of those who suffered much for their faith and remained true, than to boast the blood of kings and emperors.

My father had buried two wives and four children. Mother had buried her husband. So those sorrowing souls found consolation, faith, hope, and comfort in each other. Father had five children still living, and mother brought two children into this union, to which my brother and I were born. So our family was cosmopolitan. We learned to love and respect each other. My sister said I was never a robust child, but I have survived them all! After my mother's death, Father married a fourth wife, who had two children by her previous marriage.

My father was born in old Steinfeld, but due to frequent floods, the village was relocated to higher ground—about two kilometers south from the flats of the Sansaghan River. My mother, Anna Froese, was born in Schoenenberg, southern Russia. In the loss of their earlier mates they sought the Lord and were found by Him. They were one in faith and fellowship when they married.

My father was of short, stocky build, about five-feet, three-inches tall, weighing 170 pounds. He was physically strong and healthy.

He was frugal. So much so, that today we might brand him "a bit stingy." If we consider his earlier economic hardships, we can understand and even appreciate this characteristic.

I recall a domestic stir when he discovered that my sister had given leftovers to the pigs. Mother came to her rescue, and the occasion resulted in a spirited discussion. Actually, this is the only disagreement I recall in our home. The next morning at the breakfast table a scene took place that has been a benediction to me all my life. After the meal and before the Bible reading, Father spoke a few words to the family, explaining that the atmosphere of the night before was not becoming to a Christian home. My sister apologized, so did my mother. And so did Father. What a healing we all experienced as Father led in devotions that morning!

Father was a hard worker. He felt that sports and recreation were a waste of time, therefore a "no-no" for a Christian. He felt that energies expended on such follies could be better utilized in productive work. And he was a constant worrywart, seeing always the darker side of situations. Why venture? Play it safe.

Father was very sincere and serious. He felt that humour belonged to "foolish jesting," and had no place in Christian conversation. Mother's optimism and sense of humour provided a perfect balance. Though I sensed that Father did not always appreciate a situation, still he would respond favourably, and often entered into family fun and laughter.

Father was a stern disciplinarian whom Mother backed wholeheartedly, while seeking to temper the severity. I recall many a time when the rod was not spared! Let me share a few incidents—serious but humourous.

Our parents were retiring one evening when my sister asked about David and Henry. "What, not home at this hour?" Father roared. That situation was to be settled immediately. It happened we were swimming in the pool at the steam mill, a frequent practice. None of the gang had a watch, and time went by much faster than we realized. After the swim, we remained near the pool entrance visiting. Suddenly a man appeared out of nowhere and asked, "Are my boys here?" puffing between words.

"Why, yes," replied my brother, David.

"What!" shouted Father.

David sensed evil was determined, so he hightailed for home. While Father chased after him up the middle of the street, I followed—for safety's sake—on the sidewalk. Father could not see me, for electricity had not yet been installed. I heard Father puffing and scolding, "When I get home those boys are going to learn fast!"

I beat it for home as fast as I could, and when I arrived, my brother was already in bed. I said, "David, I am not undressing because Father is going to give us a good whipping." He did! Then all was quiet on the eastern front. We did learn fast.

On another occasion, we knew that discipline was coming—usually on the seat of our pants. At my brother's suggestion, we agreed that padding might temper the impact. I went first, yelling as the stripes fell. David's suggestion worked fine. It did not hurt. I thought that we had finally discovered a way to ease the sting of the whip. Next, my brother was called. As he stretched over the chair, Father saw the end of the scarf poking out above his pants. I heard, "What's this?"

David got his spanking, without the scarf, and this gave me time to dispose of mine. I expected to be called back for inspection.

Sure enough. "Heinrich, I want to see you!" But Father found nothing, so he dismissed me with the words that we heard when he was pleased with his boys, *"Schmocka Yung."* Judging from the restrained spanking David got, and from the twinkle of Father's eye when he inspected me, I suspect he must have enjoyed our little stunt.

Many incidents of "Mutt and Jeff" and their father come to mind, but this will suffice to show that ours was a very human family.

The story would be incomplete without words about my mother. She was a beautiful lady, clothed with strength and honour. She matched the description of a virtuous woman given in Proverbs 31. She was the perfect complement to my father. Like Father, she had buried her first love. She knew the burden of widowhood with small children.

When she married Father on that cold February 8 in 1909, she brought wisdom, love and understanding to a family bewildered by bereavement. "She looked well to the ways of her household, and did not eat the bread of idleness." Picture the family in its discouragement. The older children had suffered the death of two mothers and four brothers and sisters.

In God's love and providence, He brought this wise and wonderful lady to Father and his household. With her she brought two children who too had been bereaved. How well they all fitted together, how she opened her heart of wisdom, and how her tongue revealed the law of kindness, until her husband was "known in the gates, sitting among the elders of the land." It is material for a lovely picture book, a life for the women of our land to emulate.

Father could safely trust Mother's economic insight, counsel, and drive, so that he had no fear of spoil. She did him good all the days of his life and attended to all the varied household needs. She wove the members of four different groups into a solid union. We were one family.

Mother was proud of her family, and we knew it. How she would encourage us when we did right; how she would chide when we did wrong! When we performed well, she said so. When we performed not so well, she would lift us up.

The Hildebrand home became a model that was respected and honoured by the village and church fathers. I thank God for both Father and Mother.

Father was born on a village farm. He began his own farming as a young man and he made an honourable livelihood. But it was not until 1910-11 when he purchased the farm and farmyard on the main street, that he began to move ahead. The farm work was left mostly in the hands of my mother, his boys, and hired help, for Dad was at heart a miller.

In his younger years he had worked in the windmill, and when the opportunity came, he purchased it. The windmill served chiefly to grind grain for animal feed, rye for bread, and wheat for whole-wheat, brown bread.

Dad knew his trade. A windmiller had to read the weather accurately or lose his windmill. Dad had developed a sixth sense that kept him ahead of dangerous winds. A good deal of skill was required to set the grindstones properly to produce the best results. The windmill augmented Father's farm income considerably, so much so, that he was able to buy one-third of the shares of the village steam mill.

Operating the steam mill was like moving from a Ford to a Cadillac. This mill produced fine flour for all sorts of breads, including white bread.

Along with the mill, my father and his partners purchased generators that provided electric light for the homes and streets of the village—a first in that entire region. Imagine! Lights in southern Russia, in the early twenties. Did Canada have electric lights in its villages and farms in those days?

Later, when the family had moved to Canada, Father tried farming. He worked so hard! It was pitiful to see a man, who in the old land had made an excellent go of it and who had earned a place of honour and respect with dignity, having to begin over. He had to work as hard as in his younger days.

In all this I never saw Father bitter or regretful that he had come to Canada. What mattered to him was a homeland with religious liberty for his family and his grandchildren. Father saw to it that we would have the freedom to worship God. For that freedom he was grateful. For that, we his children, grandchildren and great-grandchildren must be eternally grateful.

Our parents were religious people with a deep and personal faith. This carried them over many rough spots. Their faith was to be tested in the deepest stresses of life. As these came, they only strengthened their faith in the God whom they loved with deeper and deeper insight.

Sunday school and church attendance were never options. We all understood that church was where the family belonged on the Lord's Day. Family devotions at breakfast and before we retired at night were as regular as our meals. If we were pressed for time, we could miss the meal, but not devotions. How often a promise from the Word sustained all of us in the times of trial that soon came.

The Revolution struck in southern Russia. Our parents, who were seen as *Kulaks* (land owners) belonging to the bourgeoisie, were marked for plunder. They were forced into hiding. In the upheaval that followed, they were stripped of everything. The Reds and the Makhnovse (roving bands of robbers) came in waves, receding, only to return with greater fury.

During one of the lulls, Father and Mother came out of hiding and called the family together (some of us younger members stayed with our in-laws while our parents were underground). After a hastily-prepared meal in the summer dining room, Father, as his custom was, reached for the family Bible. I can see it yet—I always will. I do not know the passage he read, but after the reading, he committed his family to God's care and closed with the words of Job, ". . . the Lord gave and the Lord hath taken away; blessed be the name of the Lord." Thereafter, Mother and Father kissed each of us and went underground again, hoping to see us when it was all over. In all this, my parents did not sin nor charge God foolishly.

One more incident that demonstrates the living faith in Father's home will have to suffice. Revolution is often accompanied by famine and pestilence. Pestilence, like the revolution, raged, but spared our lives. The famine remained for several years.

When it was at its worst—strangely—Father had the finest crops and garnered in a bountiful harvest. People came from far and near to borrow or beg grain. The scene is by the grain bin in the large threshing floor *(Scheune)*. The people would literally fall upon their knees and plead for another *pud* (40 pounds), or a few more pounds. Father would sink to his knees, crying to God with them to undertake. Then they would rise from their knees, and Dad would give them more grain. Later, in the kitchen, I heard Mother plead with Dad to keep at least enough for the family. But under those circumstances, how could he? That year, though the fields yielded a bumper crop, our family suffered, but survived. We saw faith demonstrated in our home. It had an impact on us for life.

In later years, worldly-wise professors were unable to dislodge my spiritual convictions, though they tried so often to explain them away as pretense or mere profession. I had seen *genuine* faith at work. In the gravest economic crisis, I saw how detached my parents were from the things of earth, and how bound they were to things eternal.

I remember our family for its singing. We were a singing family—not in public, but in our home. Father would play his flute, my sisters played guitars, my brothers the mandolin and violin. We younger ones joined heartily in song. Often it was spontaneous—when rain kept us indoors, or in the evenings. At times friends came with their instruments, and our large parlor would be filled with young people and music. I suspect that some young men came because a songfest was the nearest thing to a date they could get with my sisters—Dad was strict! But he loved to see the young people sing, and Mother enjoyed it. Although not a singer, she too would join in with enthusiasm.

I enjoyed a very happy childhood, notwithstanding the tragic upheavals of the ruthless revolution that soon came upon us.

"When fathers are tongue-tied religiously, need we wonder that their sons are sin-tied?" Spurgeon

2

The Russian Revolution—Through the Eyes of a Child

I . . . quieted myself, as a child. Psalm 131:2

I was born in a secure Christian home and raised in a settled "well to do" community. My boyhood days were at first secure and serene.

At the age of five, I was bundled up and sent to our village school with my older brother, who preceded me by a year. From the first day I loved it. I loved the classes, I loved the studies, I loved my teachers. I found it all so interesting. I have been so fortunate to have excellent teachers all my school life! Some were better than others, but I have not had a single poor teacher.

As I reflect now, I am not so sure that my love for school was Simon pure, for when we were not at school, we had to do chores at home. Of the two, I preferred school. I was an average student and my grades were usually near the top. My favourite subjects were history, arithmetic and drama. After I completed grade school, I had to wait a year, because the opening of the junior high *(Fortbildung-schule)* in Gruenfeld, our neighbouring village, was delayed due to political uncertainty and economic stress. That year of waiting was not very pleasant.

At school, I enjoyed a good mixture of studying and playing. We enjoyed ball, soccer, and plenty of swimming. We romped through the hills and bushes of the *Baikush* west of our village and on the river flats. In winter, we had plenty of sledding, building snowmen and forts, and skating. If ever I was in danger from playmates or otherwise, my older brother came to my rescue and guarded me well.

Sunday school and church attendance was an accepted practice in our home. I do not ever recall that any family member ever questioned this practice. No one in our home faced that weekly decision. That decision had been made by our parents long before any of us realized that there might even be a choice.

I recall how our Sunday school teacher, on one occasion, explained to us young boys how God created us out of the dust of the earth. Just then I rubbed my hands—a bit damp—and showed the particles of dirt as proof that we were made out of dust. (I understand my Sunday school teacher chuckled about that presentation the rest of her life.) We were introduced to the Saviour from earliest childhood. "We heard with our ears, O God, our Fathers have told us, what work thou didst in their days, in the times of old" (Psalm 44:1).

As children we enjoyed life. We were really not conscious of the serious times in which we lived. We were far removed from the scenes of World War I that began when I was only three. Rumours of unrest and danger were floating around, but we had no newspapers, radio or TV in those days. We were sheltered from war fears until one day German soldiers entered our village and announced their victory on the eastern front.

A month later the Russian revolution reached our area, and the Reds sacked our village. On the morning of that day, we went peacefully off to school as usual, although our parents seemed apprehensive, kissing us good-bye several times. But we were off to school in our usual carefree manner, planning our strategy for recess play.

School began as usual, but the first recess was different. Instead of gathering on the playground, we were drawn toward Main Street. It was full of soldiers, horsemen, and carriages. Several riders came to the sidewalk where we were enjoying their demonstration. Then, suddenly, one horseman drew his sword, flashed it, and darted toward us. We scattered like frightened rabbits. We fled through the gates to the safety of the school. A short-cut led through the open window of our classroom. My brother climbed the ledge and crawled through. I attempted to do likewise, but had difficulty. I panicked, frightened that any moment the sword would chop me to pieces. Trembling, I sank to the ground in a heap. These few moments seemed like an eternity. Next, I became aware that my brother stood beside me, trying to quieten me. "Don't fear, Henry," he said. "The horseman was unable to ride through the gate." The horse had balked.

Our teachers sought to carry on a normal routine, but we learned little that day. Our minds, if not our eyes, were on the street teeming with soldiers—an unusual occurrence in a Mennonite village. Rumours floated in abundance, and whenever possible, we huddled in groups to hear the latest. It was a fearful walk home. We were accosted by soldiers several times. They seemed so undisciplined and crude, so unlike what we thought soldiers are supposed to be.

My brother and I reached our gate to home and safety. But we were yet to experience the greater shock. There were no cheerful activities about the house, no warm greeting by Mom and Dad. Instead all was quiet. We entered our large kitchen—but no one was there. We looked in the family room—no one there. We found the living room silent but confused. Our orderly home was topsy-turvy, as though someone had ransacked the house. We called for Mom and Dad—no answer. An eerie feeling enveloped us. What do we do now? The security and laughter of home was gone. We ran from room to room, but there was no response.

Finally, my oldest brother showed up, and he too looked scared. In a hushed tone he explained how Father and Mother and our sisters had gone into hiding. He could not tell where. But they had left instructions for us. "After school go to your oldest sister's home who will be expecting you."

"But they live at the other end of the village!" my brother and I protested.

It took a while for us to get sufficient courage to walk past the soldiers to our sister's home. The way seemed so long, but no one molested us. Henry and Elizabeth welcomed us warmly, reassuring us that all was well with our parents and that they would call for us perhaps in a few days. Until then, they would care for us. We did not know at that time that Father and Mother were hiding in our sister's basement shelter.

After a week, the Reds left. Our parents called for us and things returned to normal, up to a point. From then on our lifestyle would be drastically changed. School opened the next day, and we resumed our studies. That evening, however, after the family altar, our parents explained as much as they dared what had happened. They said that it would likely reoccur, but they believed that God would take care of us all.

This was the first of many sackings by Reds and Whites as the battle for that area seesawed. Worst of all, there was a third party of roving bands, led by Nestor Ivanowich Makhno, who was determined to keep the situation as fluid as possible so he could carry on with robbery, rape and murder. When the Whites gained the upper hand, he would help the Reds. If the Reds appeared to win, he would help the Whites. Finally, he cast in his lot with the Reds, and these in turn were joined by the Red Regiments that had gained the upper hand in the northern areas. And so the Whites were defeated and driven into the Black Sea.

The pillaging, plundering, burning, and murder that took place when the armies sacked the villages have been recorded by Russian Mennonite writers. Rumours usually preceded it, an incursion, which gave our parents and sisters time to go underground and pack the two of us off to our sister's place. But sometimes the *Makhnovs* (roving bands of robbers) pounced upon our village without warning.

One pleasant summer afternoon, a large number of horsemen approached from the east. They rode down the street when suddenly one band turned up our driveway. Now what? They seemed to be in a pleasant mood, in keeping with the day. My older brothers greeted them, and after a few pleasantries, they asked for our father. When Father came, the captain identified himself. "You don't remember me, do you?" he asked Father.

Dad thought he looked familiar but could not recall for certain. The leader gave his name, and Father knew him as a younger man who had worked for him one summer. Dad wondered, as he confessed later to us, had he come to settle a score, as so many had ruthlessly done in our village? Or was he just coming to display his new status in the proletariat?

It didn't take long to find out. He had enjoyed the summer with us, but he reminded Father of an incident when he was very rough with him for failing to attend to a certain task. "But," said the Captain, "you apologized to me the next day." Had it not been for that, his attitude and conduct would have been different.

While my brothers looked after their horses, the soldiers enjoyed a cup of coffee and some goodies Mother served in the summer house. The captain assured Dad that as long as their regiment was in the village he would be protected. Then they climbed proudly into their saddles and rode off.

On another occasion, the Bolsheviks pounced upon our village. My sisters disappeared to their hiding nest, but my parents were not so fortunate. They were interrogated and tortured in our large living room. Knowing that Father was a *Kulak,* they assumed that my parents were hiding many valuables. They threatened, "Come forth with your gold and silver or you will lose your head!" Dad had been stripped of all of these during the many previous raids; he had hidden nothing he insisted. They ordered him to lay his head on a chair, and they drew a sword over his neck. I panicked. Mother had tried her best to get me out of the room and so shelter me from this horror, but they wouldn't let her, insisting that I stay. Apparently my screams added to their sport.

Disappointed and frustrated that no valuables were to be had, they cursed and demanded that Father curse his God. Father would give up all that he had, he would share his faith in God his Saviour, but give it up and deny his Lord? Never! No, not even in the face of the sword.

On another occasion, they tested my oldest brother. A loaded gun was put to his forehead, but he would not yield. He too stood true.

I shall never forget the anguish of another sacking by the roving bands. Our parents went underground, my sisters fled. I too sought shelter in an outhouse among our fruit trees. I did not feel too safe, so I fled to our neighbours east of us, only to discover the robbers were there as well. The torture of fear when parents are away in such circumstances can hardly be described. When I see the children in Beirut scatter, fleeing in terror, not knowing where, my heart goes out to them. How grateful to God we can be for a stable society in our land. But we know, "it can happen here," if we continue to reject God.

You can hardly imagine the aftermath of each sacking; the filth, the lice, and the vermin we had to contend with. With the revolution came two equal evils—famine and pestilence. A plague of typhus fever, tuberculosis, and cholera swept through our area killing many. Though seriously hurt as a family, we survived both.

We were plundered and stripped of all portable wealth, but the houses in our village were not destroyed. Our farming implements were left intact, as were some of our cattle and horses. Since the famine was so severe and the new regime needed grain to feed its vast population, they let the farming villagers return to their lands. Order was slowly established, and the *Kulaks*—although heavily taxed—were allowed to restore their farms, and the production of grains resumed. In fact, considering the upheavals through which the people had gone, the recovery was remarkable, with fair prospects for the future.

The communists had their hands full to establish their new regime, and since food was desperately needed, they decided to wait with collectivization. My father, however, fully understood their intentions and was not fooled with their temporary considerations. He knew the aims of Marxist-Leninist Communism. He knew it was atheistic, therefore, anti-Christian, and he foresaw the evil that was soon to be imposed upon the entire land. He had heard of the religious freedom enjoyed in North America. After he listened to Herbert Hoover, who, as the American Administrator of Relief, visited our area, Father took courage and felt that our only hope was to emigrate. He began to pray, plan and prepare. He became excited, if not obsessed, about the possibility of life in North America.

3

Emigrating to Canada

The Land of My Opportunity

By faith Abraham . . . sojourned . . . in a strange country.
Hebrews 11:8-9

Father dreamed about Canada as a refuge for persecuted Christians and a land of religious liberty. Its doors began to open for our people in 1923, but we were delayed for two years. My Father had all the papers in hand. All that he needed was a health certificate for each of us to complete the entrance requirements, that he felt was only routine. He was disappointed but not discouraged when the medical examinations revealed I had trachoma, an eye disease about which Canada was very sensitive. Fortunately, that could be treated with bluestone. Each treatment was painful, but it was cured. By the summer of 1925 all was ready.

We made our way to Kolotschevsky, our nearest railroad station, accompanied by the pastor, relatives, and friends, singing as we went. We travelled by train to Alexandrovsk, the meeting place of the Mennonite emigrants for Canada in 1925. Most of us had a few days to get settled in the freight cars that were waiting for us. Each car held two or more families. Straw was provided for beds, and our baggage trunks served as seats. The cars had no heat and no conveniences. The emigrants filled a full train of freight cars, and we were on our way to Canada and freedom via Smolensk on to Riga, our first port in Latvia. Father literally shouted with praise when we passed through the border gate, the Red Gate—later called the "Freedom Gate" between Russia and Latvia.

In Riga we were delayed a few days. Again we had medical examinations, which our family passed with flying colours. All our clothes were fumigated. Ironically, although we were fighting lice in Russia, our first experience with bedbugs was in the port barracks of Riga. We boarded the ship Baltara and headed out to the Baltic Sea. We passed through Kiel Canal and the North Sea to Southampton, England. There we were cared for in a clean army barracks and we enjoyed excellent food, although some of us missed our *borscht*.

We waited over a month in Southampton until Canada was ready. The swift, smooth train ride from Southampton to Liverpool was exciting. Arriving at Liverpool, we immediately boarded the ocean liner Montnairn and headed across the Atlantic for the land of liberty.

We encountered no storms, experienced little or no seasickness, and so we enjoyed the entire trip immensely. We had made plenty of new friends and had a lot of fun investigating every nook and cranny of the ocean liner that we were allowed to enter.

Six days later, on October 24, 1925, we arrived in Quebec, Canada—the land of our emancipation. In Quebec we took the passenger train to Winnipeg, enjoying the rugged countryside of the northern, more direct route through this vast land. In Winnipeg we bade good-bye to our many new friends of the journey, and we travelled by local train to Winkler, Manitoba. There two of my sisters and their husbands, who had emigrated to Canada two years earlier met us. My Uncle, Peter Froese, who had been an industrialist in the Old Land, greeted us saying, "You will have peace and liberty in this great land, and you will find it so different." After a welcome meal in my uncle's home, we travelled by horses and wagon ten miles south to Blumenfeld, our relatives' temporary home. So much seemed so different! The farms, the implements, the clothes. Actually, I soon discovered that we were the ones that were different, a curiosity to the Canadians.

The village school was next door to the Blumenfeld house, and the following day I enrolled as a thirteen-year-old in *grade one!* The teacher was a Christian and understood my situation well. This made the adjustment less difficult, but she left me in grade one. Early in the spring we moved to a farm southeast of Deloraine and my education was interrupted again. It was a good summer economically, but there was no church home, and, after all, that was the main reason we had immigrated to Canada.

In the fall of 1926 our folks purchased a farm near Myrtle, Manitoba. We found a good school, and our new home was only about eight miles from a Mennonite Brethren Church in Kronsgard. My parents perceived that, "the Lord had called the child," so they enrolled me immediately in school. Myrtle had a consolidated school with horse-drawn vans to provide transportation. I shall never forget my first day in that much-larger school, with grades one through twelve. In the Mennonite setting, the winter before, I had learned very little English. Now it was exclusively English; really the best thing for me.

The pupils in the van asked me what grade I was in. I said, "grade one." They looked at each other, but dutifully took me to the grade one room. As I waited at the door for the teacher, I soon discerned that I was the curiosity of that morning. Fourteen years old and only in grade one! Two grade nine students introduced themselves and wondered if I meant first year in high school. "No," I insisted, "Just grade one." They shook their heads as they left.

Finally the teacher arrived and provided a desk for me in grade one. It was a humiliating but healthy experience. With the grade one students, I learned to write English and say the nursery rhymes: "Tom Tinker had a dog; it said, 'Bow wow.' " Even more humiliating was the experience of using crepe paper to make dolls. Within a month I was promoted to grade three. After two months, to grade four. By now I had a handle on the language and began to read freely, and even to speak it.

Within the goodness of God, the superintendent visited our classroom in grade four. My teacher explained why this fourteen-year-old was only in grade four and introduced me to him. After a few encouraging words, he had me read and then write a paragraph. The last hour of the morning, he set an exam for grade six in geography. He asked me to write it too. Fortunately, it was on Siberia and the far east. In the afternoon, he had me take a test in grade eight mathematics. Eight grades in six months! You will agree that is at least modest progress.

Things were going well for me, and I had almost caught up with my age group in grade nine. From novelty to questioning, both teachers and students accepted and respected me for my persistence. I loved school once more.

But clouds of disappointment were gathering on the western sky. Unusually heavy rains and runoffs from the Pembina Mountains flooded our land, now seeded, and destroyed my parents' hope of economic success and independence. Mother had an attack of a recurring illness, and within a few days, she went on to be with the Lord. With the loss of Mother, my father and family floundered, but faith in God and hope for a blessed reunion sustained us through our severest loss.

Father managed to rent land with a few buildings north of Horndean and there we resettled. Mother's death disrupted our life-style. Once again I had to quit school to earn a livelihood with Father. In many ways, it was a pity to see my father, now in his sixties, work so hard. He, who had been so honourable in the Old Land—one of the village fathers whose word carried weight—had become in Canada a "hired-hand" without the years left for recovery and prosperity.

Had Canada disappointed him? Did reality fail to live up to his dream? He felt the loss of my mother keenly. He saw no prospect for economic success. But at no time was he bitter, and at all times he was grateful that God had led him to Canada, "the land of Religious Liberty."

The more recent immigrants from Russia confirmed what Father sensed was the aim of communism: economic collectivization and religious persecution that was imposed in the Old Land within a few years of our departure. The *Kulaks* and Christian leaders were hunted down and deported to Siberia as slaves, where they perished. We in Canada were free to worship God and earn sufficient for an honourable livelihood.

Canada proved to be the home of many refugees from Eastern Europe. With them they brought their skills, their Judaeo-Christian work ethic, and religious convictions. It took a while before the different ethnic groups began to fuse, but their sons continued to work hard and prospered. To us as a whole, and to me in particular, Canada became "The Land of My Opportunity." That is the story of my conversion and ministry.

4

My Conversion, Commitment, and Call to the Ministry

Thou art the God of my salvation. Psalm 25:5

It was my turn to go out as a "hired hand" and earn money to help my dad get re-established in his small but practical farm. This was a new experience for me. Although I had worked away from home on special jobs, this was a commitment for a year. I had so much to learn at the Anton Heppner farm, and I was a slow learner at times. My boss became a bit impatient and had reason to be disgusted, but before too long we understood each other, and the family was very kind to me. We built a friendship that has continued to this day, another mark of God's goodness for which 1928 is remembered.

Then followed a year of decision, for which 1929 will remain fresh in my memory. I had known the Gospel from childhood and lived in the comforts of my parents' Christianity. Though I wanted first to taste this world and its pleasure, there was a deep inner longing for personal reality, for forgiveness of sins, and for a hope of life called the conversion experience. Time and again I wished some young Christian would speak to me about the Lord. Outwardly, though, I gave the impression that my spiritual relation to God was nobody else's business. I mixed freely with Christians but schemed to avoid a personal conversation about conversion.

A fascinating speaker who had more recently come from Russia was due to visit our home. My brother and I decided to walk to town. On our way, we passed a horse-drawn sleigh bearing our local deacon and this Russian preacher. We felt sure they were on their way to our home and that we had eluded them. We continued on our way, attended to our business and walked home, feeling certain that by now they had left.

But no, there they were, waiting for our arrival. It was a friendly meeting. With his captivating stories from Russia and his miraculous escape he won our interest. Tactfully he approached us about our personal relationship to God, but he sensed that as yet we were not quite ready. He left a copy of his book, *Under the Red Cross,* with stories of his witness in communist Russian jails. Then he turned to me and said, "Heinrich, when you become a Christian, you will become a teacher of God's Word to many in Canada."

I was puzzled. What could that mean? Surely he could not be serious, and yet he was so sincere. My brother at first teased me and had a little "schputt" with me, but then too began to wonder how this could be. I have since learned that clergymen on a collecting tour are often impressed by the high qualities of the children of their hosts! I soon forgot about the prophetic word until I was asked to reflect upon the things that led to my conversion and ministry.

That same winter, early in March, I learned of the Canadian Sunday School Mission's Scripture memorization contest. A contestant was to memorize 500 verses selected from the Gospel of John and say them to the local school teacher before the end of April. Thereby he could earn a free week at summer camp. Finances were low in our home. How else could I get to a week of summer camp?

I inquired of the teacher at Rosenheim School for details. Mr. Jantzen informed me that the contest closed the end of April, but he was willing to hear me, providing I really went to work. To work I went! I recited the 500 verses in three sessions before the April deadline. As he listened, he asked if I had ever considered going into teaching or drama? He too started me thinking.

The CSSM camp that summer was held in San Susie of Matlock situated on Lake Winnipeg in Manitoba. I enjoyed the week, even though the camp workers singled me out daily to point me to Christ. Before too long, whenever a camp worker came near me, I would make sure I was in plenty of company and so escape being buttonholed. I was successful until the last night of camp, when God spoke to me. The closing hymn was "When the Roll is Called Up Yonder, I'll Be There." I knew that in my state I would not be there.

The hymn was still echoing in my ears when I was gently approached by Miss Grace Furness. She spoke to Rev. Jalmer Erickson, our tent director, who led me to the Lord. I yielded and believed the

Word. The following day on the way home I had misgivings. Others testified that when they came to Christ they felt a heavy burden roll off their breasts. Like Pilgrim who saw in his dream that "just as Christian came up to the cross, his burden loosed from off his shoulders, and fell from off his back, and began to tumble, and so continued to do till it came to the mouth of the sepulchre, where it fell in, and I saw it no more." I had felt no such rolling off of my burden. Was my conversion for real or just make-believe?

My father greeted me upon my return home with the words, "Has the prodigal come home?"

"Yes," I replied, "but I hope no more as a prodigal."

My father was ecstatic. "I knew it, I knew it!" he kept repeating. "I prayed that God would save you at camp."

It was great to see my father happy about his 17-year-old son, but in my heart doubts still lingered. That Sunday evening after the *Yugendverein,* in Melba School, I sought counsel from Rev. David K. Derksen, a godly teacher of that school and preacher at the Mennonite Brethren Church. We went for a walk in the meadow while the evening sun was setting. I shared my concerns. I wanted reality. I wanted real repentance and not "easy-believism." Since I had felt no remarkable easing of my burden, was my conversion real? He respected and appreciated my concern, but faithfully pointed out once more that Jesus had borne my burden of sin, that He had died for me and was raised on account of my acquittal. He reminded me that "God so loved the world, that he gave his only begotten Son, that whosoever believeth in him should not perish, but have everlasting life" (John 3:16). We knelt in the meadow beside a barbed-wire fence where I committed once more the saving of my soul unto God. It was not my notion of what should take place during my salvation, but faith in Jesus and His Word. Assurance that began to filter into my heart grew as I read and studied the Word of God, believing in the Lord Jesus Christ.

The Bible reading and teaching of our home made it clear to me that the cross called for unconditional surrender, and when I accepted Christ as my Saviour, I also accepted His Lordship. Yet in the light of failure, I have often had to confess my sins to Him and reaffirm my commitment. As the Scriptures continued to speak to me and new truths of His wondrous grace were revealed, they called for the response of obedience in my heart, for every truth of God becomes a trust. Moreover, in the hours of my conversion I became conscious of God's hand upon me, commissioning me to be a witness. Truly, "in keeping His commandments there is great reward."

Like Gideon's army, I was tested by the water. This was the heart of the message given by Rev. John Heide, leader of the Grossweide Mennonite Brethren Church at the baptismal service two weeks after my conversion. This took place in our own community, at David Hiebert's farm dug-out, about a mile or so from the local church. I understood baptism's significance as a public confession of my identification with Christ in the likeness of His death and resurrection.

The people received me warmly into the fellowship of our church and encouraged me to become actively involved in the work. They appointed me as treasurer of the Sunday school, and invited me to assist in the *Yugendverein,* the Young People's Association. It has been said, "As you grow in grace, your powers and talents become unified and coordinated; if not, they go warring to destruction."

I soon learned how to store my mind with words of wisdom right from its source—the Word of God. Harvest was early that year, and Henry Rempel, my brother-in-law, got me a job with a farmer near Domain, Manitoba. As a young convert, I mingled with hard-core harvesters from Winnipeg. We slept in a bunkhouse. A dim, flickering oil lamp provided what little light we had, and that was further dimmed by heavy smoking by the crew. It was not too difficult to say no to tobacco as I had never developed that habit. But my test came as I was about to retire.

Loud laughter and filthy talk filled the evening. What should I do? Should I retire quietly, turn over toward the wall and pray so no one would notice? Or should I take my New Testament and read a portion, then kneel by my mattress and pray? I felt I should declare myself immediately. They looked at me when I read from my New Testament and joked a bit. When I knelt, some boots came flying in my direction. But I continued, and rolled into bed and slept well.

As this practice was continued each night, fewer boots dropped by me and the ribaldry toned down. By the end of the week, they quieted down completely. By the middle of the second week, they apologized and asked me to read aloud and pray for them. By the third week, several wanted to know about my Saviour too. When we parted at the end of the harvest, they were thankful for the Bible reading and prayer. As for me, I returned home strengthened in the faith and was grateful I could hand over my earnings to help Father pay his debt.

The CSSM Bible memory contest taught me two very valuable lessons. I have not lost the gift of memory which has served me so well over the years. More important was the storing of the treasure of God's Word in my heart. The Mission required 200 Bible verses for the second camp and a correspondence course for the third year. I enrolled as a worker for the third year.

Meanwhile, I was being armed and prepared for battle. Bible school training was placed upon my heart immediately after my conversion. Winnipeg Bible College seemed to be the only possibility. Rev. Lloyd Hunter, Superintendent of the CSSM, felt he had a job lined up for me for forty dollars a month, and a Christian home that charged only twenty-five dollars a month for board and room, Isaac Wiebe, my brother-in-law, loaned me ten dollars to get me started.

I settled in the home and set out to investigate the job, only to discover it was selling Christmas cards. One salesman had made as much as forty dollars one month a year ago. The man required my ten dollars as a down payment. I declined, and so ended the job.

Two young men were batching next to my room. Mrs. Jack Arnold, my hostess, saw my predicament and agreed to rent the room to me with sufficient equipment to make my own meals. A schoolmate and I conceived the idea of washing windows and putting on storm windows at 25 cents each. We would take a couple of hours on Monday after classes to line up a week's work in advance, preferably in the same block, for we carried our ladder, pails, and equipment from place to place. This, plus digging gardens and cleaning furnaces and basements, earned me sufficient money to pay my way through school, to repay my brother-in-law, and to secure a nest egg for the following year. In those days, bread could be bought for three cents a loaf, and small earnings seemed as holy as David's water from the well of Bethlehem. The idea of quitting when disappointments and hardships came never entered my mind. God had saved me for a purpose, He had led me to Bible school, and He would see me through.

City life, though it can be exciting if you are there in the will of God, really never attracted me. I came to the city as green as grass. Back in the home community, people assumed the Bible was the Word of God, though they sometimes differed as to its interpretation. In the city, I met rank atheism, smug modernism, and all sorts of *isms.* Even at school there was a group of aggressive students who claimed to have special spiritual gifts, whose worship was anything but decent and in order. Some of their manifestations reminded me more of heathen worship than Christian worship. In fact, I could not conceive that they even attempted to go under the umbrella of Christianity.

The principal of the school was Dr. Sweet, an elderly, godly man, but too soft to hold the reins. He was a good teacher. I loved this gentleman, as I loved all my teachers, and he loved me.

The Board of Directors pressured him to clear the air, teach sound doctrine and establish order. He felt the pressure and asked a number of us to join him for prayer in his own home. As we arrived, he took us into the attic, I suppose to create the upper room flavour. His wife did not join us, and this raised a flag in my mind. In our home, Father and Mother were always together in spiritual worship.

As the meeting proceeded, the praying got louder and louder and uncomfortably close in bodily contact. I opened my eyes and saw a ring was formed around me. I had become the object of their prayers. The over-zealous folks felt that the power should come over me and so tried physically to push me back and down. The scene reminded me of Elijah and the prophets of Baal on Mt. Carmel.

I got up and walked away, all the more determined to study what the Bible had to say about this well-meaning, very earnest, but often erring movement. I remembered Paul's instructions to young Timothy, "Take heed unto thyself, and unto the doctrine; continue in them: for in doing this thou shalt both save thyself, and them that hear thee" (1 Timothy 4:16).

The principal was replaced at Christmas time by his assistant, Mr. Leo Lapp, and the rest of the school year was meaningful and productive. The following year was even more profitable. Rev. Simon E. Forsberg had become the principal at WBC and led the students in sound Bible teaching for my next three years—two years to complete my diploma course, and a one-year post-graduate course. I owe so much to this dear servant of God, who with his wife, Anna, consolidated and established my faith in God and His Word. I will always feel the impact of his dynamic teaching of sound doctrine and practical Biblical exposition. Truly, spiritual grounding is a prerequisite to being placed in a seat of honour.

That second year I worked my way through school by selling homemade candies for Mrs. Jack Arnold, the lady who had been so kind to me the first year. I cannot ever forget how kind the people of God have been, especially at the most critical periods in my life.

For the next three years the Lord opened the way for me to do the house chores for Mrs. Margaret Thompson and her helper, Miss Christine Lumsden, both up in years. They were two beautiful Christian ladies who welcomed me into the home as a son. My stay with them was most pleasant, enabling me to continue my studies while giving summers to the CSSM to work in rural Saskatchewan and Manitoba. Those were very important years for the undreamed-of ministry to come at BBC. My doctrinal convictions were being formed. Also, Henry and Evelyn Budd were born during those years.

City lights had their glamour and appeal to a young country boy, but I was not taken by outward glitter. True, the city provided opportunities for learning, but its sophistication had little appeal. Before I would commit myself, I wanted to know what was beyond and beneath the glitter, for so much of it seemed to lack reality.

The student body at WBC was organized into small groups for Christian service. This gave me the opportunity to participate in services where we provided testimonies and music, and sometimes we were asked to take complete charge. Our group was responsible for the Friday evening service at the Lighthouse Mission—a rescue mission in the red-light district of the city. It fell to my lot to preach, my first sermon!

Mrs. Forsberg, my teacher in speech, was present at the service. I spoke on Romans 6:23, "For the wages of sin is death; but the gift of God is eternal life through Jesus Christ our Lord." All seemed to be going reasonably well until I brought my fist down on the pulpit to emphasize the point. I hit the collection basket. It flew into the audience, and so did the pennies and nickels. My teacher blushed a little and smiled. I completed my sermon and the response at the conclusion was good. My teacher was gracious, for in our next class she found something good and encouraging to say about my first try.

In my home church I was asked to give a lecture to the whole church on "The Person and Ministry of the Holy Spirit." Again the response was favourable, but it was my Father who placed his hand on me when we arrived home and said, "Son, I believe God wants you in the ministry. Thankfully, I learned a lot this morning that had not been clear to me. Henry, go ahead. You have my blessing and my prayers." To have Father's blessing seemed to me like the seal of God for the ministry.

A real test came during my last summer at home. The Melba Yugendverein Committee asked me to speak on John 15:1-8. At the time I was not aware of their strategy. They had also asked Mr. Abraham Hiebert, an elderly brother, to speak: He was sparring for a good debate. They had heard that I was leaning toward the awful doctrine of "eternal security." This occasion would bring it out in the open and I would be corrected publicly.

Innocently, I spoke on the Christian and progressive fruitbearing, pleading for an acceptance of the Father's discipline in our lives until we bring forth much fruit to His glory. The speaker that followed could only confirm my positive approach. Contrary to the fears of those who were aware of the plan, the evening proved to be heartening to the people of God. And so I began to learn by trial and error to dwell on the positive aspects of our Christian faith. Much more was yet to be learned out in the fields of service during my years of preparation. We will look at that in the next phase of my development.

5

Circuit Riding Preacher

They that sow in tears shall reap in joy. Psalm 126:5

Missions abroad? That was my first consideration for a life work. Pastoral ministry? My second choice. Teaching? Possibly. But founding a Bible college? Impossible. I never gave it a first thought.

Missions was presented to us periodically in Bible College. The challenge was clear and moving. Beside the stimulus of regular missions classes, I sought information about the different fields. I studied missionary literature and became interested in the Sudan of Africa. During an interview with Mr. Whitman one day, I was advised, that in view of the depression, it would be better for me to gain a few years experience serving the home field. Following that, economic conditions might improve sufficiently to warrant further consideration for missions abroad.

I considered the advice sincerely, and, at the time, it did not occur to me that it might have been a polite brush-off. Whatever, I knew God's hand was upon me for some ministry, and I was anxious to get the recommended experience in the homeland before I reconsidered the foreign field. But where? With whom? All I wanted was opportunity to serve my God.

That opportunity came from the Canadian Sunday School Mission (CSSM) in Saskatchewan which was led by Rev. D. R Aikenhead. I was invited to serve in summer ministry in the rural areas west of the South Saskatchewan River, around the towns of Birsay, Dunblane, Tichfield, and Lucky Lake.

This would be a new experience for me. I was excited about the possibilities, yet apprehensive about entering a completely new and unchurched area to begin my first summer ministry. But I took life by the hand and romped with it sincerely and simply; praying, believing.

A schoolmate friend from Saskatoon with considerable experience in Christian work was returning home after graduation and offered a ride to another schoolmate and me. So the three of us, Andy Elliot, Edwin Backlin, and I, were on our way early in May, 1933. The trip introduced me to Saskatchewan, which would become the province of my lifelong ministry.

On the way, services were arranged at Maryfield and Trossachs. I could not know that people I would meet on that trip would become my lifelong friends and supporters.

Edwin led the gospel services while Andy preached and I sang, accompanied by my guitar. At the Trossachs service, I had an experience that I had never had before nor since. Not being used to travelling and visiting late nights, I grew so sleepy, that while I was singing, I dropped off into dreamland for a moment! I awoke with a jerk and carried on. Most in the service noticed something had happened, but only a few knew that I had actually fallen asleep while singing. I have heard of audiences falling asleep—but a soloist while performing?

On our way to Saskatoon we stopped to see some of Andy's friends in Moose Jaw. They later became our regular supporters. At Saskatoon, the provincial CSSM Superintendent welcomed us warmly and introduced me to Walter, his son, who was a young boy. Walter and his wife, Edith, led our music department at Briercrest for 17 years. Rev. Aikenhead briefed me about the field. As far as the CSSM was concerned, it was virgin territory. Reaching "the otherwise unreached in Canada" was the aim of the CSSM. Rev. Aikenhead gave me the name of Mr. Jim Bagshaw of Birsay, in whose home I was to become welcome whenever I was not busy away in the field.

Andy Elliot was engaged by the CSSM to minister that summer in the schools west of the South Saskatchewan River near Outlook, a field about 40 miles north of my designated territory. He graciously offered to take me to the Bagshaws at Birsay, stopping on the way to visit friends near Outlook. A warm welcome awaited him in the Ankermans' home. Again, when Briercrest Bible College began, the Ankermans became ardent supporters. In time, Dale Ankerman, a son, enrolled in our school. At this writing, I cherish the friendship of the remaining members of the family. Since the above-mentioned ministering brethren were called to other fields, and I was to return to Saskatchewan two years later for my life's work, they rallied around my ministry.

After a few days of refreshing Christian fellowship, Andy took me to Birsay to meet Mr. Jim Bagshaw and his family, where I would make my home for the summer. I was graciously received by the Bagshaws, who shared the CSSM vision for "reaching the unreached." Mr. Bagshaw had heard about the CSSM ministry in Saskatchewan through Chapel Chimes, a radio broadcast led by Mr. Aikenhead. As a result, he made contact, and now the young, inexperienced lad from Winnipeg had arrived. If he had any misgivings, he concealed them. That night apprehension exceeded anticipation, but I committed everything to God and slept well.

The test came the following morning. The evening before, we had attended to the formalities and the generalities of the work. The time now came for specifics. Mr. Bagshaw gave me the names of a few people to contact in the hills northwest of Birsay. He offered me his horse—a staid old-timer known as Tom. We figured out how to strap my guitar to the saddle, as well as a briefcase containing my Bible, notes, and reading material. I was now set.

At 10:30 in the morning I rode out with feelings of fear and faith. Today I advise students on such a venture to do their homework. Get a map from the municipal office with every farmer's name. Get the names of the trustees of the little red schoolhouses, the names of those who are likely to be interested in Sunday school, etc. Armed with Bible, a guitar, a few tracts, and a few names (but no experience), I headed into the hills.

My first contact was a churchman who assured me that there were already too many churches in the area and there was no room for another religious organization. The next farmer had no interest in religious matters. The third was doubtful, but assured me that his neighbor, by the name of Dahl, had a larger house and barn and would likely accommodate me for the night.

About 8:30 in the evening I arrived. Remember that old Tom was steady, but slow of foot. He gave me plenty of time to bathe my next contact in prayer. Although a bit cool to the proposition of a Sunday school, I found Mr. and Mrs. Dahl hospitable. They gave me an evening meal, which tasted great after missing dinner. Fortunately they had a family, and the children asked about my guitar. A breakthrough! The children loved the choruses, and soon they sang them with me. I read a brief Scripture and prayed. The parents were delighted and sent me on my way the following morning with their wish that sufficient interest might develop for a regular Sunday school in their district, although they doubted it. They gave me the names and locations of the chairman and members of the local school trustees, men who might be inclined toward my project.

I visited the trustees and obtained permission to hold Sunday school in Finland, the name of their school. Then I visited the school during recess and talked with the teacher about my plans. She gave me permission to speak briefly to the pupils. Recess over, the teacher introduced me, and I sang a song and taught the children a few choruses. They loved it! I explained the possibility of a Sunday school, hoping to return before the weekend to announce the time.

The next school I came to was Westpoint in the beautiful wheatlands that led toward the breaks of the South Saskatchewan River, north of Dunblane. A Swedish family, Forsbergs, had homesteaded there. Their sons with their families were well established on their farms. The depression, which had reduced most farmers to poverty level, had not quite erased the evidences of their success. They and their neighbors were interested in the welfare of their children and welcomed me into the district.

Fortunately, the school teacher loved music and had a very fine voice. She introduced me to her pupils and gave me as much time as I wanted to sing with the children. She joined heartily. With permission to hold a Sunday school readily offered by the trustees, I announced the Sunday school for the following Sunday morning. I invited everyone I met to join us and was warmly received into each home for singing, Bible reading and prayer.

On Wednesday I returned to Finland to announce the time for their Sunday school the next Sunday afternoon.

Rockpoint, some 13 miles west of Finland, presented a possibility for Sunday evening services. This would complete my circuit. Twenty miles on horseback with two Sunday schools and a service each Sunday would make it a full day! I worked. I visited in that district on Thursday and Friday mornings.

The experiences of Finland and Westpoint repeated themselves. Permission was granted to hold services in their school, but they felt to a man that it would not work. Several denominations had tried and given up.

The children in school loved the choruses and the guitar—and that was long before the guitars became popular. It served as the most practical and mobile instrument at a time when many country schools did not have pianos. The parents loved my music too. So a service was announced on Friday for Rockpoint that coming Sunday evening.

Friday afternoon I returned to the Bagshaw home. Arriving late in the evening, I announced to their joy that on Sunday I hoped to have two Sunday schools and an evening service at Westpoint, Finland and Rockpoint. The following circuit became routine. Early Saturday afternoon I would saddle Tom and head for Westpoint, about 14 miles north and east of Birsay. I would stay over night, usually with the Forsbergs. They would prepare a picnic lunch for me so I could leave immediately after the morning Sunday school for Finland.

The attendance at Westpoint was encouraging—usually 20, and even up to 30. Finland in the afternoon was not so good. A mile-and-a-half west was a communist hall which sponsored all-day Sunday entertainment, so eight to ten faithful children attended the Finland Sunday school.

Upon completing the afternoon sessions, I would leave for Rockpoint, thirteen miles west of Finland as the crow flies. At Rockpoint, the evening service took priority over supper. The kind people would serve me later. My first service in the Rockpoint School was well attended—about 50 people, but the atmosphere was tense. While the children and young people responded favourably, the service turned out to be a disaster. I was afraid to announce its continuance next Sunday. I will explain the problem in a later chapter.

However, God gave me the courage to announce a service the next week, and while the following Sunday's attendance was only about 40, the atmosphere was good. Thereafter, the attendance at Rockpoint doubled and about as many were outside looking through the door and windows as were inside. God gave me favour, and the response for decisions was excellent. Before long, word got around, and other schools invited me to their districts. Some I served with only an occasional visit, but the Newbank School District, some eight miles south of Rockpoint, invited me to teach the book of Romans. As a result, Thursday evenings were added to my weekly circuit. Friday mornings, I would return to home base—Jim Bagshaw's.

As mentioned before, the people of Westpoint were mostly of Swedish descent, while at Finland and Rockpoint, they were Finnish. At Newbank, the people were mostly of British background. (I spoke of the Forsbergs' hospitality at Westpoint; I must mention the wholehearted reception at Rockpoint. The Olsons, Johnsons, Gales, and many more were oh-so-kind and generous.) Some of the older folks confessed that their faith had been restored, while a number of young people and children responded to the salvation invitation and learned to love the Lord. Two churches were later founded in those districts that continued gospel services for years. One church is still in progress and very well attended, while the other decided lately to join hands with friends and worship in town. While a number of my generation have passed on, we have dear friends whom we love to this day. Some of them and some of their children have attended our college. Isn't the Lord good!

Birsay, Sask.
August 8, 1933

To the Canadian Sunday School Mission, Winnipeg, Man.

Brethren:
It gives the people of Rockpoint great pleasure to be able to express to you their appreciation of the wonderful work done here by Henry Hildebrand. He has proved worthy of the trust you placed in him and has faithfully performed his duty at all times.

Like all missionaries he has had difficulties, but his cheery disposition has overcome these. He has enlightened many in the work of God and proved a blessing to them. It has been a wonderful summer for Rockpoint and many have been enlightened and helped. He has opened the way for a great work here, which if carried on, will prove a blessing.

In conclusion, we express our sincere thanks for this privilege you have afforded us, and we hope you may see fit to have him come back next year to complete his wonderful work.

Beautiful life is that whose days
Are spent for others in various ways;
Beautiful life when you have labored for good,
And heard God whisper, "You have done what you could."

Respectfully submitted,
Rockpoint District
Chairman—Olaf Johnson
Sec. Treas.—L. LaBar
Trustee—Arvid Raisor

The CSSM policy provided help for their missionaries' expenses up to $5 a month if they needed it. My total expense account to the CSSM that summer was less than $4, though we took no offerings and I had no outside support. How did I manage? I learned a lesson for life that summer: I needed friends more, much more, than I needed dollars.

At each place I served they took a love-offering for me at the closing service. Moreover, in the river flats, the farmers had a crop that year, and I earned a bit during harvest. Since I could earn my board and room in Winnipeg upon my return to take the post-graduate course, these friends provided sufficient spending money, so that winter I lacked nothing.

It had not been my wish that first summer, nor was it to my liking, to eat in different homes and sleep in different beds most nights. Still, I never looked upon this inconvenience as a sacrifice, but rather as an opportunity. I visited every home in the community to sing my way into their hearts, to read the Bible and pray, and to teach and testify "publicly, and from house to house."

The thing I found difficult, if not well-nigh impossible, came during my excursions into other, poorer districts. On occasion, night after night, I was afflicted—bitten by bed-bugs! They feasted on me until I was plastered with welts. Often I had to sleep with a lad in the same room or bed, and I had to endure the bugs without letting on. At times they teased me about how mean the mosquitoes had been to me that night. I discovered that, if there was one bed-bug in the whole house, it would find me. If I was in the room alone, I would sit on a chair to escape. Even then they would find me. Though my experience was difficult, the kindness of the people, even in these poor districts, was overwhelming. I cannot help but thank God for them. Only once was I called upon to burrow into an old strawstack to escape the night drizzle. But God "gave his beloved sleep," and I woke up, rested and grateful.

An account of this first summer ministry would not be complete without special reference to the kindness of Mr. and Mrs. Jim Bagshaw and family of Birsay. I knew I was welcome in their home, though I must have caused inconvenience, for they needed the bedroom. They listened with interest and prayer to my experiences each week. They made sure my laundry was clean before I started on my circuit each Saturday. It was so dry and hot the summer of 1933 that the Bagshaws harvested no crop. Instead of chafing about it, they accepted the drought as from a Higher Hand and sought to make the most of it.

Each Friday evening they planned a picnic lunch with friends by the River, where we could romp around and swim. The picnic provided the anticipation and relaxation without which I might have been a dull instrument! Their love and their kindness kept me in the field and helped set my destiny. Without them, on the human level, I might not have made it. Dad and Mom Bagshaw are in glory now, and I felt honoured to speak at their funerals. Their children are my friends till this day, supporting our work as did their parents. The reward for refreshing one of God's servants will be theirs in glory.

The second summer mission centered around Carman, Manitoba. The CSSM had pioneered these fields earlier, and I stepped into others' labours. Mr. George Barkman, a schoolmate, took over my appointment of the previous summer in Saskatchewan. This left me free to choose a field nearer Winnipeg. Why nearer Winnipeg?

Mr. and Mrs. Adam welcomed me into their home for the summer. They and their friends invited me to assist in their Sunday schools and lead the preaching services to follow. One school where these services were held was about four miles northeast of Carman, while the other was a few miles west of town. I was welcome also in the Cockburn home west of town. My transportation that year was by bicycle.

It was more of a pastoral ministry that summer. But since the fields were not large, I had opportunity to visit neighbouring districts to introduce the CSSM camping program and the Bible Memory Contest in preparation for it. In some districts I ventured to hold evangelistic services. The Lord gave the increase and added believers to the little flocks. The climax that summer was the baptismal service in the creek that flows through the town. Rev. Lloyd Hunter, the founder of the CSSM, performed the service. It was encouraging to see young believers walking in the obedience of faith. They became the nucleus of two evangelical churches that now serve Carman and its community.

Some of my bicycle excursions led to Winnipeg, a 40-mile distance. A lovely brown-eyed Norwegian "gazelle" was the attraction. That was the lure of Winnipeg! The Adams and Cockburns were kind enough to loan me a car for ventures farther afield.

The surprise, if not an outright shock, that fall was a letter from a Christian businessman in a town called Briercrest in Saskatchewan. It seemed to come out of the blue. It was addressed to me in care of Winnipeg Bible College and forwarded. In the letter a Mr. Whittaker wrote on behalf of a number of Christians who proposed to begin a Bible school and wanted me to lead it. Pioneer missions—yes. Pastoral ministry, by now desirable. Teaching the Word—perhaps, possible. I could trust God for such. But, the founding of a Bible college? Impossible, unthinkable! I concluded that it must have been a matter of mistaken identity and returned the letter.

My cousin and classmate, Rev. Peter Wiebe, took over the Carman field that fall, which released me to return to the city to continue studies for my missionary entrance requirements, so that when the opportunity came, I would be ready. And you guessed it, to cultivate the interest of my bright, brown-eyed, Norwegian sweetheart.

The names of some of God's people to whom I was introduced earlier in my ministry represent so many who became life-long friends and supporters. They sent their children to Briercrest and stood by us over the years. This is true also of many of my colleagues from school days. God gave me friends! The only explanation I have is that God meant to do a work, and He gathered the truest of His people to stand by it. Our God was laying the foundation of a work that is the marvel of the following chapters, a work that all specialists declared could not be done. But God did it!

6

The Birth of a Bible College

The steps of a good man are ordered by the Lord. Psalm 37:23

And so Briercrest Bible College, today one of the largest Bible Colleges in Canada, was born. It derives its name from the village in which it was born—Briercrest. A casual glance at its location would suggest that it just could not be. It is one of the smaller towns of one of the less populated provinces. No wonder visitors to Briercrest shake their heads.

However, a closer study of its people and the believers who gave birth to the school may suggest good reasons why God selected and honoured them with the birth of a Bible College. When I arrived, I noticed that the community was rich in talent, highly cultured, well educated and many had deep religious convictions. God was doing a work among them and drew out a nucleus of people that sought after Him.

Miss Annie Copland, "a high-spirited, strong-minded young woman, a teacher from Ontario, had come to teach in the Sunny Hill School, located a few miles northeast of Briercrest. She was a fine Christian, well-taught in the Scriptures. She had been a missionary candidate to Bolivia but was not permitted to go to the field because of a lack of a traveling companion. This precaution in her case seems doubtful." (See *Miracle on the Prairies,* pp. 16-17).

In the months that followed she met and married one of the finest young men, Walter Hillson. She began a Sunday school in her school until a community church was built in the village—later known as the United Church. Here she faithfully taught the Bible to the adult Sunday school class, but opposition by the liberal wing of the church would not accept her clear Bible teaching of the gospel. This caused her to withdraw from any active part in the local congregation, but some of that class believed and continued to search the Scriptures.

When the Hillson family moved to town from the farm, Annie began to call on a friend who was bedridden with arthritis. Mrs. Fraser loved those visits and especially the Bible reading they had together. "Should we not invite a few more ladies to get like benefits from these Bible studies?" Mrs. Fraser wondered. They did, and the ladies came. The studies developed into evening Bible classes. And so in 1922 the Home Bible Studies began, a good preparation for the birth of a Bible College thirteen years later.

The Bible studies had their impact upon the community. Augmented by good Christian literature and visiting speakers, clear Bible teaching led many to become dissatisfied with the liberal trends of the Sunday school material of the local church. Mr. Sinclair Whittaker, a Sunday school superintendent of many years, introduced the lessons of the Sunday School Times—an influential, evangelical magazine that enjoyed a large circulation. This was resisted, and the only course open to believers of like persuasion was to begin a Sunday school of their own.

A small evangelical church was established, comprised mostly of people converted and/or influenced through the Bible studies led earlier by Mrs. Hillson. The young church had a fine blend of people; some Easterners, some Westerners, some from Central Canada, and some Americans. The church included farmers as well as professional people, educators, businessmen, and members of the Legislative Assembly in Regina. There was also a fine blend of British and Continental Europeans. But they all had one thing in common—they loved the Lord, and they loved His Word. This was the common bond that drew them together.

As I look back, I see a microcosm of what BBC was to be. Moreover, they stamped an imprint upon the College that is evident till this day. They looked to the Lord to send someone to lead them, but they knew not who it might be.

Meanwhile, God was preparing me for this task. Fifty-two years ago, on the second Sunday of my first year in missionary work God began to speak to me. The morning service at Westpoint was very encouraging. It was well attended and the response was excellent.

Then I was on my way to Finland Sunday school in the afternoon, and to the Rockpoint service for the evening.

I was apprehensive, frightened. I feared what might happen that evening. The experience of the first service a week earlier at Rockpoint worried me. The attendance had been good. The children and young people had responded well. They loved to sing choruses and hymns, and they loved the Bible story. But when I proceeded to address the adults, confusion developed. While the younger folks listened with respect, their elders showed disfavour by turning their backs, forming several groups, lighting cigarettes and talking to each other. They turned once in a while to me to laugh out loud. I hardly knew if I should announce another service for the next Sunday, but after some deliberation, I did.

I could not figure out what caused the adults to be so rude. They had given me a friendly welcome into their homes. As I got to know the people of Rockpoint, they turned out to be wholesome, true, and gracious. They were some of the nicest people I had ever met. Now, some 52 years later, their children are friendly and kind to me, and I love them. But why the reaction of the adults that first night?

I learned later that there was not only a communistic hall on the east side of the district near Finland School, but also a like hall on the west side. A few communist representatives determined to wreck my first service and laugh the young preacher out of the community. But it backfired! The Rockpoint people would not stand for such rude conduct.

I did not know this as I made my second circuit. As I reflected on the service the Sunday before, I anticipated all kinds of evil disturbances. What did I do? I stopped the horse at a lonely curve. I can still see the place. A few years ago I took my bride of forty some years and pointed it out to her. I still recognize that bend of the road in the valley west of Dunblane. Although a new road has been built, some of the curves of the old road are still recognizable. I said to my wife, "Honey that's the place where the seed of the Briercrest Bible College was conceived in my heart." I told her the story.

Inger asked, "What did you do after you stopped the horse?"

"I got off and learned to do what I have done so many times in an hour of crisis. I cried to God in my fear and He delivered me. He assured me that He would accompany me, 'My presence shall go with thee, and I will give thee rest.' "

Calmed and reassured, I asked the Lord to give me the opportunity to teach His Word to young people. I was but 21. As I rode and walked from house to house and from district to district, I sensed the awful famine of the Word of God. The old people, I felt, were not listening. The younger at least had remained respectful during that memorable first service. Moreover, I felt as a young man I could identify with young people, and if our country was to hear and know the Word of the Lord, my hope and prayer was with young people. I recalled the command, "And the things that thou hast heard of me among many witnesses, the same commit thou to faithful men, who shall be able to teach others also."

With His reassuring presence, I rose from my knees and swung up on my horse, determined to remain faithful to God's Word. That afternoon and evening God blessed His Word and continued to give the increase spoken of in the previous chapter.

I had cried, "Oh God, give me the opportunity to teach young people the Word of God." At that time I knew nothing of Briercrest, and Briercrest knew nothing of me. But Briercrest gave me the opportunity two years later, and growth was immediately evident, so from that time on we have hardly been able to build big enough or fast enough to accommodate the young people coming in increasing numbers to study the Word of God. Truly God means to be good to their generation. That is the unfolding story.

7

Briercrest Discovers Him

Thou hast been faithful over a few things, I will make thee ruler over many things. Matthew 25:21

Fresh from the experiences of my first summer's ministry, I returned to Winnipeg Bible College for further preparation. The fields I served were handed over to Mr. George Barkman, a classmate and first tenor of our school male quartet. The continuation of the ministry was assured, so I could give myself unhindered to the study and ministry of the Word which I enjoyed.

As I reflect, I marvel how most, if not all, of my opportunities for service swung open on ever so small hinges: commonplace duties discharged with delight.

In the fall of 1933 the College organized its student body into small groups for student ministries in and out of Winnipeg. Since I was a senior, I was selected as a group leader. A pianist, song leader, and five other students were assigned to my group. We worked hard both semesters. The team clicked. By spring we had, I believe, a credible ministry, and plenty of outlets for ministry were entrusted to us. After graduation, we regretfully separated. How often have I witnessed that scene repeated here at Briercrest!

To my delight, I was assigned by the CSSM to the Carman field southwest of Winnipeg. It was exciting to experience the fellowship and enthusiasm of young Christians, climaxed by their baptism that summer. In autumn, another schoolmate accepted the invitation to the Carman field, which freed me to continue with my studies in Winnipeg. That fall the following letter from Mr. Whittaker of Briercrest was forwarded to me.

Sept. 5, 1934

Mr. Henry Hildebrand
Winnipeg, Manitoba

Dear Christian Friend:

For some time past we have felt that the Lord wants a Bible School at Briercrest. As the days go by, He seems to put it more and more upon our hearts. We have discussed this matter on many occasions during the past year with outstanding Christian leaders. With scarcely an explanation, they discouraged us with the undertaking. All seem to think that we should enlarge the capacity of the schools already established. We are, however, anxious to obey God rather than men. If He continues to lead us in this direction, we will follow, regardless of man's opinion.

We fully realize that under the economic conditions prevailing here it will require a great deal of faith to proceed. We have had six crop failures. Ninety percent of the people are on relief. We are, however, blessed with some dozens of praying Christians who are endowed with enough faith to move mountains.

We have prayed if it is His Will that we proceed, that He send us a man to take charge of the school. Your name has been mentioned repeatedly. Our reason for writing is so that you may know what we have in mind, and so that you may give the matter much prayer too, and then report to us His orders.

It has been suggested that we might only be able to take up first-year work for a start. I imagine that six or eight from our immediate vicinity would avail themselves of the opportunity to attend if we go ahead. We have buildings that would be available with little expense, aside from furnishings, and some way may be found to get these.

One reason we have delayed writing to you has been that we hesitated to suggest that you come here when we cannot see our way clear to offer you even a decent living. However, if you are led in this direction, we could only remind you of His promise to the faithful. We can assure you that we will do all we can to make you comfortable.

I may add that I'm taking this matter of writing to you upon myself. I have no authority from the others in our group to contact you in this manner. However, I thought it no harm to let you know what is upon our minds and hearts. Then you can let us know your reaction. Let us both pray earnestly while we await the outcome.

Anxious about lost souls,
Sinclair Whittaker

I felt that the letter belonged to another man, so I returned it with a brief explanation why I thought so.

The second letter from Mr. Whittaker assured me that they had not been mistaken and wanted me to visit Briercrest. By then I had committed myself to further studies in Winnipeg for the winter, so I was in no hurry to answer. I wondered why they felt that I was the man for whom they were looking. How were they even aware of me? I later learned how.

> Our first pastor, Henry Hildebrand, has always been a "special" person to us. It was my privilege to be a student at WBC the year he took his post-graduate work, and I was pianist of the little group he led for Outreach Services. Having been much impressed with his ministry, it is no wonder that we were led to suggest that he be contacted and invited to come to Briercrest . . .
>
> Genevieve Tysdal
> (now Mrs. Alton Blager)

In the meanwhile Mrs. Hillson's Home Bible Studies were shifted to evening Bible studies to allow men and young people to attend. Soon Mr. Whittaker, a prominent businessman and politician, became a Christian and supported them. The Whittaker conversion to the Lord is recorded in the *Miracle on the Prairies.* His home, with its beautiful, spacious lawns, hosted periodic Bible conferences. A number of young people became excited about the Bible studies leading, if possible, to a Bible school. But *there* was the hitch: "if possible."

Canada was in the midst of the great depression. On top of it, the severest prolonged drought was plaguing the prairies, adding greater burdens. The Moose Jaw area became a dustbowl, and Briercrest lay in the heart of it. There was no money for young people to go to school and no jobs to occupy them profitably. Yet interest in daily Bible studies increased, but who would lead them? It was this situation God used to stir Mr. Whittaker to write a third letter in which he enclosed five dollars, hoping I would visit Briercrest to see what God was doing.

Five Dollars—Wow! That was the biggest donation I had received up to that time. Fellow students had testified how they had received monies—large amounts—in answer to prayers. But somehow I had to work for my money at menial tasks. Was it a lack of faith, or was God teaching me the value and accountability of stewardship for the days to come?

I informed Mr. Whittaker that after completing my course in the spring I planned to investigate the possibilities of a summer ministry in the Saskatchewan countryside west of Renown and Watrous. If it was desirable, I could visit Briercrest sometime in May, 1935.

Upon further inquiry, Briercrest began to tug at my heart, where a fine work was going on. The home Bible studies had developed into a regular Sunday school, with occasional preaching services in the evening. The Bible conferences on Mr. and Mrs. Whittaker's lawn were unique. A pastoral ministry by an older, experienced man of God might work, but a Bible school? Impossible!

I was further cautioned that I was too young to shepherd that flock. The group was led by one or two strong-headed women who would make it difficult for me. (Wrongly appraised.) My informants were not so sure that those ladies could even work with each other! What about Mr. Whittaker? they cautioned. He was a politician, and you wouldn't know where you were. Discouraged? I should have been, but the more I prayed about it, the more I was drawn to the saints at Briercrest. So I waited for the unfolding of God's plan.

I travelled to Renown where I was warmly received and offered a home from which to operate. Since no travelling means were offered, I walked from one school district to another, as many as 30 miles a day. I saw good possibilities, with a fair measure of interest in beginning Sunday schools.

One evening when I arrived after a day's walk, I found a letter from Mr. Whittaker welcoming me for a visit to Briercrest. Any time in May would suit fine. Then he informed me that a friend, a Christian businessman from Moose Jaw, Mr. James Miller, was holidaying at the Watrous Resort. He had room in his car for me on Wednesday when he planned to return to Moose Jaw. (I had been introduced to him when we first passed through the city in 1933.) But how to find Mr. Miller in Watrous? No address had been given, and Watrous was famous because of its mineral waters.

I was not daunted however, and searched for the Millers at Watrous. I first checked the Post Office, which was closed on Sundays. I located the postmistress, but she was not disposed to help me on her day off. Besides, I had no street address, and Watrous had many holidayers—how could she know?

Now what? I could pray for guidance.

Why not resort to inquiring from house to house, looking for the Millers as I had looked for customers in Winnipeg while working my way through school (when I chanced to meet my beautiful, brown-eyed gazelle answering one of the doors)? But on which street should

I begin? There were too many. It was like searching for a needle in a hay-stack.

God guided me to look for a street with the type of cottages that a reasonably successful, depression-era businessman might choose for his holiday. Having selected the street, I knocked at the first door, but they had not even heard of the Millers. I looked at the second cottage, but before I stopped at the door—would you know it? I saw the Millers on the veranda of the third cottage. What a relief! They too had been wondering if I would find them. Truly "The steps of a good man are ordered by the Lord . . ." (Psalm 37:23).

The following Wednesday Mr. Miller took me to Moose Jaw to meet Mr. Whittaker in front of the Harwood Hotel. After the introduction and a few friendly exchanges, Mr. Whittaker introduced me to his daughter, Jean, who had been in Moose Jaw for music lessons in preparation for her exam in ARTC. Off we were for Briercrest!

On the way it seemed to me that Mr. Whittaker was a little disappointed with the prospective Bible school leader. His expectations may have been too high and my bodily presence was not too imposing. He hinted that Briercrest may not be the place of my ministry after all. He enumerated some difficulties and felt that perhaps the Renown field might prove to be easier.

Enroute to Briercrest we stopped at a teacherage to pick up Genevieve Tysdal for the Bible study that night which was held in her mother's home, two miles west of Briercrest. We arrived too late for the Bible study, but as we entered, the saints at Briercrest were in the midst of a spirited discussion (a row!) about who should do the baptizing. The living-dining room was fortunately packed—so was the kitchen; we were seated near the back entrance, out of sight. One of the leading ladies of Baptist background wanted the Rev. Hind, pastor of First Baptist Church in Moose Jaw, to do the baptizing. She had already talked with him and he had responded favourably. Another lady of Presbyterian background favoured that an interdenominational minister should do the baptizing. They attempted to draw me into the debate, but I declined. After much discussion, the matter was dropped. Mr. Whittaker then introduced me to the gathering, and I met each person in turn as they filed out.

That was my introduction to the saints at Briercrest. Some of them were embarrassed. Others feared I would be driven away by their heated debate. But I gave much thought to it. I had been cautioned. Now I had seen it with my own eyes. I wondered, "Could they be led?"

But there was another side to the evening. Some commented on the rich Bible study they had enjoyed. I sensed a genuine love for the Word. The more I thought of it, the more positive were my conclusions. The people seemed interested in obeying the Word of God, and I knew of districts in Canada where people cared nothing about the Bible, did not know enough to debate its teaching, and cared less about its requirements. After all, the saints at Briercrest, though from different denominational backgrounds, had agreed on the mode of baptism. It was only a matter of who should do the baptizing.

The Whittakers took me in and gave me excellent hospitality during that visit. I was asked to teach the adult Bible class on Sunday. The lesson was on Ruth chapter 1, following the Sunday School Times lessons and pattern. A chalk-artist would copy the picture from the magazine, summarizing the lesson. One of the class members gave a short talk on the lesson in conclusion. The lesson presented Naomi as a missionary soul-winner, who at tremendous cost to herself and family had brought Ruth, the Moabite, to the people of God.

Never one to look for a disagreement, and equally unwilling to pretend an agreement when conviction and conscience dictated otherwise, I chose to teach the lesson as I understood it. The story concerned the restoration of a backslider. I traced the steps of her backsliding until she had lost all. Then she bethought herself and returned to the people of God, bringing Ruth with her.

They liked what they heard. At last a preacher who believed the Word of God and fearlessly taught it. It fell to Mr. Whittaker's lot that Sunday to explain the chalk artists' picture. He was equal to the occasion. He said, "After what we have heard this morning, this picture, though beautiful, has little meaning. But I'll go through it as I'm supposed to, even though I wholly agree with our new preacher."

I remained in the Whittaker home for two weeks ministering the Word at the Wednesday Bible studies and Sunday adult Bible classes. I was overwhelmed by the way the people loved the Word and loved the Lord. It was a delight to teach a well-taught class. True, there was room for growth in loving one another, but they were most sincere in seeking to obey that Word. Such a people could be led to follow the Lord, I concluded.

I do not recall that an official meeting was held to give me a call, where I received a unanimous vote. That's an ideal we leave for great men! For us common mortals, that stipulation would close most doors. We proceeded by common consensus (Psalm 109:30-31). We agreed that I would proceed with the pastoral ministry and postpone the matter about starting a Bible school.

8

The Founding of a Bible School

Be blameless and harmless, the sons of God, without rebuke.
Philippians 2:15

The saints at Briercrest were unique. What Dr. Cedar said about rural America, I say about rural Saskatchewan. "One of the great things about rural America is that people expect you to be authentic. If you are not, they recognize you from afar." I have often said that our farmers have a sixth sense. They detect a phony at once. But with that discernment there's often a limitation. When they find a minister who is genuine, they hesitate to pay the price for reality. They compare his salary with that of their hired men, and if near it, they wonder where's the spirit of sacrifice? Our people were genuine, and they expected you to be likewise—a most reasonable requirement.

They were also unique in their gender. Beginning with a Ladies' Home Bible Study, the original assembly was comprised mostly of women well-instructed in the Scriptures. The few men we had did not avail themselves of the Home Bible Studies and so, in contrast with the women, knew little of the Bible. Still they were to be my elders.

In fairness to historical accuracy, Briercrest Bible College owes a great debt to the Christian women of Briercrest. Let me refer to just a few:

Mrs. Walter Hillson founded the Home Bible Studies. How she suffered at the hands of religious people who were modernists! She was excommunicated from her adult Sunday school classes by both churches. They could not stand her teaching. Excommunicated, she began Home Study Bible Classes to meet the need for true Bible teaching in the community. She was the dominant figure in the early group, but this does not mean that she was arrogant or dictatorial. She was valiant for truth. I found her most supportive, loving, and loyal at all times. Mrs. Hillson appreciated a true Bible ministry.

Mrs. Sinclair Whittaker had studied the Bible with the help of Scofield's Correspondence Course offered by Moody Bible Institute. She was sound in her thinking and living. She was blessed with a delicious sense of humour. She deeply trusted the Lord and sought to follow His teaching. She too was an excellent Bible teacher and an inspiration to younger Christians.

Mrs. Andrew Glen was well educated and a capable Bible teacher. She was a woman with a fine culture, noted for her integrity and steadfast abounding in the work of the Lord. Her family was a credit to the Christian testimony, two of whom became missionaries to Africa.

Mrs. Ernie Sanderson was one of Mrs. Hillson's first converts. She was an outgoing person and vocal about the Lord and His Word. She was musically talented, leading junior choirs and thrilling her audience with a rich, melodious mezosoprano voice.

Mrs. Hazel Tysdal sought the Lord and found in Him salvation and healing of a broken heart (Psalm 34:18). She loved to do personal work and loyally assured us of her backing. She was both Mary and Martha. She waited much upon the Lord, and she faithfully served the servants of God in particular and the people of God as a whole.

These women were well instructed in the Word, and the men could profitably ask questions of them at home as to the deeper meaning of the Word. They loved the Word, and the servant of the Lord with his handmaiden. We could count on their prayers and loyal backing in all ventures of the Lord. The women's devotion to the Lord and to us was an example for elders and church members to emulate. As Spurgeon put it, ". . . if they would follow a broomstick as they followed me, the work would have succeeded."

This is how these early saints looked upon their youthful pastor. (The reader should remember how graciously the Gospel heals responsive memories.)

> Never did any of us feel that our pastor was not qualified to teach our group . . . If she had felt comment was needed, Mrs. Hillson would have

offered advice or assistance, as would any of the others . . . The attitude was, "Let no man despise thy youth." We all felt our pastor had been sent by the Lord, and I can remember no criticism of him.

We appreciated his positive attitude—his tact in dealing with some of the more impetuous members and wisdom in the goals and standards that were set. In all that was done, as we look back, we can see that the Lord took a small, unimportant group of people and used us for His glory in a way we could never have foreseen, and we praise Him.—Mrs. Genevieve (Tysdal) Blager

* * *

. . . I remember him playing the guitar and teaching us choruses, and directing the male quartet in which he sang. We respected his diligence and . . . knowledge about the Bible. He enjoyed sports and encouraged us to have games . . .

Some of his stronger points: His German thoroughness and self-discipline, his keen mind and willingness to learn, his knowledge of the Bible and his love for the Book, his courage and ability to adapt and to get along with difficulties, his strong personality.

Some of his weaker points: His limited education and German background . . . at that time there was still prejudice regarding those of German descent.—Mrs. Jean (Whittaker) Rohde

* * *

It was a profitable summer with Sunday school in the suite above Mr. Whittaker's store and Sunday evening services on Mr. and Mrs. Whittaker's lawn. Mid-week Bible studies were held in different homes. The men responded and identified themselves with the work and with the Lord. Their wives and children who had prayed for them were ecstatic. This accounts largely for the favour that God gave me with them.

The saints at Briercrest truly, "gave the bonnie lad their hearts without reserve." More than a dozen of our people were baptized by the Rev. S. E. Forsberg during the summer conference. By fall we had rented a former hardware store and converted it into a meeting hall for Sunday evening services. All was going well and we were happy together with the people of God.

On Wednesday nights I would teach the book of Romans. We had come to Romans chapter 10. I pointed out the difference between salvation by works and by grace. Somehow I felt the rowing that evening was difficult. It had been hard work and I did not enjoy the usual freedom in the lesson, but I prayed quietly that God would honour His Word. After the service, one of my leading deacons took me aside and said, "Tush, tush, Henry, that's dry stuff. Folks won't come out to hear such. Select more interesting topics on prophecy such as, 'Is Mussolini the Antichrist?' "

While he was admonishing me, there was a knock on the door and in stepped Reg Hubbel. Reg could neither read nor write at the time. He was a heavy smoker and drinker with a fierce temper and foul tongue. With tears in his eyes he stuttered out, "I always thought youse tried to get to heaven by good works and keeping the ten commandments. I knows youse was hypocrites because youse couldn't do it. Tonight I learned for the first time the difference between law and grace and that youse expect to go to heaven by grace because Christ died for your sins. If there is grace for youse, there must be grace for me; how can I get saved?"

By now my deacon had exited by another door. Reg became a Christian right there and then. He threw his tobacco away, gave up his drinking, learned to read and write, enrolled in our Bible school, studied hard and became one of the most effective witnesses in the Canadian Sunday School Mission, and later, the most welcome speaker at the rescue mission in Vancouver. The director said to me, "When Reg is due to speak, the house is full."

The following morning my elder apologized to me and said, "I sure made a fool of myself. I claimed your lecture was too deep and dry, when the village bum who can neither read nor write can understand it. Carry on, Henry!"

Harvest time had come, and the farmers wanted all hands to harvest. I was approached about stooking by Mrs. Sanderson after one prayer meeting. I mentioned I was free Thursday and Friday, Monday and Tuesday, but Saturday and Wednesday I needed to prepare for my lectures. I stooked Thursday and Friday for them. When they asked about coming on Monday and Tuesday, I told them I had promised to help the Hillsons. So I moved about helping different farmers, but taking no wages of them, much as I needed finances. I felt Briercrest would likely develop into a long-time ministry, and I did not want anybody to make a hired man out of me. They could put what they liked into the offering box on Sunday. They knew I was not afraid of hard, physical work. The farmers found the preacher's sermons were then more welcome.

The nearer we came to fall, the more frequently the question kept cropping up, "What about opening classes for Bible studies this fall?" But now I was enjoying my pastoral ministry thoroughly, and I had plenty to do. I had plans for an extensive outreach. But what about classes during the winter? We had to face this question head on, so I called some of the leading brethren to consider this matter after a Wednesday Bible study and prayer meeting.

We agreed that if we could get a certain young man to come and lead the Bible school we would proceed. I would continue to lead the young church and assist him in the school. We contacted our prospect, but he had other plans. We met again the following Wednesday and agreed that we should postpone opening regular Bible classes indefinitely.

On Thursday morning Mrs. Hillson phoned, asking for an appointment. She and Mrs. Whittaker wanted to see me about a very important matter. At two o'clock, the last Thursday in September, these two godly women came to see me. After a few formalities, Mrs. Hillson came to the point—her chin quivering a bit, a sign that she was deeply agitated. "Isabel phoned this morning and said that the news was not so good. You men have decided not to go ahead with Bible classes, is that correct?"

"Yes," I replied, "that's true."

"Are you sure you have the mind of the Lord?"

"We think so," I replied.

"Why?" she asked.

"Because we were unable to get the right man to lead the school."

"We have the right man," she retorted. "We prayed for the right man for a number of years and God answered our prayer and brought you to us. You are God's man for us. We will stand behind you in prayer and will give you all the help we possibly can."

I began to respond favourably, for I did want the backing and prayers of these godly women who I highly respected.

"Will you men reconsider?" asked Mrs. Hillson. Together we committed the all-important question to the Lord. As they left, Mrs. Whittaker gave me counsel that I have often sought to follow: "Trust in the Lord with all thine heart; and lean not unto thine own understanding. In all thy ways acknowledge Him, and He shall direct thy paths" (Proverbs 3:5-6).

I was left pondering the issue. The women were committed; the men would likely go along, but what about the young people? Would anyone have sufficient confidence in me to enroll? I waited on the Lord and kept my ears open. The answer was soon forthcoming.

It sprinkled that Sunday so we had to retreat from the lawn to the Whittaker home for the evening service. After the service Odd Brygmann edged up and shyly said, "I hear we may open the Bible school after all."

"Depends," I replied, "will anybody want to enroll and study with me?"

"Sure," came back his spontaneous answer, "I will."

"So will I," answered Reg Glen who had moved closer.

"And so will others," they assured me.

Armed with this response, I went once more to the Lord pleading, "but what and how can I teach? I love to teach thy Word, but I'm not trained to organize and lead a Bible school." The Lord assured me that He required nothing more of me than to pass on the things I had learned from the Bible at home, at church, and in Bible school. "And the things that thou hast heard of me among many witnesses, the same commit thou to faithful men, who shall be able to teach others also" (2 Tim. 2:2).

Now fully assured in my own heart, I had one concern, "Would the men reconsider?" They did! The decision was made to go ahead with the Bible school that fall. I made one request of them, that they would consider my youthful inexperience and pray for me. A house for classes and residence was rented for $5 a month, known as the Nichols House. Several had indicated that they wanted to enroll, but Monday, October 19, registration day would be the test.

It was a bleak, cloudy, blustery day with snow flurries off and on. The house was spic and span. The rooms were furnished, and I had moved in to take possession of one bedroom that would serve as a study, library and office. We were ready—we didn't have to wait long. The first registrant was Percy Hazelhurst, about twice my age. Others followed and settled in that day. Tuesday morning we opened the school with 11 eager, enthusiastic students.

The faculty was more apprehensive in those days than were the students. Mrs. Hillson and Mrs. Whittaker assisted me, along with other experienced teachers who had diligently studied the Bible. Jean Whittaker, with an ARCT in piano, taught music, and Margaret Rusk, also a teacher by profession, taught English and doubled as secretary-treasurer. The five of us led the infant school. The board of directors was not organized until the fall of the third year, when such was needed for incorporation with the province. Growth was immediately realized. By the second semester, 17 students had enrolled.

You can imagine our struggles. I was teaching Bible, Theology, and Church History, 16 hours a week, all of the courses for the first time around. I also continued leading the local church, ministering Sundays and Wednesdays as well. But everyone was so helpful and would participate in turn, which made the load so much easier and more pleasant. To my relief, Donald McMillan came, another WBC graduate, who joined us the second semester. The presence of God was evident, morale remained high, and we had a profitable year, a good omen for things to come.

9

Early Years at Briercrest: Those Were The Days!

Let them shout for joy, and be glad. Psalm 35:27

Life at Briercrest Bible College in the early years was filled with fun. The studies and course development are best described by Rev. Orville Swenson, a student that first year and one of the first three graduates. He became one of many Briercrest graduates who received the school's highest honour and expression of confidence. He was invited to join the faculty.

Mr. Swenson joined the staff in 1937 and has been with us for 48 years, including 40 years as principal of the Bible School Department. How well he filled his position and how he stood with me for four decades are discussed in a later chapter. You will enjoy Rev. Swenson's description of those early years.

My Introduction to BBC

Personal Reminiscences by Rev. Orville P. Swenson

The opening of the Bible school in Briercrest in the fall of 1935 proved to be the providential answer to my need. Although I had been able to attend the Winnipeg Bible Institute the previous year, the economic conditions affecting our family made it impossible for me to return. Upon hearing of Mr. Henry Hildebrand's arrival in Briercrest, and, learning that he, in association with some local folk, was endeavoring to provide Biblical and theological instruction for a number of others in similar circumstances to mine, I felt that I should try to enroll, which I did. Arriving two weeks after classes had begun, I was promptly assigned to my work detail as assistant to the male cook, Percy Hazelhurst, with whom I shared a room just off the kitchen.

The rented house in which we lived and studied had neither plumbing nor electric lighting, and was heated by two coal burning stoves. The dining and living room areas were partitioned off to serve as classrooms, and the upstairs bedrooms housed the other five fellows beside Mr. Hildebrand and his associate, Donald McMillan, who joined the faculty the second semester. Thus entrenched in our all-male domicile, we not only survived, but thrived in our masculine domain, taking some degree of pride in our ability to keep the place "relatively immaculate," and in the main, presentable to the ladies who came during the day to study with us or to attend the mid-week prayer meeting.

That weekly prayer meeting was a blessing in more ways than one, for it was the time of replenishing our larder with edibles that bore the feminine touch—pies, cakes, cookies, fruit preserves. Staples such as meat and vegetables were brought in by the friends and supporters of the infant school. This supplied the needed variety to supplement our otherwise unexciting rations composed of bread, pancakes, and hash (this last named delicacy was called "Houchemagouchs" by the creator of the concoction).

And speaking of pancakes, these gastronomical delights proved to be not only edible and "fulfilling," but amazingly durable, as on at least one occasion their tensile strength was tested to the limit of their elastic and adhesive quality by some joker (who shall remain unnamed) who cut a 3-inch diameter hole in the middle of several and played ring-toss on the knob of the kitchen door!

One evening, the patience of our elder brother, the cook, wore thin through constant interruptions from some less-studious residents of our normally quiet dormitory. He decided to lock the door between his kitchen bastion and the rest of the house, to ensure privacy. That constituted a challenge to the rest, who decided that entrance must be gained to that now-forbidden sanctuary at any cost. Reginald Glen, known to many for his ingenuity, came up with a plan. Why not smoke him out? He would have to open the door in order not to suffocate.

Knowing that a ladder was leaning against the house, Reg went outside, positioned the ladder for easy access to the roof above the kitchen, and, taking a square piece of board, proceeded to the rooftop and placed it over the chimney. Not long afterward, a sputtering, coughing cook unlocked the door and came out, wondering what ill wind had caused his normally clean-burning kitchen stove to backfire—that evening, of all times!

Indeed, we had our times of hilarity, frivolity, and fun! But these were periodic, not continual, for all of us were at school for a serious purpose, with an over-riding holy motivation. God had called each of us to this place to study His Word, and this became the dominant factor in our daily routine.

Mr. Hildebrand and Donald McMillan, both trained at Winnipeg Bible Institute during the presidency of Simon Forsberg, were scholarly and well-disciplined. Together they mapped out a course of studies very similar to the one they had completed upon their graduation. The subjects included Biblical Theology, Bible—both analysis and exposition, Spiritual Life, Personal Evangelism, Missions, Church History, Homiletics, Speech, Pastoral Theology, and Music. The men were aided by some local women, some of whom were former school teachers. The classes at first met four days per week, later five. In the process of time, other subjects were added to round out a well-balanced curriculum. We had regular chapel services, and from time to time, we were challenged through the ministries of visiting pastors and missionaries. They, as well as our regular instructors, held before us constantly the challenge of the ministry, at home and abroad. In the hearts of many of the students that was destined to bring forth a spiritual commitment. This commitment would eventuate in a commissioning from on High, putting both men and women into the Lord's service. At the close of many a class, chapel, or worship service on the Lord's day, many of us were led to pray sincerely, "Lord, what wilt Thou have me to do?"

A highlight in my life, and in the lives of two of my classmates, was our graduation day. It was in the spring of 1937, after we had completed two years of study in Briercrest, each of us having taken a year in Winnipeg. Instead of arranging for a visiting speaker to give a commencement address, we three were given the staggering responsibility (or so it appeared to us at the time) of addressing the conference audience.

To this day I have not forgotten the awesomeness of that assignment. For me, a crowd-shy, intensely nervous farm boy, to face a hundred or more guests whose expectations were very high (or so I thought), and to deliver a message without forgetting what I had prepared to say, seemed an insurmountable task indeed. I had no fears for Margaret Rusk or Reginald Glen, for they appeared to possess a poise in front of people that I did not have. But God saw me through that eventful hour, and in the process, taught me that I could trust Him to give special grace for special responsibilities—a lesson I badly needed in view of what He had planned for me for the days ahead. Incidentally, the text I used that day was Colossians 1:27-29 which reads, in part, ". . . Christ in you, the hope of glory: whom we preach, warning every man, and teaching every man in all wisdom; that we may present every man perfect in Christ Jesus: whereunto I also labour, striving according to His working, which worketh in me mightily." If I had only listened to that text and grasped its import, I might have saved myself from bordering on nervous collapse.

Following graduation, I went that summer to the Lucky Lake area to preach and teach Sunday schools in several school houses. One day a letter arrived from Mr. Hildebrand asking me to consider coming to Briercrest to teach, beginning in the fall of 1937. Again I faced a crisis, for this was something I had not so much as dreamed of. Yet, in my heart I had settled this much, months before, while at school: I was willing to go where God wanted me, and do whatever He asked of me. But to teach and to preach at Briercrest! This was too much. So I argued, "But Lord, that will mean facing in the classroom several who have been fellow students, in some cases, classmates in courses we took together. And then there are family problems. My father's health is failing, and my help will be needed on the farm." I prayed, committing the prospects and the problems to God and asking for clear direction by the time I needed to reply to the invitation.

One factor in the invitation appealed to me—Mr. Hildebrand specified that I would be asked to teach theology. That was my favorite subject from the start of my Bible school training, and the prospect of handling a comprehensive course in that area captivated my imagination. I talked it over with my parents, and my father assured me that he would be able to obtain hired help and so released me to Briercrest, if I so desired. Despite my fears, the prospect of teaching intrigued me, and with some trepidation I sent a letter to Mr. Hildebrand stating that I would come.

The opening of the 1937 fall term found me in Briercrest, beginning a teaching career in the field of theology that has, at the point of writing, lasted for 48 years. As time went on, other subjects were added to my area of study, such as Dispensational Truth, Pastoral Theology, Christian Evidences, and some Bible analysis or exposition courses. I found all of these subjects challenging, for in every case there was opportunity to amplify and make practical the truths that are inherent in systematic and Biblical theology. Both Reginald Glen and Margaret Rusk returned to teach for a time, until Reg went to Africa as the first Missionary out of BBC, and Margaret was led to enter the teaching profession in our Saskatchewan public school system.

Although there were other Bible schools or colleges in existence that offered courses in a variety of specialized fields, our administration felt that in those early years of struggle and growth, a proliferation of courses would prove to be premature, so we continued to emphasize the basic three-year program which seemed best adapted to the needs of the greater percentage of the students who looked to us for training. In due course BBC has expanded its curriculum to include a number of specialized majors, but it continues to offer the time-tested and time-honoured foundational program leading to a diploma. I am convinced that the multiplication of course offerings too early in the development of a Bible college can put too great a demand upon the teaching resources and ultimately weaken rather than strengthen the total academic and spiritual impact of the institution.

Early in my career, I became firmly persuaded that sound doctrine and holy living are inseparably bound in the purpose of God for His people. The pastoral epistles of Paul are replete with declarations of the value of sound doctrine and with corresponding exhortations to godly living as its natural consequence. For example, Paul counselled Titus, "But speak thou the things which become sound doctrine . . . in all things showing thyself a pattern of good works, in doctrine showing uncorruptness, gravity, sincerity, sound speech that cannot be condemned" (Titus 2:1, 7, 8). He instructed Timothy, "Till I come, give attendance to reading, to exhortation, to doctrine . . . take heed to thyself and unto the doctrine; continue in them: for in doing this thou shalt both save thyself, and them that hear thee" (1 Timothy 4:13, 16). In chapter six, Paul refers to "doctrine which is according to godliness" (v. 3), and in his second letter to Timothy he gives that positive imperative, "Preach the Word: be instant in season, out of season; reprove, rebuke, exhort with all longsuffering and doctrine, for the time will come when they will not endure sound doctrine" (2 Timothy 4:2, 3).

I encountered these plain and powerful pronouncements of the apostle early in my teaching ministry. I faced their implications for the work to which I had been called and adopted as a primary goal for my life the task of indoctrinating my students in the truth of God. I have never said to a student, "Here are some fine teachings that you may accept or reject as you feel inclined," or "Here are a number of options; look at them, and then make up your mind as to what you want to believe." On the contrary, I have dared to affirm without apology or hesitation, "This is God's unchangeable truth. This you must believe!" This approach to indoctrination I profoundly believe to be in keeping with the apostle's tone, "Teach these truths, Timothy, and encourage all to obey them. Some may deny these things, but they are sound, wholesome teachings of our Lord Jesus Christ, and are the foundation for a godly life. Anyone who says anything different is both proud and stupid" (1 Timothy 6:2-4, *The Living Bible Paraphrase*).

A healthy dogmatism based on a firm insistence on Biblical truth, I hold to be the right approach, and I have had occasion to witness its benefits in the lives of many. It has been most gratifying to receive letters from students of yesteryear telling how they are still using the theology classnotes in their Sunday school teaching, and expressing appreciation for my insistence that they understood the terminology and definitions I gave them. One note received from an appreciative student reads,

> Mr. Swenson: Thank you very much for teaching me Theology. I was brought up in a Christian home, but I never knew many of the things I learned this semester, and last. I used to believe that salvation could be lost, and that there would only be a partial rapture, and many other things that caused me to live in constant fear. Now I really do know the peace and love of God—the way I always hoped it would be, but thought it was too good to be true.

I am not alone in receiving such encouraging notes from students who have benefited from our instruction, but this is one of the rewards a teacher receives in this life which makes us feel that all the effort we have put into our preparation is very much worthwhile.

To clarify the present purpose, let me say that this chapter is intended to present, not a comprehensive summary of my lengthy tenure as teacher or principal, but rather, as the title indicates, merely a resumé of the earliest days that marked my introduction to BBC.

One final word—if ever I had aspired to popularity or fame, I should have to confess to failure. But if I have helped a goodly number of my students to a better knowledge and appreciation of the age-abiding doctrinal truths of the Word of God, I shall be grateful and content to accept an epithet given me by some appreciative soul: "Mr. Theology." I accept it as a compliment and honour, and I covet no other.

Messrs. Swenson and Glen were asked to join our faculty after their graduation to replace the McMillan brothers who had assisted us so ably the first two years.

To accommodate the incoming students in 1936 and '37, we rented the Jamieson Building. It served as classrooms, kitchen/dining hall, administration office and the upstairs as women's dorm.

The year 1937 was the driest and most difficult year of the depression. Even the sloughs failed to yield grain or feed. Talk about duststorms! It took the heart out of the staunchest of Westerners. "It may be the wisest move to close the school for a few years, everybody will understand. This is the toughest year of all." This suggestion came from a thoughtful but discouraged businessman. But we stayed with it, and school opened that fall with a slight increase to 35 students.

It proved to be a great year, and my enthusiasm was contagious. Believing now in the future of the school, Mr. Whittaker proposed incorporation with the Saskatchewan government, which required the organization of a board of directors. Mr. Whittaker was chosen to be chairman and Mr. Andrew Glen and I as members. In due time more were invited to the board to give counsel and direction to the school. The board's development, composition and contribution is also exciting.

Mr. Whittaker defined its responsibility very simply, "Henry, it will be your duty as a faculty to get the students, and it will be ours as a board to make sure we have adequate room for them." This proved to be a great undertaking, but over the years the Board of Directors has risen to the challenge.

Briercrest Bible College became known to the Christian public for its survival, enthusiastic students, and its radio broadcast, which began in the summer of 1937—another story of great interest. To provide for the anticipated space needs, Mr. Whittaker had his eye on every vacant building in town. The old Yale Hotel, if renovated, would make a great place. It did. A deal was made with the town fathers, and we built a town hall (still standing) in exchange for the hotel. The hotel required a lot of renovation, but when the students, now double in number, arrived, all was ready. The details of the hard work that summer and God's preservation from fire is told in *Miracle on the Prairies.*

On opening Sunday of the semester it became evident that if the new town hall was good for the town, it was even more useful for our public rallies. Dr. Lowry, a very effective radio evangelist, was guest speaker for the dedication of our newly-acquired facilities. The old Yale Hotel was the first building the school owned.

As the years passed, the students continued to come and we purchased or rented all available space in town to accommodate them—110 precious lives, each with tremendous potential. The war years soon took their toll, however, and the student body shrank to 51 during the last year of the war. Mr. Whittaker foresaw the influx of students after the war and made preparation for it, which ultimately led to Caronport, our present home. But the 11 years at Briercrest were precious and will remain as a fragrant memory. Those years laid the foundation of the college and stamped its imprint upon it.

If under God I helped to shape BBC, the college also shaped me and prepared me for the years ahead.

10

Enter The Heroine

Whoso findeth a wife findeth a good thing, and obtaineth favour of the Lord. . . . and a prudent wife is from the Lord.
Proverbs 18:22; 19:14

Two shall be born a whole wide world apart
And one day out of darkness they shall stand
And read life's meaning in each other's eyes.
P. S. Beniter

Enter the heroine, the Madonna of Elm Crescent—a woman of marked character and devoted godliness, most exalted among the daughters of Eve. This is the story of the person who became the first lady of Caronport for over 40 years.

Inger Soyland Hildebrand was born in 1914, the year that World War I was ravishing Europe. Befitting the beauty and grace of Norway, the first darling of Olof and Kari Soyland of Aalgaard immediately captivated them with dancing hazel-brown eyes that sparkled as if anticipating a great future. Four brothers and one sister soon followed. The children were heirs of a good father and a godly mother whose Baptist convictions were infused early in life. Inger was converted at nine during evangelistic services in her school at Opsal. Her mother took her by the hand and led her to the Saviour. She was later baptized by Pastor Jensen of the Norwegian Baptist Church in Winnipeg, Canada.

Travelling and seeing other countries is in the blood of most European young people. Inger, with her cousin, decided to visit her aunt in Canada. Canada was pictured to be the land of promise, but the depression struck, which at first delayed and then eventually cancelled her return to Norway.

It happened this way. While the return trip was delayed, she met a young bride and her husband by the name of Ella and George Sinderson, graduates of Winnipeg Bible College and missionary candidates to Africa. During a service in the Norwegian Baptist Church, their fervent testimony touched the young lady, recentiy from Norway. She too was constrained to consider missionary work. To prepare for it, she enrolled at Winnipeg Bible College in the fall of 1931. Her struggle with the language and study courses in a strange land soon gave way to a different struggle, one that was much more exciting and more difficult to understand.

She wasn't long at school until "Prince Charming" to be, a second-year Bible college student, took notice of her. When he first saw her, she had the unspoiled sweetness of a young lady that led him to pray with the poet, "God keep her so natural, so lovely, so nice." Sometime later, at the foot of the stairs on her way to a prayer meeting, there was that "embarrassing yet delightful collision of the eyes." He thought he saw the adorable grace of marked luster coming into her hazel-brown eyes when interest was challenged. He later called it, "that twinkle of a Soyland's eyes." She was a man's woman—every bit of her five-foot-four. For him, it was love at first sight.

After this first encounter, I knew that I was not gifted for the single bliss. Visions of what was to be surged through my mind and stirred every recess of my heart. Still I lost not my mind. It has been said that if you expect or demand perfection or nothing—you end up with nothing. Even in my dreamiest moments I never fantasize perfection. I was too practical for that. I kept my feet on the ground. I lived with reality. Hence I experienced no disappointments after the wedding. Partially because I discovered that I *had* gotten perfection; well—almost. At no other point was "the unreasonable grace of God more to be observed than when God brought this adorable young lady into [my] life." Truly God guided all the way.

There was only one problem. Fair lady had responded favourably at first, but then she had second thoughts, and those second thoughts disturbed me. I tried to dispell them, but to no avail—she said "No" to my wooings. She felt she was being rushed. She was young and had plenty of time, and she was preoccupied with her schooling and sense of mission.

But I wasn't about to settle for "no." I discerned further that each "no" left the door a bit more ajar for future consideration. Each letter ended up with a beautiful Bible promise—which I took to be as an encouragement. But I was not content with a half-opened door. I decided to test the waters. I had one date to a musicale with another school mate, and the next thing I noticed, the door was opening, with a welcome mat to boot.

I had one more concern. I sought my father's blessing. To marry outside the Mennonite fold was frowned upon in those days. Dad had but two questions: "Is she a Christian?" and "Is she baptized?" Assured of both, he gave his blessing. When I brought her home, he loved her at once and said, "Son, God has led you to a wise and gracious lady. She is just like your mother." Then I wrote to her parents in Norway, who likewise gave their blessing.

And so loving looks, tender tones, and clasping hands gave way to verbal confessions and commitments to each other and to God. In spite of the depression and my busy school days, I was able to slip a diamond ring with all its significance onto the finger of that graceful hand. The distance between Briercrest and Winnipeg seemed so long! I was not able to span it too often, perhaps three or four times a year. The two years of waiting until Briercrest was willing to support a married couple served to test our love and gave my Madonna opportunity to evaluate how she would fit into the life of one leading a struggling Bible school. Some of God's gracious dealings in preparing both of us for that awesome task are precious, but too sacred to allow to become common property. Again God was leading all the way.

The wedding took place on August 12, 1937 in the Norwegian Baptist Church in Winnipeg. It was a simple, moving wedding. Pastor Swennung married us. Inger's cousin was the maid of honour, while my brother was the groomsman. The men of the congregation had decorated the church, and the ladies provided a tasty meal at the reception. My father and all my immediate people were able to be with us, and we felt God honoured the occasion.

Kind friends had provided for our honeymoon, a lovely cottage at Victoria Beach on Lake Winnipeg. Away from watchful eyes of well-meaning friends, we set out to deepen our relationship, and blend our lives together for the task that awaited us at Briercrest. We have continued to build that relationship, and the honeymoon continues into our 49th year with deeper meaning. How good the Lord has been in preserving us for each other and for Him these precious years.

Back in Winnipeg, we packed our belongings into a 1927 Chevrolet that Mr. Whittaker had donated to the cause. This car served us well and took us over the dusty road to Regina and Briercrest. The year 1937 was the driest year of the great depression, and Inger had her first look at the dust-bowl of Saskatchewan.

Arriving at the Sanderson home near Briercrest, our people gave us a warm reception. They loved my bride and took her into their hearts for keeps. They discerned that she would bring taste, dignity and fidelity to the Hildebrand home and to the young college. The bachelor's suite above Whittaker's store was transformed to be our first home, and what an inviting home it became! We loved it. The second year we moved into a two-room suite at the Yale Hotel, acquired by the School the summer of 1938. We spent a few delightful years in this second-storey suite in the dormitory area of the school. For the remaining five years in Briercrest, we lived on the lower floor of the dormitory known as the Gilroy House.

When the School moved to Caronport, the firehall became our home for 14 years. This building has been declared a "Heritage Centre." Since then, the new house on Elm Crescent has become our home. Each of these places soon felt the elegant touches of the hostess, and we have grateful memories of each. So do many of our guests. During the first 15 years, the School had no guest accommodations. The Hildebrand home was the guestroom. Of this world's goods we had little, but we were rich in Christ, and rich in each other. I hope I don't do violence to the Scriptures when I apply part of Jeremiah 2:2 to my young bride, "I remember thee, the kindness of thy youth, the love of thine espousals, when thou wentest after me in the wilderness, in a land that was not sown." She faced a life of possible poverty, with no prospects that it would ever be otherwise, yet found a life of fulfillment beyond the fondest expectation.

She sank her interests into mine in our home and school. Often upon my return from ministering to our constituency, she would brief me as to what happened in the chapels which she attended regularly, or what took place on the campus, its atmosphere, etc. She found her place in the home, and, as one person wrote,

> (her) greatest joy (was) in the circle of her home and family, yet when duty called her to the responsibilities of social life, her natural grace and culture were admired by everybody . . . She made her home the best place on earth for her husband and family. Everybody understood that her wise counsel and support was one of the secrets of her husband's success.

But she knew just where to stop, never crossing that mystic boundary where "Mrs. True Helpmeet becomes Madam Married Interference." She deliberately hid herself. Her modesty was a copy of the great wives of the faith in the Bible. Her love never made her a mere unthinking echo of myself, but she always spoke out in Norwegian independence. Her practical wisdom and common sense helped us to face reality, and so look to God for His help. This was all part of that fully surrendered heart which makes the living sacrifice acceptable to God and daily life so pleasant. She had chosen to walk by the side of her husband clear to the gates of glory.

Five times she made the pilgrimage of pain and came home holding tiny bundles—Marcia '38, Evelyn '40, David '44, Paul '51, Glen '57.

She looked well to the ways of her household. When I was in journeyings often, she stayed by the stuff. She would lead the children in Bible reading and prayer. In turn, each of our five children ascended "the bright staircase of Mother's prayer," unto eternal salvation. When Glen, on one occasion, complained that there was no democracy in our home, I promptly explained to him that when Dad was away, Mother had 51 percent of the votes. There remained no accounts to settle when Father came home from long journeys. As a result, the children looked forward to my return. On one occasion Marcia said to her Mother, "Dad must be about due home because he must be running out of laundry." Laundromats were not so accessible those days.

And when I was home, I was often on the platform leading or speaking at the services, while she was alone in the audience, struggling with our children. Without a murmur she accepted that difficult job. The children belong in church. In a family class, a mother insisted that junior could not be expected to be in the house of God. "As soon as the service starts, my boy fusses and frets until I take him out." I answered, "My wife has the answer."

"Oh, please, tell me what it is!"

"When Junior fusses until she takes him out, she makes the outside so uncomfortable that he is anxious to get back into church—he verily finds the house of God a place of refuge."

In our home the children felt free to discuss issues of interest and even debate them at the family meal. All five are natural-born talkers. They must have gotten it from their Mother! She gave her's away. I kept mine. When she does open "her mouth, there is wisdom, and in her tongue is the law of kindness" (Proverbs 31:26). At no time would their mother allow them to answer saucily or debate indiscreetly. Heated as debate might get there must be respect for Father and for each other. Indeed, she looked well to the ways of her household.

Do not feel that I have gotten carried away in this chapter. You shouldn't hold that against me. I have good reasons. Since my Madonna of Elm Crescent deliberately chose to submerge herself in my life, that the labours in this college may be more telling, I believe that this chapter should set forth her labour of love so that our age can see that she belongs among the historic wives of the faith. Her quiet spirituality, calm and common-sense outlook on life, and her fine Norwegian restraint formed a perfect balance to my impulsive, active personality.

It was not until 1956 that a trip to see her people in Norway was possible. All her immediate relatives reside there. When the Bergensfjord made its maiden voyage and docked in Stavanger Harbour, many, oh so many, of Inger's relatives were on hand to welcome us. It was a moving experience to see her parents, sister, and brothers welcome Inger home with her husband at her side—after so many years. The wedding breakfast in her father's house was a heart-warming experience. Norway compares well with beautiful British Columbia, and the people are so gentle and gracious. We love our people and they accepted me fully at Inger's side. The parting at Stavanger and the trip home to Canada was not as difficult as I had imagined. There was another welcome waiting for us in our own family in Regina—all a parable of parting here and greeting the members of our family someday on the golden shore.

In later years the financial pressures have eased and the people of God have taken care of us very well. Since the family has flown the "coop" and all have married fine Christian mates, Inger travels with me most of the time, and both of us are enjoying good health. Inger's hobbies are reading and knitting. She reads more books than I do.

Mrs. Sanderson of Briercrest loves to tell how well Madonna took care of her children in difficult financial times. A number of women had gathered in the hardware store at Briercrest. Inger, with our two little girls, walked by. Said the proprietor to them, "Look, ladies, that's the kind of a young mother our children need. Would we had more of them!"

When Mr. Gladstone was asked as to what he ascribed his great capacity for work, he answered, "I am happy at home."

All her life Inger has maintained the captivating combination of physical charm coupled with a deeply spiritual nature. The current of our love has deepened, becoming more exalted as the years roll by. "She seeks no renown for herself; his honour is reflected upon her, and she rejoices in it. She will defend his name with her dying breath; safe enough is he where she can speak of him . . ."

I could never have done the work without this understanding, godly woman at my side. She has been a good wife to me over all these years and a good mother to our children.

> The heart of her husband doth safely trust in her, so that he shall have no need of spoil. She will do him good and not evil all the days of her life. . . . Her husband is known in the gates, when he sitteth among the elders of the land. . . . Strength and honour are her clothing; and she shall rejoice in time to come. She openeth her mouth with wisdom; and in her tongue is the law of kindness. She looketh well to the ways of her household, and eateth not the bread of idleness. Her children arise up, and call her blessed; her husband also, and he praiseth her. Many daughters have done virtuously, but thou excellest them all
>
> Proverbs 31:11-12, 23, 25-29.

11

Trials and Triumphs

Remembering . . . your work of faith, and labour of love, and patience of hope. 1 Thessalonians 1:3

"If thou faint in the day of adversity, thy strength is small" (Proverbs 24:10). The life of faith is not a plateau where one can coast along with ease. It is, rather, an incline leading up to the hill called Difficulty. and to the house called Beautiful, and to Valleys of Humiliation with Springs of Refreshment. Once, while travelling in central Canada to challenge prospective Bible college students, I received a letter apprising me of serious difficulties that we could not possibly overcome. I was advised to return home to preside over the dissolution of our Caron Airport venture. I replied that I was reading again *Pilgrim's Progress*—Christian's flight from the city of Destruction to the Celestial City. I had come to the place where Christian was climbing the hill called Difficulty on top of which was the house called Beautiful. Pilgrim was discouraged by Timorous and Mistrust who were running down the hill crying, "The lions! The lions!"

The only danger I felt we were facing was losing the scroll from our bosom. Christian returned to find it at Pleasant Arbor. He retrieved it, read it for comfort and encouragement, and proceeded up the hill. Sure enough, the lions were there, on either side of the narrow path. Pilgrim was afraid, but the porter of the house called Beautiful beckoned him on, "Fear not the lions, for they are chained, and are placed there for the trial of faith where it is, and for discovery of those who have none: keep in the midst of the path, and no hurt shall come unto thee."[1] Truly the closer I grew to this ministry, the more certain I was that God was in it.

The great depression continued and with it the constant need to rely upon God for survival. World War II followed upon its heels and our young men were called to the battle front or to duties directly involved with the war effort. A Bible school was not considered part of the war effort, therefore it could be phased out. But God saw us through those difficult years as well.

The problem of water is acute on the Prairies, and more difficult for small towns that lack a reliable source of water, perhaps not even enough for limited use without a regular sewer system. This was the problem at Briercrest, and it proved to be one of the main reasons for looking for a new site, one with sufficient water. It seemed so unfair to impose the sewage problem of a growing institution upon a small town.

And a problem it was for the school itself! Assigned to empty the toilet pails in the women's dorm every night after everybody retired, a young man could not take it. He quietly stole away for home in the night in the middle of the first semester. Since our suite was in that dorm, it fell to the lot of the young president of BBC to attend to this duty every night for the rest of the year, without anybody knowing it.

We were miraculously preserved from the ever-present danger of fire that threatened the tinder-dry, match-box dormitories, at first in Briercrest with its scant water supply, and later at Caronport. We came close to being wiped out several times by fire.

At Briercrest, we had just moved into the Yale Hotel—the opening weekend of school. Three days later a fire broke out in the local pool hall three buildings to the west of us on the same side of the street, and a strong wind was driving the flames our way. The telephone building next to us was aflame, when suddenly God changed the wind and blew the flames away from us. On Friday morning after that dangerous Thursday night, we read Psalm 103 in our chapel, humbly thanking God for preserving us.

At Caronport the furnace room of the classroom (now G Dorm for high school young men) was smouldering, ready to ignite, but again God spared us. Several years later a double failure of automatic electric switches occurred. The furnace room of the large gymnasium was afire, with a strong southeast wind threatening to sweep away the heart of our campus. God undertook and guided our fire chief, Mr. Irvin Rodin, and his men to direct the water effectively, and even the gym was spared. After both instances we read Psalm 103 and thanked God for sparing our campus.

Another night the sirens screamed and our service shop was on fire. Had we taken all the precautions necessary to prevent it from starting? It burned down with some of the equipment. The next morning in chapel we read again Psalm 103 and thanked God for enabling our firefighters to contain the destruction to one building. Most frightening to us was the fire in a hangar suite during Youth Quake night. Again the fire was contained to that one room of the hangar suite, and again we lifted our voices in thanksgiving to God, our Preserver. Truly, ". . . except the Lord keep the city, the watchman waketh but in vain" (Psalm 127:1).

You can understand why, during special events on our campus, we have one or two watchmen on night duty on every floor of each dormitory.

We also experienced a fuel shortage during the first winter at Caronport. Carloads of lignite coal were piled in rows, a sufficient supply we felt for several winters. But winter set in early that fall, and the thermometer dipped. For two months it hardly rose to above 25 below with the winds howling. These airforce buildings, not yet insulated, demanded a lot of heat. Our supply of coal dwindled. We had put in our order for coal long before, but so had the cities and towns. We were advised to close down and send the students home to conserve coal for homes—it was an emergency. For regular schools that meant closing for just a little while, then opening after the emergency. For us, with dormitory students from most of the provinces of our Dominion, sending them home would mean closing the school altogether. But God supplied through Christian fuel dealers who directed sufficient of this precious mineral to us so we could continue to operate. He supplied all our needs (Philippians 4:19).

Financial burdens, like the poor, "always ye have with you." This applied to us personally as well as to the school. Let me share one incident of how God remains no man's debtor. We were involved in heavy renovating expenses at the Port. The airforce buildings, though serving us well, were built to be temporary and needed a lot of attention. How would our God meet that need? There came to our campus one holiday weekend a woman, by profession a school teacher. She had asked to see me personally. She could wait till Monday morning for I was due to return late Sunday night from weekend services.

On Monday morning she arrived in my office as arranged. She had in her hand what looked like a shopping bag. She didn't need to introduce herself. I had known her and her family for about 21 years, since the 1938 summer Bible conference led by Rev. Lorne Gillett in the Forest Edge-Hazel Valley Districts south of Kipling.

Miss Marguerite Long opened her bag and heart, "I have some papers or 'whatevers' that my mother asked before she died that I give to you as a memorial." I quietly prayed that I would respond with true appreciation, for folks had sent all sorts of trinkets and gadgets (including a Napoleon hat) in appreciation for services rendered, things that meant much to those dear ones, but little to us.

However, my enthusiasm for the papers on behalf of her family increased as I saw her pull out Dominion Government Bonds one after another, the savings of many years. God supplied the serious need the School faced at that time. Gratefully acknowledging this sacrifice of the family, my mind went back to the Bible conference where I was introduced to that community of friends who have stood with us over the years.

Twenty years earlier, during my second visit to the summer Bible conference, I ran into a problem. I had stopped in Kipling at a B/A gas station. I had only one hour before the first service at which I was due. The conference was some 15 miles south of Kipling. If I ran out of gas, I would be late. I checked my purse again and found only 24 cents worth of postage on hand. I asked the attendant whether he could give me 24 cents worth of gas to be paid in stamps. "We usually don't do this, but if it helps you out, fine." I arrived in time and enjoyed communicating the Word of life. The response was genuine.

From Forest Edge I had motored to Langbank, some 20-plus miles east and north for another three-day Bible conference. Again God honoured His Word and we were introduced to friends and helpers who have stayed by us until this day.

The honoraria from these conferences were sufficient to fill my gas tank and a little left to take home. The pastor asked if I wouldn't mind taking a Salvation Army lassie along since I had to pass through Regina anyway. We motored our way to Regina on what is now Highway #48. As we approached Vibank I felt the steering become difficult, so I stopped at the garage. "Yes, one of your tires is giving way. I think a boot may tide you over for a while." (Ask your father or grandfather what a "boot" meant to the tire.) The cost? One dollar and thirty cents. I paid the bill and still had 10 cents left in my pocket.

All was well, except the Salvation Army lassie was getting hungry. I did not want to let her know that I had little for a meal at Vibank, hoping she would be all right till I dropped her off at the Salvation

Army Home in Regina. She was—at least, she fainted not.

I still had 50 miles to get home. As I drove south, out of Regina, I noticed again that my steering wheel was not responding naturally. I stopped at the gas station and another tire was low. The attendants, and they were so considerate, felt that the valve was leaking. A valve cap may get me home. It did. Cost? Ten cents!

I arrived home to the usual warm welcome. I shared with Inger how graciously the people had received me and how God had blessed His Word. She shared with me—the cupboard was bare, only enough for a meal tonight. You see, the saints felt that the pastor had been out for conferences and must therefore be well cared for. With a likeminded wife who had sunk her life into mine, we knelt beside the crib of our firstborn who smiled cheerfully because Daddy was home. The baby seemed to sense the feelings of her Mother. We committed ourselves and our need to God. He did undertake! The following morning a letter proved to be God's Epaphroditus (Philippians 4:18).

The friends we gained during those conferences covenanted to stand by us. They offered prayers for us, sent their children and grandchildren to us, and poured thousands and thousands of dollars over the years into this ministry. "God is no man's debtor." Potters, Robertsons, Dakus, Butes, Crosses, Stenders, Borwatzkes, etcetra. God keeps a book of remembrance, and I want to preserve the memory of these saints for the archives of our library.

However, the greater trials during the earlier years were spiritual—doctrinal. The infant School was interdenominational, evangelical. Men of different persuasions sought to capture our school into their orbits or to infiltrate us with their teachings. What was so difficult was that some were so sincere in their effort.

The Oxford Group visited us with the intent to speak and testify to our student body. Since I understood them to say that the blood of Jesus was not necessary to cleansing, and that the therapy was in the confession itself, I could not in good conscience open the chapel or the student body to them. I could not equate their sincerity with sound doctrine. The pressure of having to say "no" when they were all ready for their program only few can understand. If they had been invited to come, I knew nothing of it. I suspected that they must have been, and this made it doubly difficult.

On another occasion, a speaker of an extreme charismatic persuasion and hot temper showed up for conference. At first he expected and then demanded to be heard. He was ready to battle with the two leading men of God scheduled to speak at the spring conference. Since the spring conference is our last opportunity with the students for the summer, I was especially cautious to make sure that no false note would be struck. To let that person loose could destroy our testimony and eventually the entire work, and we already had had some sad and harmful experiences in these areas.

The Monday after conference, at 5:00 in the morning, I was awakened and taken to task for setting myself as judge. Mr. Whittaker insisted that I had denied audience to a good man. I learned then who had invited the visitor! "A servant is to obey his master," and since I had disobeyed, the hired servant wasn't even allowed to resign. He was fired right there and then—no if's, no but's. I asked, if I was a hired servant, where were my wages for the first five years? I had received none from the school. Moreover, the board was scheduled to gather later that day, and if the board decided so, I would yield. But if the board supported me, I would continue as the servant of the Lord.

After we cooled down, we had a clear and profitable discussion of the issues involved. I was asked to forget about the earlier part of the discussion and not even refer it to the board. In all this we remained true to each other and partners of a common cause.

The difficulty had stemmed from a lack of clearly defined guidelines as to who would do the inviting. Future consultation avoided such confrontations. I may add that many guest speakers addressed the chapel, even if I had not been aware of their coming, and they ministered with blessing. But we were guided in all these matters by several Scriptures in Romans, Thessalonians, the Timothys, Titus and 2 John 10-11, "If there come any unto you, and bring not this doctrine, receive him not into your house, neither bid him God speed: For he that biddeth him God speed is partaker of his evil deeds."

> By human standards, Briercrest Bible Institute should not exist. It should not have survived its tottering first year, or the second, or the third. It should not have been permitted to buy the RAF Airbase at Caron without priority or money. And, assuming that staggering financial load, Briercrest should have faltered and gone out of existence like so many similar schools that sprang up in Canada during the same period.
>
> That it did none of these things, but instead forged ahead to new heights of service, can only be explained in one way. God has a purpose, a task for the school.[2]

Through fire and water our God has brought us unto a large place (Psalm 66:12). The problems of the earlier years prepared us for greater problems later, but God was equal to every test. Truly, if the hand of the Lord had been withdrawn from us for a moment, we would have fallen apart.

12

The Growth of a Work of God

Enlarge the place of thy tent, and let them stretch forth the curtains of thine habitations: spare not, lengthen thy cords and strengthen thy stakes. Isaiah 54:2

The story of BBC is one of expansion and consolidation. Not the flash of a comet, but the growth of an oak. Not a fitful spurt, but the rising of a building, brick by brick, until it has become one of the larger Bible colleges of North America.

Mr. Whittaker felt very strongly about a Board of Directors' responsibility to provide adequate space for students. In spite of the prolonged depression, the college had grown to fill every available building in Briercrest. It was also surviving the drain of young people during World War II. Mr. Whittaker accurately foresaw the influx after the war, when many veterans would return to complete their studies.

Some of our young men were engaged in the war effort as carpenters, building airports for training pilots. They described to Mr. Whittaker one such airport, complete with water and sewage facilities. "Perhaps they can be used as Christian training centres after the war," he said. The centers had the room and the water supply so sadly lacking at Briercrest. Royal Airforce Base #33 was being built at the time. Its possibilities intrigued him.

"Henry," he said one day, "From all I know, an airport is what we will need after the war. Let us pray that God will give one of them to us and we will have room and water facilities for all our students." This was well over a year before V-Day. True to his British disposition, it was not a question if we'd win the war, it was only a question of how soon.

About six months before the war ended, Mr. Whittaker said to me, "Henry, we have been praying for an airport after the war. Our boys are doing well overseas; the war will soon be over. Let's put legs to our prayer and thread our way through the red tape so that when the airports are disposed of, we'll be on the ground floor, ready to buy one." And to work he went!

It is a fascinating story. Mr. Whittaker knew government procedures, and he was guided by a Higher Hand. I went with him on a number of trips just for moral support. I marvelled again at the vision, courage, and sagacity of a man who overcame insurmountable obstacles to gain the interest of officials in charge of disposing of war assets. God gave Mr. Whittaker favour with Mr. Eisenhauer, the liaison officer between Federal and Provincial governments; the Honourable Mr. Sturdy, Provincial Minister of Reconstruction; and the Honourable Premier Douglas. The one-million-dollar Caron Airport was made available to the School for five percent of the original cost—fifty thousand dollars!

In the meanwhile, the spring conference was upon us. It was well attended. Although we had nothing in writing, and our Board of Directors' meeting was not due until the Monday after the conference, Mr. Whittaker consulted with most of us and then announced to the conference the proposition. Fifteen thousand dollars were needed immediately. If we could raise it at the conference, the bank would loan the remainder. The people of God grew excited and gave liberally.

On Monday the decision by the board was positive, but our people of Briercrest who had given birth to the College were stunned. It all went so fast that we could not properly brief them about the developments. They loved the school and were loathe to see it move away. We loved the people, and had become part of them, and were not too excited about a move, except that it seemed to be the only way out for a growing work. I had further concerns, "Were we clear about the transaction?" We all assumed it was Briercrest Bible College that would buy the airforce base, but had that been clearly spelled out? We were soon to find out.

The real test was yet to come. A group of Christian businessmen invited us to a special meeting in Regina the following week to discuss the airport project. The group was impressive; most of them were owners of businesses that had weathered the depression and the war. One of the men was a leading lawyer. All of the group were unusually interested in the purchase of the airport. As the discussion progressed, I discerned that they had formed a committee to purchase the airbase and hoped BBC would be one of the tenants along with other Bible colleges and Christian organizations. The project was too big for a small school like Briercrest to undertake, they suggested. They wanted me to fall in line and lead our people into their scheme.

After I recovered from the shock, I protested, stating that our board understood that we were purchasing the airport and knew nothing of becoming tenants. I agreed that it was perhaps too big an undertaking for us, that I had said so on several occasions, but their proposition was a "horse of another colour." I could not agree with their plan until a decision was made by our board.

Here was our dilemma. Our board and our people had committed themselves to obtain the airport. We had gone public to do so and raised the immediate money needed. But now, after all, it was not to be. In good conscience I could not commit our people to this new scheme without consulting with them. That to me seemed a most honourable course.

The new committee in Regina insisted upon an immediate commitment. I sensed that without BBC's backing they were not so sure they wanted to go ahead. I'm not sure they could have because the government officials also understood that the airport would be taken over by BBC.

Then came the crunch. I was given the pauper treatment. Said Mr. Stuart Champ, "Hildebrand, you haven't a dollar to your name, still you want to run it. You want our money but not our control." Silence followed for a moment. I felt like a mouse scurrying for cover. Then the spirit of the Lord came upon me. I straightened up and said, "Thank you Mr. Champ, you are right. After eleven full years in the ministry I do not have a dollar to my name. Any of you gentlemen could pay for the airport without touching your lifestyle, but God enabled me to gain the confidence of the people of God for eleven years. In going ahead with this venture of faith, I place this on the line, not only the eleven years but the whole of my life. If we were to fail, who would trust us in the future?"

They listened respectfully. The atmosphere changed and we could discuss the whole affair constructively. Some felt that if we changed our doctrinal statement some of them could join our board and really support us. One suggested he then would give ten-thousand dollars; another, twenty-thousand dollars. I responded that a human document is not absolute and subject to refining. If, under wholesome circumstances, our board and faculty wanted to restudy their doctrines in the light of Scripture, that could be justified. But to sell our conscience for money was unthinkable. It was too great a price to pay.

They respected our convictions, and they asked for time to reconsider the whole affair. I offered to consult with the chairman of our board and call a meeting with them as soon as possible to review the whole venture. They thought it might not be necessary, but would remain in touch with us.

For several days we waited for word. Instead, Mr. Eisenhauer phoned on a Wednesday afternoon asking us to come in on Thursday and clinch the deal. There were other organizations who had much more political clout who were bargaining for the same airport. He was anxious to complete the transaction before it could become a political issue.

Mr. Whittaker and I agreed to leave Thursday morning for Regina, see the businessmen at noon, and meet Mr. Eisenhauer at two o'clock. That was a dark night for me! How could we proceed without a clearcut understanding? But God undertook.

I rose early Thursday morning to seek the face of God. In my Bible reading I had come to Romans 15. I paused a good while at verses 5 and 6, "Now the God of patience and consolation grant you to be likeminded one toward another according to Christ Jesus: that ye may with one mind and one mouth glorify God, even the Father of our Lord Jesus Christ."

It was God's reassurance to me, the God of patience. This petulant, perturbed soul needed His patience. I said, "Thank you, Lord." With His benediction we could go to Regina.

But how could we swing so big a deal? My faith was so small. I continued reading until the second benediction, verse 13: "Now the God of hope fill you with all joy and peace in believing, that ye may abound in hope, through the power of the Holy Ghost." Joy, peace in believing, plus an abounding hope through the Holy Ghost. The God of Hope! God would undertake.

This was great, but how could a small school like ours possess so large a place without falling apart? The answer came in the third benediction, verse 33: "Now the God of peace be with you all."

Thrice blessed that morning, I went to Regina believing God would overrule. He did. According to His Word, all came to pass. At the dinner table the businessmen urged us to go ahead and they would back us, donating and/or loaning, if needed, substantial sums of money.

That afternoon Mr. Whittaker and I were ushered into Mr. Eisenhauer's office to make the required down payment and sign the contract.

We took immediate possession of what had been the Royal Airforce Base #33. On July 1st, 1946, we had the official Dedication Service. The recreation hall was used as a chapel. The people of God filled it. Rev. Bradley of Garside Gospel Church, Hamilton, Ontario, and Rev. Roberts of the Metropolitan Tabernacle, Vancouver, were the speakers. East and West met at Caronport. Students from those areas have been meeting here ever since.

The linguists of Wycliffe Summer Institute, meeting on the 'Port, enjoyed the dialects of the preachers—Irish, Scottish and yours truly. The Christian public was delighted and God honoured that first service by saving precious souls. When I expressed my concern over our heavy financial obligations, Mr. Fulmore, a member of our board, said, "Henry, don't worry, God is here. Just make sure God is with you and the finances will come." We needed another twenty-five thousand dollars to refurnish the 'Port. In four years God enabled us to pay our bank in full.

Students in increasing numbers enrolled in the fall. A grade school for children of the faculty and married students who lived on the campus and a resident high school were added to our ministry. This has added pressures, but the ministry yields some of the greatest victories. There are now 150 in attendance in the grade school and 300 in the high school. In 1984 the enrollment in our Bible college reached 748 students. What a precious ministry.

In a sense, numbers don't count, but if one of the number is your son or daughter, surely you want us to count them in. With good intentions, Mr. Swenson said, "What do I care whether its 50 students I teach or five, as long as I have quality students?"

"True, we want quality. We aim for excellence. But how many will you teach if you don't have those five?" I answered. The Holy Spirit was not afraid to number the converts in the books of Acts. Should we fear, as long as each student is received as a trust from God for whom we must give an account?

We accept this growth of our student body as a gift from God. Again, humanly speaking, it should not be. How can the open prairies provide such a phenomenon? While it is God's miracle on the prairies, He does use human means. Our people are not sitting on their hands, hoping students will come. They pray for them and then go out and scout for them. I believe student interest is built on a solid foundation—building the home and the church, and seeking out parents and pastors who are influential in directing the type of students our way that we want and God can use.

Let me illustrate. A young lady was sent into my office for information. Knowing that she came from Minnesota I asked, "Cindy how did you ever hear of BBC?

She smiled and replied, "You may not remember, but about 21 years ago, you with a school quartette visited Tri-State Bible Camp. My mom and dad were just married and spent their honeymoon there. They made up their minds that if God gave them children they would like them to go to BBC. Now, here I am, the oldest. My sister is coming next year, and my brothers are also interested." I remember the camp and the four young men who were with me, and here is one classic illustration of parental influence.

Is it any wonder then that a large percentage of our students are what we affectionately call "second generation students?" Their Moms or Dads or both were students here before them. For the last three or four years, third-generation students have been enrolling. Not only were their parents students at BBC but also their grandparents! It is so interesting, so exciting, to see our prayer in the language of David literally come true. "O God, you have helped me from my earliest childhood—and I have constantly testified to others of the wonderful things you do. And now that I am old and gray, don't forsake me. Give me time to tell this *new generation [and their children too]* about all your mighty miracles" (Psalm 71:17-18, Living Bible).

The summer after Stanley Collies ventured farther north to witness to our native people and settled in Buffalo Narrows, Mr. Whittaker, very interested in this mission of faith, proposed a visit to the Collies. Before our flight left Buffalo Narrows, Mr. Collie had but one concern, "When we get converts—will you accept them into your school?"

"Yes," replied Mr. Whittaker without hesitation.

We did—with excellent results. Think of the testimony these lovely people are bearing to their own people: Rene Caisse, principal of a large northern school; the Shackleys, pastoring their own people; the Moses, he is an elder of the Native Evangelical Church; the Stephensons and the Jollys—Joe Jolly is president of the Native Evangelical Fellowship, and many others.

When we opened BBC on October 19, 1935, we could not have dreamed about the phenomenal growth of the school we experienced. We sought to be true to the trust that God gave, "And the things that thou hast heard of me among many witnesses, the same commit thou to faithful men, who shall be able to teach others also" (2 Timothy 2:2). We still honour that trust.

With its growth, the School has become much more visible, hence much more exposed to criticism and unkind attacks. Though the archers grieved Joseph, and shot at him, "his bow abode in strength, and the arms of his hand were made strong by the mighty God of Jacob" (Genesis 49:24). Pray that in humility we will, like Joseph, draw upon the strength of the Lord.

To meet student growth, BBC has engaged in continual building programs, with major projects before us as we face our Jubilee Year.

A New Mission for Royal Airforce Base #33

Mr. Whittaker's vision of converting an airport into a Christian training centre led BBC into its boldest venture up to that point in its brief history. There, where pilots had been trained to rain death and destruction from the sky, a new kind of sky pilot would be trained. Young men and women by the thousands would spread throughout the world bearing the message of life.

The following letter, written by a flight officer trained at Royal Airforce Base #33 points up the transition of missions from death to life.

"Stonehaven"
25 St. Johns Hill,
Ryde,
Isle of Wight,
PO33 1ES.
England.

12th November, 1980.

Dr. Henry Hildebrand
Briercrest Bible Institute,
Caronport,
Saskatchewan,
S0H 0S0,
Canada.

My Dear Dr.,

You may recall that in September 1976 my wife and I paid a brief visit to the Briercrest Bible Institute at Caronport, staying in the recently completed "guest house" overnight and being entertained on campus until early afternoon the following day. In October of 1980 it was my pleasure to visit Briercrest Bible Institute again, this time accompanied by my wife, my daughter Marilyn, and my niece Celia.

So that you may understand more easily my reaction to these two visits I ought first to declare my "stake" in those few flat isolated acres of prairie, 15 miles or so west of Moose Jaw, that were then identified as No. 33 Elementary Flying Training School R.A.F. Caron.

You will recall that in the early years of the Second World War when the United Kingdom was suffering the full force of the German air attack both by day and night, there was a desperate need to recruit young men in the skills of flying in order to counter this German threat and further to turn a defensive stance into one of offence. It was at this point in 1940 that Canada, Rhodesia and the United States of America offered their wide open spaces and peaceful skies to create what was to become known as the British Commonwealth Air Training Plan. If the record before me is accurate, it states that between 1940 and 1945, from 111 schools in this plan, 131,553 men qualified in one of nine possible flying trades.

Undoubtedly, without this vital contribution, the final outcome of the conflict might have been quite different, and one might reflect that under a more oppressive regime, R.A.F. Caron might never have been permitted to blossom into Briercrest Bible Institute, Caronport.

If you wanted to establish a valid link between the R.A.F. Station and the Bible School, you will find it in the few headstones surrounded by a low hedge in Caronport cemetery—men killed in flying training accidents—pointing to the cost of the freedom we now enjoy.

It was then at the age of 20 years that I disembarked from a C.P.R. train at Caron railway station (long since dismantled) after darkness had fallen in the early January of 1942. The crisp snow crunched under our boots as we marched the two miles north to this R.A.F. station in the making, for contractors were still busy erecting buildings and setting out roads.

To appreciate a little of our feelings, you should know we had left England shrouded in its cloak of darkness to embark on a troopship from Barry in South Wales. We had suffered the cramped conditions aboard for 15 days, being only allowed to remove our boots when sleeping. From the port of Halifax we were entrained to Moncton, N.B., formed into groups for posting to the schools of our destiny, which for me and 29 others was Caron, and the resultant 3 days and nights aboard a C.P.R. sleeper.

We were tired from our travels, a little bewildered at our surroundings, but relieved to be in a place of peace and security. No more sleeping nights in air raid shelters or subject to the tension of air raids.

So it was a welcome sight to find supper prepared for us in the Dining Hall (no lack of meat, eggs and butter here) and to enjoy the first full night's sleep in 3 weeks, on First Floor of what is now "C" block.

The daylight next morning was to expose us to the huge mantle of prairie sky—the 360° of uninterrupted horizon—and, what we would miss most of all, the total absence of trees.

For the next 12 weeks we were to know all the excitement of learning to fly in that super little aeroplane that D. H. Tiger Moth, applying ourselves to the academic subjects of airmanship, navigation, theory of flight, meteorology, etc., enjoying the incomparable thrill of a first solo flight and spending some 60 hours in learning to master this little bi-plane and become proficient in all the exercises we were taught to practice. There were regular tests, periodic assessments of progress, examinations to pass and an enthusiasm to work hard and achieve success.

There was a great spirit of competition and comradeship among our coursemates, and as we worked hard so we played hard too: basketball in the gym or ice hockey on the "home-made" rink.

The Chapel of 1980 was then the camp theatre where the Hollywood "greats" would flicker on the screen, or we would be entertained by our own auditioned concert party—and there was always Saturday nights under the bright lights of Moose Jaw!

I was to remain in Canada a total of 16 months and taste the life of the Maritime Provinces and Prince Edward Island, in addition to the prairies, but these first 3 months were unforgetable.

I feel it is necessary that I record this sketch of my R.A.F. Caron memories so that you can get the measure of my reactions to the contrast which my 1976 visit was to expose.

Your welcoming letter of August 1976 indicated briefly the extent to which Caronport had changed in its task and the popularity it enjoyed by staff and students. However, this did not really prepare us for what we were to see and hear on that first visit.

We were totally ignorant of the "Port's" history since the take-over of the base in 1946—and of the Hand of God as it had touched Lloyd Hunter, the Whittakers and Hillsons and the establishment of a Bible school at Briercrest.

Orville Swenson was our host and settled us in the guest house (what an honour—had we only known!)

However the Holy Spirit does not depend upon history—He makes it, and there is no doubt of His presence witnessing to our own spirits that this was a very special parcel of land. I had the distinct impression that Caronport was illuminated by a "spotlight" from Heaven—an example of men and angels of what a man's faith can exact from an omnipotent God.

Daylight now gave us the sight of trees, of original buildings now painted white, of neat domestic dwellings, of new school buildings and modern equipment.

There was a breakfast to be enjoyed in that same 1942 Dining Hall and shared with high spirited students, though one sensed with a different spirit to that which activated the 1942 variety. Unforgettable too was the sight of assembled students and tutors at morning chapel—the joy of their singing and their response to this "phantom" of a past generation who had come to add his "thanksgiving" to theirs and was trying to measure the multiplication of seed from that first sowing in 1935 at Briercrest.

There was no denying the loving atmosphere and generous welcome, but the full significance of the honour that had been paid us was not to be fully understood until our presentation copies of "Beacon on the Prairies" and "Miracle on the Prairies" had been read. It was only then as the story unfolded that the real significance of Briercrest Bible Institute, Caronport began to dawn. The early faith of a few tenacious men was now bearing fruit in quantity and quality they would never have believed possible. I guess they grasped the kingdom Jesus insisted was "at hand"—only an arm's length away—there for the taking by an open hand. John 14:12—"Verily, verily I say unto you, He that believeth on Me, the works that I do he shall do also; and greater works than these shall he do; because I go unto my Father."

Jesus trained and commissioned only 12 men as missionaries (or 82 if you include the 70 of Luke 10). What's the latest count from Briercrest? Greater works? No doubt about it! The Hildebrands, Swensons, Brygmanns, Whittakers, Hillsons, Memorys, etc. believed on Jesus and greater works than He did bear testimony to the faith they placed in Him.

So I am rightly thrilled when I remember the 23-year-old Lloyd Hunter acknowledging his call to a ministry among children in 1913, for his influence upon a young Russian lad expelled from his native land due to the faith of his family who refused to deny the Lordship of Christ. I think of the 22-year-old Henry accepting the pastorate of Briercrest Church in 1935 and the Bible School the Whittakers inspired him to lead, and I see today, 45 years later, a flourishing school staffed by men and women of faith *and* scholarship, standing firm upon the Word of God *and* well qualified in the skills of teaching. How typical of our God to take the most unlikely of men and use them in the unlikeliest of places to bring Glory to Himself—but that's how I see Briercrest Bible Institute, and that's why in 1980 I came again so that Marilyn might see for herself and Celia, whose father also came to R.A.F. Caron, might taste its present delights.

Thank you for extending to us as a family the warmth of your welcome, for the kindness of Dr. Budd in allowing me so large a slice of his Chapel assembly, for the fellowship of the student body who agreed to join in a song of worship with me. They were indulgences I had savoured for months, and in their discharge I received much blessing.

If in 1976 I was welcomed by Orville Swenson, a pillar of the Briercrest Bible Institute, then in 1980 my thanks go to David Nadeau for his warm and friendly reception and hosting our two-day visit, a younger generation upon whom B.B.I. is finding support. A word of thanks too to Odd Brygmann who readily agreed to carry in his car our heavy cases to the gas station. We hadn't met before but I guess "Father" made this the icing on the cake—to be farewelled by another of the "original" graduates from Briercrest's first student intake.

We give thanks to God for the association we have shared with you over the past four years and as we continue to receive literature from time to time, will be better informed to appreciate it.

God Bless Briercrest Bible Institute—Briercrest Bible Institute Bless God.

Yours in Him,
Leonard Smith

13

Christian Education: Grade School—High School

That they may teach their children . . . the good and the right way.
Deuteronomy 4:10, 1 Samuel 12:23

On the prairies, a number of our friends lived great distances from high schools. The grid roads and school bussing system were not yet in operation. Parents found it difficult—during the extreme winter months, impossible—to make the daily trips to school.

A greater problem was the secularization of our educational system which filtered from our universities to the high schools and down to grade schools. Christian values were eroded, and godly parents became concerned. They approached us, hoping we could provide a high school education in a residence setting where their young people could study.

During the war years we began to experiment in supervisional dormitory living while young people attended the local public high school. That served reasonably well as a makeshift provision for some. After we obtained the Caron Airport, we believed we could provide a Christian high school with supervised boarding facilities.

We felt it should be a fully accredited high school education from a Biblical perspective. Mr. Whittaker and I visited the Honourable Woodrow Lloyd, the Minister of Education, during the early summer of 1946. He was favourable to our proposition and assured us that his department would co-operate. He outlined the desirable qualifications for teachers and facilities. We doubted whether we could meet these immediately and said so. He then proposed initial minimal requirements which we felt we could meet.

Assured of this possibility, we looked for a principal. Mr. Jake Neufeld, who had been teaching for a number of years, manifested considerable interest. After consultation with him, he felt that we could begin that fall. He was fully aware of the difficulty of organizing a Christian high school in so short a time, but he believed that with the help of God it could be done.

We announced these prospects at the dedication service in July, 1946. The response was immediate! Parents from the surrounding areas of Caronport encouraged their young people to apply. Seeking a good community understanding, Mr. Whittaker and I visited every home whose children had applied for admission. We explained that, although we were interdenominational, we were evangelical. We would seek the conversion to God of all of our students, but without disturbing their denominational affiliation.

Caronport High School opened in September, 1946, with Mr. Jacob Neufeld as principal. He was assisted by Hugh White and a few Bible school students who were teachers by profession. About 60 students enrolled in the high school, plus seven in the commercial course. Among them was a young, energetic student named Henry Budd. I still recall Mr. Neufeld's caution that following summer. "I understand that Henry Budd plans to enroll in the Bible school. Keep him busy, challenge him plenty. He has the potential of becoming Prime Minister of Canada, or the most clever rogue of our country!" God was good to Henry and us. He raised him up to become president of Briercrest Bible College.

The high school experienced a difficult beginning. Among other things, we lacked a chemistry laboratory, and chemistry was a required subject. Arrangements were made to bus our chemistry students to Moose Jaw twice a week. Still, most of our students passed the departmental exam that year.

While we were weak in many areas, our spiritual emphasis came on strong, if sometimes not altogether wise. Realizing that a number of our high school students were not Christians, our Bible school students looked upon them as a ready-made mission field. Some responded genuinely and became Christians. A few parents, however, misunderstood this zeal. Though we had tried to prepare them for our evangelistic goals, nevertheless they objected. About ten withdrew before Christmas, creating tension between the community and the school which has taken time to heal.

A few years later, Mr. Henry Teichrob joined our high school staff. Limited finances for summer training was given to assist the high school faculty to obtain professional qualifications. After ten years of service with us, Mr. Jake Neufeld entered a high school ministry in the city of Regina. Mr. Henry Teichrob became our principal, and we soon had a strong, qualified department offering fine high school training from a Christian perspective.

Due to financial limitations, Mr. Teichrob felt that—after leading the school for two years—he could not continue. The high school teachers served at tremendous salary cuts. So did the other departments, but their allowances were not as easily pro-rated. It was argued that the financial burden of a high school ministry should not be borne mainly by its teachers, but since the finances were not forthcoming, that sacrifice was necessary to get this department going. We pause to acknowledge the tremendous contribution the high school faculty has made to this cause of Christ.

But perhaps the greatest contribution was made by our high school's third principal, Mr. Julian Grymaloski. He came to us with professional qualifications as a high school principal and years of experience. More than that, he brought a genuine appreciation for Christian values. He was a single man at the time, and he took at least a sixty-percent cut in salary. God rewarded him with a lovely bride, Miss Joan Armstrong, who had come from Toronto to study at Caronport. Even then, it was at great sacrifice that year after year Mr. Grymaloski continued to lead this department. He retired in the spring of 1984 after 25 years of committed service.

Mr. Robert Adam, Jr. served as assistant to Mr. Grymaloski for many years. When Mr. Adam was selected to take charge of the Public Ministries of the College, Mr. Robert Boughen took his place. Upon Mr. Grymaloski's retirement, Mr. Boughen was promoted to the principalship. He invited Mr. Grymaloski to continue to teach part time. As assistant to the superintendent of the Dauphin School in Manitoba, Mr. Boughen came with excellent qualifications. Bob Boughen and Ruth, his wife, are committed to the Lord and this task. Our high school has an enrollment of 300 and continues to be in good hands.

To me, these gentlemen are special. God gave me opportunity to minister the gospel to them, and to have a part in their conversion to the Lord. Our broadcast, then known as the Young People's Hour, reached the Grymaloski home. Two sons, Julian and Anton, responded and trusted in Jesus. Then, while I was ministering at the CSSM Youth Camp south of Dauphin in the Riding Mountains, Robert Boughen accepted the Lord as Saviour. It is so precious to see these men with their families serve the Lord.

The high school years are usually the years of emotional instability which inevitably causes problems. But it is in this ministry where we also experience some of our greatest triumphs. When a son or daughter insists on his or her way, we have to take action. Seldom do parents and their communities understand. As a result, the reputation of a school suffers. However, we must take these risks believing that risks are needed.

The high school also witnesses many noble decisions for God. Most of our students resolve to follow the Saviour. You will appreciate what I mean when I name just a few of our high school grads.

I mentioned earlier our president, Dr. Henry Budd. I could add Dr. Lorne Penner, Dr. George Goertzen, and Jack Stenekes, to name a few. Then there is Dr. Erwin Lutzer, senior pastor of Moody Memorial Church, Chicago, Ill. With them are hundreds upon hundreds who continued with their training and are now witnessing a good confession of Jesus Christ in vocations, professions, and on mission fields. How thankful we are that God led us into this great ministry. To all of you who have contributed so much to this work, thank you!

The following letter expresses the gratitude so typical of our appreciative alumni.

Dear Brother and Sister Hildebrand,

My purpose for writing is to encourage you in the work of the Lord, and to say thank you for *you*, and the Briercrest Bible College.

I vividly recall the autumn afternoon in 1951, when my mom and dad left me leaning against the Administration Building as they drove back home in a cloud of Saskatchewan dust.

They had brought an awkard, academically slow farm boy to B.B.C., and said, "Take care of him, and *learn* him real good!" I had failed grade 5 and again in grade 7. After grade 8, I quit school and did not take grade 9. When I came to B.B.C., I was the only kid in high school who weighed 200 pounds and could vote in the election!

They were six difficult years. The academic acceleration, the social adjustment, the Biblical instruction and the spiritual dedication were dimensions unfamiliar to me. I recall the "hassles" I gave my teachers and the constant correction I received. I am convinced that I shoveled more coal, manure, and rotting vegetables in extra gratis than any student in B.B.C. history. Please understand that this is only a subjective value judgment! I also recall the encouragement and instruction. Outstanding in my mind was Mr. Jake Neufeld, high school principal at that time. Outstanding in my mind it was, because our discussion terminated in my expulsion! As I recall the conversation, it went like this, "Wilf, we have worked with you and talked with you and have given you every chance, but your behaviour gives us no other alternative but to ask you to leave."

With tears in his eyes he continued, "Wilf, you have to change."

I thank God for teachers with patience and wisdom! I thank God for your vision and B.B.C. For indeed, change I did.

Walking home (dormitory) that evening in sub zero temperature, I looked heavenward, and seeing the stars I said, "Lord, you created this entire universe to work like a time piece. I yield myself totally to you. If you can't do anything with me, that makes two of us, because I have truly tried." The path to change began that night. Slowly but surely! B.B.C. took me back after full confession and penitence. I finished high school, then Bible School. Following graduation, I spent almost 10 fruitful years in the ministry, serving the last two as moderator of the Fellowship of Evangelical Baptist Churches in Southwestern Ontario.

It was at this time that I was invited to be the Conference speaker at the B.B.C. High School Conference. You will never know the thrill, the gratitude, the reward which was mine, when I was asked to minister at the very school which earlier had expelled me. Even as I write this, I weep with gratitude for His faithfulness! Thank you Lord!

Much has happened since then. I received my Master's of Science degree in Education, majoring in Psychology from St. Francis College in Fort Wayne, Indiana. It is here, where Donna, my four children, and I make our home and headquarters. I have completed work for my Doctor of Literature and Philosophy degree in Counselling Psychology at the University of South Africa.

As a Doctor of Psychology, countless doors have been opened that were previously closed to me as a clergyman. I have been accepted in almost every denomination. From the high Anglicans to the Pentecostals, Lutherans to Mennonites. Roman Catholics and Baptists have accepted me. I have been to Africa, Europe, the Near East, and from Mexico to Canada on this continent. I have on my desk invitations to lecture in Australia and South America. The message is always the same. ". . . Come, let me, I pray thee, give thee counsel . . ." (I Kings 1:12). And when they come, I direct them to thee Counsel of God's Word. Enclosed are several brochures, explaining the type of seminars that are being conducted.

I have used the personal pronoun *I* on numerous occasions in this letter. Please do not construe this as self-aggrandizement. None of this was made possible without a long chain of sequences: my parents, the Echo, the broadcast, your vision, the school, the sacrifice of countless people who pledged gifts, the teachers, etc. I consider myself as one small part of God's divine plan!

It is my sincere prayer that this letter will be an encouragement to you. God bless you all.

Dr. Wilfred Kent
Personal Growth Clinic
Fort Wayne, Indiana
U.S.A.

To serve the children of our staff and of married students, a grade school was started during the 1946-47 school term. Mrs. Hannah, a retired school teacher, was residing on our campus while her daughter attended high school. She volunteered to teach the staff children. Temporary provision was made in one of the barracks where classes were held. Within a few years the classes moved to what had been known as the Officers Mess Hall, now the Activities Building. This too became an important ministry to the campus and community.

Before too long, the grade school became a two-room school with Mr. Wally Gripp as principal. He was followed by Mr. Sidney Muirhead, who served for several years. The provincial Department of Education became interested in providing an education for the children of the campus and surrounding community. An agreement was made that BBC would provide the facilities and nominate teachers, while the Department of Education would pay their salaries.

Mr. Bill Kelsall served as principal for a few years, followed by Mrs. Brygmann. She served until her retirement in 1975. Mr. George Neudorf, who had been assistant to Mr. Grymaloski for several years, was then chosen to lead the grade school. George and Nettie, his wife, have our confidence as they lead this department of BBC.

Due to the influx of married students (now about 80-90 couples) and the increase of our staff, our grade school has grown to 150 students, with seven classrooms. Mr. Neudorf leads eight full-time teachers, plus one half-time teacher and one para-professional teacher. They are all well-qualified people and fine Christians. Our children have the benefit of studying under Christian teachers in a Christian atmosphere. The principal and teachers hope that before too long their growing department will be included in the college's building program. At present they occupy the former high school buildings as well as the Activities Building.

To see God leading us into these essential ministries causes our hearts to respond in gratitude to Him who doeth all things well. I could not possibly have foreseen that the school we launched for other children would provide the same training for my own children. At the time we began, I was still single. But Inger and I believe that this has been God's added blessing upon our home. For this too we are thankful to our Heavenly Father.

14

Fellow-workers With God

And there went with him a band of men, whose hearts God had touched. 1 Samuel 10:26

In medieval times the crops of a certain French farmer were consistently large; so large, in fact, that he was accused of magic. The farmer immediately brought forth his stalwart sons and declared, "Here is my magic."

When people ask, "Where is the secret of this college?" I reply, "Here are my associates, my fellow-workers with God." That is my magic, my secret: teamwork among men and women whose hearts God has touched. I cannot cease praising God for bringing into this ministry such a team committed to God and to the college. Loyally they give themselves, their disciplines, and their talents to the task.

When I accepted the responsibility of leading these Bible studies, I claimed for our task the promise given to Solomon, ". . . And there shall be with thee for all manner of workmanship every willing skilful man, for any manner of service . . ." (1 Chronicles 28:21). We needed strong personalities who themselves had accepted the disciplines and were skilled for the ministry. How God sent them to us is the remarkable story of several chapters.

Of the thousands that have stood with us, space permits us to name only a few. We plead for understanding from the many who well merit a large place in these Memoirs, knowing that full and public acknowledgment will be given to them at the Judgment Seat of Christ.

Mr. and Mrs. Sinclair Whittaker of Briercrest managed successfully their own chain of stores during the great depression. As an MLA, he represented his constituency in Regina and learned the art of governing in a democratic society. He became a Christian well on in life and immediately gave his life and talents to the building of the Kingdom of God.

Mr. Whittaker was very creative. Ideas of furthering the cause of Christ sprang up in his mind by the legion, and sometimes to the frustration of those who were supposed to carry them out. He was aware of this, and on one occasion expressed himself rather philosophically. "Perhaps 95 percent of my ideas are not within reach, but the Lord seems to be using at least five percent of them." Indeed He did. That five percent, plus the dedication that went with it, is the progressive story of BBC.

Mr. Whittaker was a great man. He believed in open discussion in committees and board meetings. Our debates were to focus on issues, not personalities. He would use every parliamentary procedure possible to lead the decision in the direction he felt it should go. If it went against him, he did not withdraw and sulk, but was the first to support the majority view, believing that the decision by the majority was the will of the Lord and must be respected. What a model for Christian leaders to copy, especially those who must always be right and have their own way, or quit. Mr. Whittaker set the policy for our committee and board meetings.

Mr. Whittaker believed in prayer, but, having committed the matter to God, he often said, "Now let's put legs to our prayer." He meant that literally, I soon discovered. Although I was a much younger man, I could hardly keep up with him as he raced up and down the steps of government buildings. He'd skip up those steps like a deer, wondering out loud, "Henry, we have prayed about this; we believe the Lord will answer. It will be interesting to see how the Lord will handle this official." Of course, he believed that he himself was the instrument that the Lord would use. Believe you me! it was interesting, almost unbelievable how the Lord used Mr. Whittaker.

I learned so much from this servant of God. I took courses in social sciences in college, but I learned most of it from this man of God. His enthusiasm and his commitment to the Lord and to the single issue on hand was something that you wanted to emulate. He foresaw the power of mass media and led us to minister clear across Canada by radio—more of that later. But the radio and the airport venture catapulted us forward. It introduced us to the entire nation.

Like the "house of Stephanas," Mr. and Mrs. Whittaker were

addicted to the ministry of the saints. Their example of sacrifice has gone a long way to anchor us in the ministry of the school. They gave freely of themselves and of their means. We thank God for Mr. and Mrs. Sinclair Whittaker and their fellowship in the gospel from the first day of our pilgrimage at Briercrest.

Rev. and Mrs. Orville Swenson also have a large share in BBC. Mr. Swenson has served the Lord at my side for 40 years. He continues in his teaching ministry. Due to his logical thought process and clear articulation of Biblical concepts, he was the man we were looking to develop and teach our doctrinal courses. That he fulfilled our expectations became obvious when the students called him "Mr. Theology" of Caronport. He has earned this designation and accepts the honour gratefully.

Mr. Swenson was a complement to me. I was interested in the overall plan and program. Mr. Swenson knew that if these were to be implemented, attention would have to be given to detail. Again, I was venturesome, he was cautious. If the work of evangelization was to be accomplished, we needed harvesters in abundance; he insisted on quality. Once it was clear that there had to be some quantity to realize quality our problem was solved, giving each its proper due.

Mr. Swenson also had the unique quality of speaking to me personally about areas of disagreement. We would debate the question vigorously and at times heatedly, but when we separated we were one, serving one Lord and therefore one cause. When he did not like something that was taking place in school, he would faithfully brief me about it even if it left me feeling ten years older.

Disraeli defined success as "Consistency of Purpose." Consistency is Mr. Swenson's forte, even if at times it seemed ridiculous if it were carried out to the letter. To Mr. Swenson consistency was never ridiculous. The characteristic of his personality whereby he made his greatest contribution in my judgment was that by personality and by choice Mr. Swenson was content to be an associate, an assistant. Someone has said, "It takes more grace than I can tell, to play the second fiddle well." The price of remaining loyal when one's preferences are set aside, or when they are followed and another gets the credit, must be great. But so will the reward be, when in God's light, full recognition will be given.

At no time had I any concerns that if I was away from the campus for long periods an Absalom would be allowed to sit in the gate to disaffect our people. Loyally at our side and faithful in the work, Rev. and Mrs. Orville Swenson have stood by us. BBC owes a gratitude to them. We say Thank you, Mr. and Mrs. Swenson.

Another faculty couple that cast anchor at BBC are Rev. and Mrs. Robert Adam. The Adams came to us as married students from Peterborough, Ontario in 1950 with 20-month-old Bob, Jr. They were among the earliest of many married couples that have enrolled. They pioneered the married-student department and suffered life in a makeshift suite in part of the regular dormitory. They accepted this inconvenience and stayed with their studies, graduating in the spring of 1953. We observed the quality of their work, commitment, and staying power.

As the college increased in numbers, we turned to Bob and Jean Adam to join our faculty. They began their ministry in the fall of 1953, teaching the Old Testament prophets and Church History. They lived in a suite near the northwest entrance of F dorm—the Boys' Dorm. What a life! The Adams' first child, Arlene, was born in the fall of 1954, almost three months early. She could not wait to get into this world.

When the need developed for a full-time Director of Admissions and Registrar, Mr. Adam stepped into this position. At present he is in full charge of student admissions, while he continues his work with students in the classroom. His prompt response to inquiries and his close contact with prospective students from the moment of application, provides the Deans of Faculty and Students with a fairly accurate number of enrollment prospects for each term. Mr. and Mrs. Adam have served BBC for over thirty years, giving their skills and strengths to this work of God.

Several of my associates will be acknowledged with their contributions in succeeding chapters. Here I want to mention *the secretaries*—priceless co-workers in God's vineyard. Her role lacks visibility or personal glory. Her purpose is to help another succeed—a mentor, a true definition of Biblical servanthood. I never felt that I had to make work for her, but to let her make me more effective in my work. In my secretaries over the years I was favoured with the kind that had an attitude of commitment to Christ and to the college. They brought their skills to the office. They respected their position and kept their reserve, guarding that no transference of affection took place between two people who work so closely together.

My secretaries have been loyal and have done their best to keep me from looking bad. They have been confidential while dealing with difficult situations in correspondence. They usually developed their own memory bank and reminded me of appointments and other duties I had forgotten. To these secretaries who have served out of the purity and fidelity of their hearts, we also say, Thank you.

All my associates and friends have been better to me than I deserved. They did their best to make me look good. They knew that I levelled with them as fellow-workers who had earned my trust and therefore expected reciprocation. They knew I wanted them to have cast anchor and give that quality of service that only years of experience can produce. Teasingly they would come to me and ask me for advice, "What should they do, they had been invited to a pastorate and/or to join the faculty of so-and-so for the following year?"

What do you say, how do you answer? unless it's someone you wished the blessing of moving. I learned to come back to them and say, "Unless you get an invitation or two to serve somewhere else, I'm not so sure we want you either."

Many church leaders have shaken their heads, confessing to me, "What do you do with your associates? How do you manage to tie them down? We offered them as big or bigger job for twice the salary." It's a grudging testimony to their sense of mission and commitment to this school. There is the magic we talked of at the outset of this chapter.

I have been asked in confidence, "How did you manage to last so long in one place?"

My answer is simple, "My associates loved me enough to speak to me and warn me, 'Henry, if you insist on going in that direction, you are heading for a fall.' "

Paul Cedar, senior pastor of Lake Avenue Congregational Church states, "My most painful experiences have been when I've had a problem and no one loved me enough to tell me about it. I could feel something was wrong, the walls were up, but I didn't know what."[1] Seldom have I experienced this. My associates loved me enough to talk to me.

Then again, my associates were willing to forgive. Can you imagine how in such close quarters, with people of such a variety of backgrounds, always agreeing, never saying or doing anything that hurts? Our administration was made of Norwegians, Swedes, Germans, Russians, English, Scottish, and a few Irishmen and Mennonites to boot. Imagine them always of one mind! Isn't that presuming too much? Yes, we had spirited discussions. Arguments were presented and challenged. How else can the better ideas sift to the top so you can make the best decisions? With it there were hurts, but our people forgave me and sometimes I had to exercise forgiveness too. That is the answer, "And be ye kind one to another, tenderhearted, forgiving one another, even as God for Christ's sake hath forgiven you" (Ephesians 4:32).

15

The Board of Directors

Men that had understanding of the times, to know what Israel ought to do. 1 Chronicles 12:32

Without counsel purposes are disappointed: but in the multitude of counsellors they are established. Proverbs 15:22

At Wheaton College I was introduced to President V. Raymond Edman by Mr. Pitman, the school's business manager. They explained the operation of their college and gave me a copy of their constitution with organizational charts. I studied these carefully and lifted my heart in gratitude to our God who had guided the development and organization of BBC. I discerned that we were heading in the right direction in these matters. We had so much more to learn, but I thanked God for His direction hitherto and took courage.

In its 50 year history, Briercrest has had only two presidents and three chairmen of the Board of Directors. We therefore want to share with you some of the things that have worked for us.

From the outset we tried to keep every aspect of the work Biblical, simple and practical. To conserve our strength, we offered only one general Bible course, as explained by Mr. Swenson in an earlier chapter. We organized the faculty to guide the infant school during its first three years with a secretary, treasurer and assistant. Even in those days there were too many gurus going around doing their own thing. "They are sent out by nobody and they are accountable to nobody."[1] I immediately felt that we had to be accountable to a responsible body to give a clear account of our activities.

When the School survived the worst year of the dusty thirties, 1937-38 of the great depression, and actually showed an increased enrollment, the men of our community became excited about the work. In the late fall that year we organized an official board and became incorporated with the province of Saskatchewan in 1939.

Mr. Sinclair Whittaker became our first chairman. He immediately spelled out our duties informally. "Henry," he said, "you and the faculty will be responsible to get the students and be in charge of their courses and activities, while I and the board will be responsible to provide accommodation for them." Simple, still in practice, the lines were really never that sharply drawn. I'm sure he felt he had the easier end of the bargain, for there were many empty buildings in town begging to be occupied. But when, within a few years, we packed every available space, he began to wonder. Had he underestimated the board's responsibility? But even then he took the proposition seriously.

As the school increased to its present enrollment (about 1,200 students in three departments), board members were added until they now number 25. With growth, the responsibilities of the board increased, until today it is responsible for the entire operation. The board selects the president, whose tenure is five years. The president nominates administrative officers and presents these annually to the board for approval. The president in cooperation with department heads administers day to day operations of the college, giving account to the Board of Directors twice a year.

The Board of Directors is organized into four leading areas for which each is especially responsible: the academic area, student life, plant development and finance committees. Each committee with a member of the area department head studies its responsibilities and then brings recommendations to the entire board.

God has committed the defense of the faith to the saints. With this conviction, we prayed to God to help us select the personnel to do the job. Emphasis therefore was on the choice of personnel for the entire organization—especially the board and faculty. We looked for men of integrity who were respected in their communities. We chose men who had an appreciation of a Bible teaching ministry with its possibilities, and who showed a keen interest in the school.

We looked for men of wisdom, who had managing skills and who supported us before they were asked to join our board. This support was not limited to dollars and cents, but included participation in major school functions. We looked for men who entrusted their children to us for Bible training.

We also aimed for a balanced board with different backgrounds and experience. Some advised me that we should look for younger men with enthusiasm and venture, men my own age who would understand me. I discouraged that chiefly because I was still very young. (I took my cue from the mistake of Rehoboam, Solomon's son.) I pressed for older men with experience. As I grew older, I began to look for younger men. This time we took our cue from Paul, who chose young Timothy as his associate.

We sought men from different vocations and professions, and men from different geographical areas of our great country to make a truly national school with national representation. Then, as the school continued to grow, we looked for men who had experience in larger businesses. Some well-qualified spiritual men could not handle the situation when called upon to make decisions involving more than, say, $10,000. Others bowed out when the figures began to rise to $100,000 or more.

If I have one quarrel with some business men, it is this: We sit around a table discussing the issues on hand. When asked for comment or counsel some would say something like this, "I know what I would do if it were in my business, but this is the work of the Lord." Such a man had been invited to sit on the board for his business know-how. Now that we needed it, he threw it out of the window! If a decision was honest and good for his business, then he should share that counsel for the business of the Lord.

A board that governs well must be well informed, without snowing a board member under with a paper blizzard from the office. He needs properly selected information to brief himself for decisions that have to be made. The president must see that each member receives the Presidential Report of each department and an audited financial statement, plus periodic information so he knows at all times the health of the school. Frequent visits to the school are also helpful. "An alert board member can sense the spiritual pulse and direction as well as the needs of the Institute."[2]

Mr. Memory continues to explain,

> At Briercrest committees are established which cover every area of Institute affairs. Each board member is on one committee and appointments are made so the particular expertise which a man may have is matched with the area covered by the committee he is appointed to . . . the men, being in smaller groups, are able to contribute more freely and discuss more thoroughly the business their committee deals with. Committees do the ground work and make recommendations to the board. All final decisions are then made by the board.
>
> Mutual respect and confidence must characterize the relationship be-

> tween the president and the board. The working relationship can only proceed on a high plane if the goals for the work are basically mutual. There must be agreement on basics such as financial policy, faculty, campus discipline and expansion of courses or facilities. As the president and board share together the joys and sorrows of the work, they can, as they seek God's guidance, make the Bible college a blessing to many people.[3]

It is excellent if board members are introduced to the student body, as we do once a year in our chapel. The students are heartened by their presence, and the board is inspired by the students. Both get the feel of warmth, of a family—the family of God. It is equally true when the board is introduced to the faculty and staff and they express to each other appreciation for service and sacrifice each renders.

> Board members should be men who come from an environment of prayer and dependence upon God in their own home, church and community. Their expertise, wisdom and good capabilities will fall flat in their spiritual warfare unless they are submitted to God in believing prayer.[4]

"There is nothing that makes us love a man so much as praying for him," said William Law. Prayer is the most effective weapon. Prayer to God on behalf of issues, prayer for one another, for their mates and children. "There the Lord commanded the blessing, even life for evermore" (Psalm 133:3).

One of the men that lives the requirements of a board member described above is Mr. H. Alvin Memory. He is unique in so many ways and yet representative of our entire board. A brief portrait of him and his family is valuable to give the Board of Directors representation in these Memoirs. Mr. Memory of Estevan has served on our board since 1945, thirty years of these as chairman.

> Mr. and Mrs. H. Alvin Memory have become a symbol of our continuous supporting constituency. They entrusted to BBC all of their children for education. They supported BBC generously.
>
> Mr. and Mrs. Memory have been a part of BBC for well nigh five decades, decades in which the College has grown tremendously and ministered to your hearts, your homes, your children, your communities, and on the mission fields of the world. These five decades have been extremely eventful: the Depression, World War II, the period of reconstruction, campus rebellion, and the rising costs of construction and education.
>
> It has been said that the first valid test of a man is the choice of his mate. Christine has been a faithful and supportive wife in their home, their farm, their mutual faith and in their generous interest in BBC. In all

their life they are truly one. Mrs. Memory is a wonderful mother. God blessed the Memory home with six children who love their mother. Listen to what they have to say:

"Our mother's love for God was reflected in her gentle but firm discipline of her children. She was consistently generous and consistent in her prayer for her family, her friends and missionaries. Mother was persistent in getting things well done and seeing to it that her children would likewise do their work well. She was frugal in her life style which was such a help to dad and the family in the economic vicissitudes of our times."

During our visits to the Memory home we felt their gracious hospitality. Mrs. Memory is a warmhearted hostess. As a wife and mother she fully shares in her sacrificial labour of love.

It has also been said that a man's final test are his children. They all testify to their faith in Christ and their love and appreciation of their parents.

"Our parents demonstrated a unique unity in their spiritual lives and combined that with a strong Judeo-Christian work ethic. This is reflected in all of us children."

Mr. Memory is a humble man who is content to be in the shadow of those he supports. He is a consistent man blessed with a good deal of foresight. He was a good balance for me. I was venturesome, he was cautious. I would plunge ahead, he would plan ahead. He did not proceed by emergencies, rather by thinking and planning. He did not believe we could spend ourselves out of debt. He believed we work our way out of debt. And work we did!

Moreover, he is a very generous man. His pocket book is where his mouth is. And he is a godly man.

> "Dad modelled before us a strong consistent Christian life. 'I have given a good deal of thought to this,' said Cecil, the oldest son, 'and I don't ever recall a remark or an action that was out of character with his Christian confession.' In his stewardship of time, talents and finances dad was very generous. His discipline was well tempered and consistent."

He is a great listener in matters of interest. And a talker needs a listener. With all these he is a loyal man. He is a Barnabas in his support of the College and a Jonathan as a friend to me personally. What a Jonathan he has been to me![5]

To you, Mr. and Mrs. Memory, we all say, Thank you.

Another member of our Board of Directors who exemplified our supporting constituency is Mr. Ernie Enns of Vancouver, BC.

Ernie came to us as a student from Abbotsford, BC. His rich tenor voice soon caught the ear of our music department. He became a member of the male quartet that was selected to travel on behalf of the school, representing this ministry throughout our land. He felt that God wanted him to serve in the business world. While still a student, he sensed the financial sacrifice that the faculty were making and determined that if God would prosper him, he would do his share to strengthen their hands.

God did prosper him, first in his own business, and then as president of Early Bird and later of Quest. Ernie and Martha, his wife, and their family of three sons have stood with us through thick and thin. He was invited to join the Board of Directors in 1966. He became vice-chairman in 1970, and chairman of the Board of Directors in 1980.

Steadfast and true, Mr. and Mrs. Ernie Enns have faithfully served the Christian church as a whole and Briercrest Bible College in particular. To you, Mr. and Mrs. Ernie Enns, and to all our supporters, we say, Thank you! Carry on! Great is your reward in heaven.

16

Faith and Finances

Providing for honest things, not only in the sight of the Lord, but also in the sight of men. 2 Cor. 8:21

A Christian work cannot be too scrupulous about how it handles its finances. Nor can you separate finances from your spiritual ministry. If the operating budget is not balancing, it is only a matter of time until a credit company closes your doors. Sound financing goes with a work of faith and labour of love.

It is essential that such leaders of Christian work have a clear understanding of the Biblical view of faith-financing. I want to share in this chapter how I understand the faith principles and how I sought to follow these in practice.

Christian organizations often ask me to speak on how faith provides the finances for our work. I sense that what they hope to receive is a "Recipe on Instant Financing." Some have defined a Faith Promise, as a specific commitment to a Christian work, having not the slightest idea as to how the person is to realize the sum promised. They say that if a promise is based on anticipated income, it is not a promise of faith. Fascinating stories are cited to prove that viewpoint.

The Bible has a good deal to say about this subject. Our Lord Himself said a lot about giving. "It is more blessed to give than to receive." It shall be clear to every Christian that if giving is of faith, then it has to be giving according to the Word of God. Faith is always anchored in revelation.

The Bible speaks of giving as a fellowship, a bounty, a ministry, a grace, a righteousness. The Bible lifts Christian giving to the highest possible concept. It compares giving to an act of worship, a sacrifice well pleasing unto God (Philippians 4:18).

The Bible teaches us how to give. Giving is to be systematic, personal, proportionate, purposeful and cheerful. The Bible also teaches us where to give, namely, where the name of the Lord dwells and is glorified. We are to give to those who minister to us spiritual things, to missionaries, and to special projects (1 Cor. 16:1-2; 2 Cor. 8-9; Deut. 12:11; Rom. 15:25-27; Phil. 4:15; 2 Cor. 9:7, 11; Acts 11:29-30; 1 Chron. 29:9).

We have beautiful examples that serve as incentives to Christian giving. There is the "widow's mite," a woman who gave her all. There are the Macedonian churches, who "first gave their own selves to the Lord and to us by the will of God." But the greatest Biblical incentive to giving was our Lord, "For ye know the grace of our Lord Jesus Christ, that, though he was rich, yet for your sakes he became poor, that ye through his poverty might be rich."

The Scriptures are clear as to the rewards of Christian giving. "He which soweth sparingly shall reap also sparingly; and he which soweth bountifully shall reap also bountifully." It is Biblical for the recipients of gifts to respond in thanksgiving and prayer to God on behalf of the donors (2 Cor. 9:6-15).

These principles of faith giving we first sought to exemplify and then teach it to our associates, staff, faculty, students, and the Christian public. Once we believed that a certain project was of God, we would first go to our staff and faculty to respond with faith promises. Then we went to our students, and then to our Board of Directors and conference guests to challenge them. As a result, they responded joyfully and generously.

In challenging the Christians to give, we did not apologize. We stated the need clearly. We explained the project, the estimated costs, and how the costs were to be met. We did not scold, but rather encouraged the people. Nor did we glorify small donations—remember the widow's mite was a *large* donation in the sight of our Lord.

Our Briercrest alumni are known for their generous and continuous support. The following letter, written by a missionary, may help you understnd how the alumni support has come about.

Jan. 31/77

Dear Dr. Hildebrand,

How I thank the Lord for leading me to B.B.C. I realize my life could have taken a very different turn had it not been for the loving concern of those at the school.

I'm thankful too that I first learned the real excitement of trusting the Lord for money with "pledges" while at the school. As I gradually learned how totally trustworthy our Heavenly Father is, I entrusted Him with my life, and now on furlough it's been good that He lets me trust Him for some funds for BBC again.

The $200 completes my pledge from Spring Conference.

May God bless you all richly.

Eunice

Entrusted funds always call for responsible accounting. When Daniel Webster was asked as to what had been the most sobering, searching thought that had ever entered his mind, he answered, "My personal accountability to God."[1] In the opening statement of this chapter the apostle Paul speaks of "providing things honest in the sight of the Lord and also in the sight of men." And so we looked for men of integrity to keep record of our school's finances. From the very outset I felt that the leader should be free from the actual handling and record keeping of money. We did not have to go to an outsider to find a treasurer for the first 40 years. He was home-grown—one of the Briercrest originals, Mr. Odd Brygmann.

In a true sense Mr. Brygmann and I grew up together with BBC. He was the first to volunteer to be one of my students. He said, "I was really interested in studying the Bible. When it became possible for me to do so right in Briercrest, I felt it was my opportunity and the Lord's timing." Mr. Brygmann studied hard. As an immigrant, he had a new language to master. He mastered both language and courses. He applied himself to his studies with purpose of heart. He was equally committed to any duty of the school where he could help out.

When we needed a trustworthy man, we contacted Odd. This was his response, "I joined the staff and faculty of BBC because I was deeply interested in serving the Lord, working in a Christian school with the various students available." The budget for the first year was very small ($167 for the year!). The Lord provided the daily necessities through donations and provisions by local Christians.

Mr. Brygmann's duties varied. The size of the early budgets could not occupy a person full-time, so Mr. Brygmann became a real utility member of the staff. He was not only our treasurer, but also our chief carpenter, plumber, engineer, and construction foreman. Before long, he became the trusted treasurer, teacher and vice-president of BBC. He served with distinction until his retirement.

"My goal as treasurer . . . was to be able by God's grace to meet the financial obligations in the operations of the school through careful use of funds and provisions made available, and to present accurate accounting to the administration and Board of Directors.

"As vice-president of BBC, I tried to carry out faithfully the plans and purposes of the President in the operation of the School especially during his absences while ministering the Word of God in surrounding areas.

"Since this was the work of the Lord, I felt strongly that I was responsible to do my best as a member of the Administration and Finance Committee.

"My main contribution to BBC was that I was enabled to faithfully support the plans and programs made by the Administration and Board of Directors. I feel the Lord graciously helped me with the work to do it for His own glory. I pray He will continue to bless and use BBC for His glory."[1]

Joy, Odd's wife, was a perfect complement. She was of a cheerful countenance and served in her own right as a teacher in different classes and as principal of our grade school. She had earned her Professional Teachers' Certificate at the Saskatoon Campus of the University of Saskatchewan.

Together, the Brygmanns served most acceptably. If I may paraphrase Bunyan, I would speak of them as Mr. Honest and Madame Hopeful, a perfect complement to each other. In this capacity they gave of themselves to the ministry of the School. When the chips were down I could always count on them to stand with me and with the work. They had joined the team, sink or swim. Theirs is a very important part of the story of BBC's financing. Now let me share with you the second and equally important part.

It soon became evident that we would need full-time help to manage the business affairs of the college. Because of its rural setting, BBC had to develop certain services to keep the campus functioning.

We needed a General Store to serve the students and the homes on the campus. Mr. Whittaker saw the value of it. "Henry," he said, "if we don't start a store on this place, somebody else will, and there is no need of giving this service to strangers." We began in a small way. Mr. Whittaker understood this service since that had been his life. He was away too often to supervise a store. He recommended that we should engage a store manager. Arthur and Beatrice Sundbo fitted the bill, and our store became an honourable and serviceable part of the school. The Sundbos meant much to us in the ministry.

A Post Office was obtained for the campus that in time was served by Mr. and Mrs. Gordon Olmstead. This also proved to be an excellent service. Imagine if a campus of some 1600 residents had to go daily to another centre for mail.

A dairy was started the first year we were at Caronport and with it the farm. The dairy, with its prize-winning cattle known throughout the province, provided sufficient milk for a growing campus. Though a tremendous asset to the campus, upon the recommendation of our dairymen, we sold this department. With labour laws for a school business and the need for investing finances to enlarge the barn and dairy, it was felt best that we let the dairy and farm go.

The Carpenter Shop was directed by Oscar Eliason for many years. The Plumbing Shop was led by Gordon Diggins, the Machine Shop by Irvin Rodin. The Motel—a double-purpose set-up for married students' residence in winter and motel service in summer, and the Service Station/Lunch Counter and Bus Depot was led at first by Asbjorne Amundsen. They were all essential departments of the campus. These men with their wives became fellow-labourers and close personal friends.

All of these departments served us well, but needed an overall business manager to coordinate services with the purpose of the school. The services were to assist the school in its main calling to teach the Word.

God provided the man with his family for the business manager task. Let Mr. Theodore Bergren tell about it in his own words:

> The Briercrest Bible College was introduced into our home by way of the broadcast, "The Young Peoples' Hour." Mr. Hildebrand's ministry was appreciated very much. In the spring of 1939 my parents invited him to hold meetings in our district at Viscount, Saskatchewan. He accepted the invitation and during his stay was billeted in our home. Through his meetings and in private talks with Mr. Hildebrand about the scriptures a keen desire to know more about God's Word was stimulated which led me to enroll in BBC that fall.
>
> The time of Bible study, learning spiritual truths and exposure to the ministry of many missionaries challenged me to dedicate myself to serve my Lord in some way.
>
> Dormitory life was another enriching experience of Bible school life. It was never dull. Rubbing shoulders with fellow students in close quarters helped me to be able to relate to and appreciate people more. Student work was another facet of our training which taught that the Christian life had a practical side as well as a spiritual one.
>
> A very important event for me at BBC was meeting the lady who would later become my wife, Miss Grace Envik of Frontier, Saskatchewan. Fol-

lowing our marriage we settled on a farm in the Viscount district. We developed a practical interest in missions by taking on the support of missionaries in different parts of the world. To carry this financial commitment we purchased and leased land. In 1957 all our leases were terminated. This reduced our economic base by half, which meant a considerable curtailment of mission support.

About this time, BBC invited me to fill a new position as Business Manager. There was considerable soul-searching as I had no direct experience in this field. As our mission support ministry had taken such a setback, we as a family felt that the Lord must be directing in new paths. After much prayer I accepted the challenge. Having spent the previous six winters at BBC, working with Mr. Sundbo in the store, our family felt very much a part of the campus family which helped in adjusting to becoming full time residents at BBC.

Some of the immediate goals upon assuming my new duties were to develop a more comprehensive accounting system, work toward better remuneration for faculty and staff as well as group insurance and pension plans. These goals were realized over the next few years. Interestingly BBC led the way among Christian organizations in setting up group insurance and pension plans for its staff.

Another goal was to have Sask. Power Corporation serve the campus with natural gas to replace the dirty lignite coal that was being used for fuel. In 1959 this became a reality.

Longer term goals were to develop the campus with new facilities to eventually replace the older Air Force type buildings. To some extent this has been achieved.

In retrospect it seems as though I was sort of a catalyst in bringing the ideas and hopes, of many of us, into being. Many of the challenges were staggering in the light of our human resources, such as a water supply, new office and classroom complex, new dormitories, staff housing and general campus development. Several of these projects were eligible for Government grants at both Federal and Provincial levels. The Lord favoured me in establishing good public relations with Government Departments that administered those grants, resulting in several grants for capital projects and a larger Central Mortgage and Housing Corporation, long term, low interest rate loan. Not all one's dreams come true, at least not as soon as we'd wish. One of mine was to have a new Chapel and Conference Centre erected. This will be a very large project. But the general work is being laid so that this dream may become a reality in the not too distant future.

In looking back, I am amazed and humbled to see what God has wrought on campus. How He has used professional people, business men, farmers and many others to rally around BBC in times of challenge. As examples I think of the McClintock Pitt Foundation that gave so generously toward the water line and Administration Office and Bible School Classroom Complex, R. A. Archibald who gave a large farm with equipment that has been such a great asset both in income, and then in realized

> capital when the farm was sold a few years ago. Then, too, the hundreds of supporters who rallied to each new challenge. This makes me pause and thank my Lord for allowing me and my family to be a part of His great work at BBC.[2]

Thanks Ted. You and your good wife, Grace, have been such a help to us at the most crucial times of expansion and consolidation. Your sense of fairness and uprightness in every transaction has commended BBC to the business world. Likewise, our campus family appreciated it. You and your family have been the best possible neighbour to us.

I never cease to marvel how God provided the right people for each department, who did their work as unto the Lord. For this the entire school and the supporting constituency are grateful.

Honest accounting and wise stewardship of entrusted funds build confidence, and the people of God respond. You will be excited to hear of the large share our supporting constituency has shouldered over the years.

17

Our Supporting Constituency

But my God shall supply all of your needs, according to his riches in glory by Christ Jesus. Philippians 4:19

The above Scripture is the New Testament explanation of "Jehovah-jireh"—my God shall provide.

It was so exciting as a student to read how God supplied the needs of men like Hudson Taylor and George Mueller, but it was much more exciting to witness and experience personally God's all-sufficient supply as miraculously as in days gone by. That is the joy of this chapter.

Unmentioned, unsung, and unknown will be so many who had such a consistent part in the support of this school. "Finite human beings haven't the capacity for 'digesting' the significance of a long, long list of names . . . God has no problem knowing each individual . . ."[1] In his time each will be properly named and rewarded. The few that have been selected are representatives of the whole.

There are our *prayer-supporters,* who laboured in prayer for us. My parents took up their vigil before I was born. Daily they would present their charges to God—morning and evening. Mother died before I was a Christian, but I knew Father would stay on our behalf at the throne of grace. Not a single day passed but what I thought of Dad having committed me once again to God's care in love and wisdom.

When I graduated from Bible school, a Christian gentleman assured me that he would regularly pray for me and my ministry. With eager anticipation each time I had a chance to see him he would ask about "God's work" as he called it. In 1945, during my ministry at Fair Havens in Ontario, an elderly missionary widow called me aside and said, "God has placed you upon my heart for prayer. I have covenanted with God that as long as He gives me strength, the sun will not set before I have prayed for you." With this she pressed something into my hand, saying, "This is the token of my covenant. See to it that you don't lose it." I opened my hand and saw a ten-dollar gold piece.

Some of the saints at Briercrest who knew how to plead at the throne of grace covenanted to pray for me and the school daily. My family joined in this sacred ministry, as did the school family. Many of these prayer warriors are now in glory, and we need constant volunteer replacements in this army of intercession. BBC was born in prayer and progresses as the people of God pray.

Our people supported us also by their children and grandchildren, their most sacred trust. Take, for example, the William Fulmore family of Parry, Saskatchewan. From 1935, when BBC was founded, until 1984, either children, grandchildren, great-grandchildren or immediate relatives (nephews and nieces) have been in attendance or directly involved at BBC. When I heard of this at Mrs. Fulmore's funeral, I wrote her daughter, Mrs. Copeland, of Regina. As I write this chapter, I have before me a letter documenting this fact. We were introduced to the Fulmores at one of their Bible conferences held in the thirties.

The honour of having the most children attend our School, to my knowledge, goes to Mr. and Mrs. William Baron of Fenwood. Nine of their ten children enrolled. Next come Mr. and Mrs. Gerald Frostad, who both attended BBC/CHS. Jeff, the youngest of their eight children (all who studied at BBC) is completing his senior year. Classmates of our own Bible school days have entrusted sons and daughters to BBC.

I wrote earlier of what we call "second generation students," hundreds of them. For several years there have enrolled third generation students, whose parents and grandparents were students before them. Let me mention just one, Michael Peters, son of Ted and Arlyss Peters, grandson of Oscar and Genevieve Eliason.

Grateful as we are to see them come, how much more wonderful it is to see them go forth in His name, bearing witness to the saving grace of God as missionaries, pastors and Christian workers.

With their prayer and children, the people of God also supported us with their means. From the earliest days of the great depression,

Circuit riding preacher, summer—1933.
Below: My hosts: Mr. and Mrs. Jim Bragshaw and family, 1933.

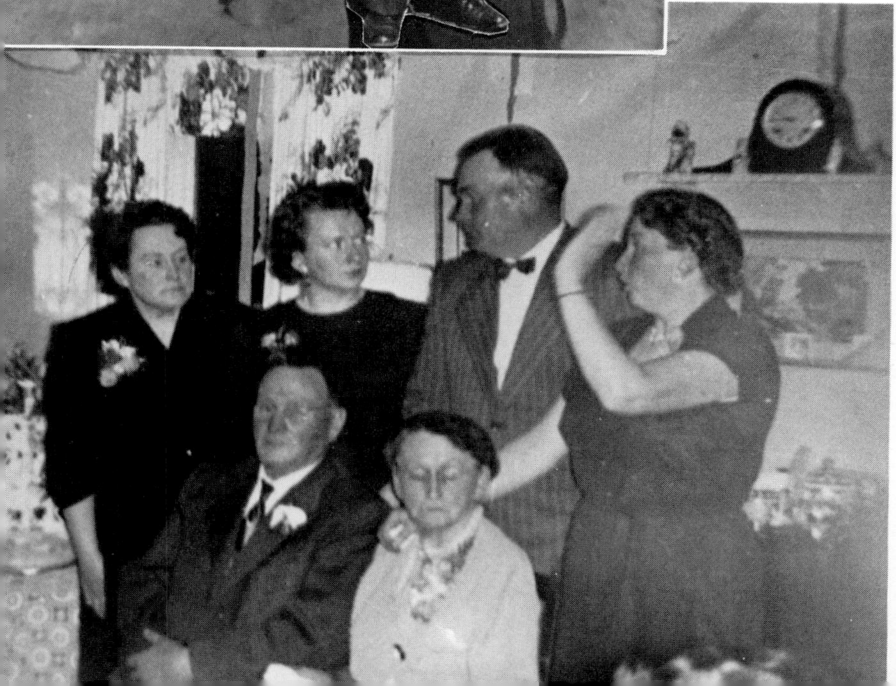

Inger in 1929, age 14.
1935, age 20.
1967, age 52.
Our wedding, 1937

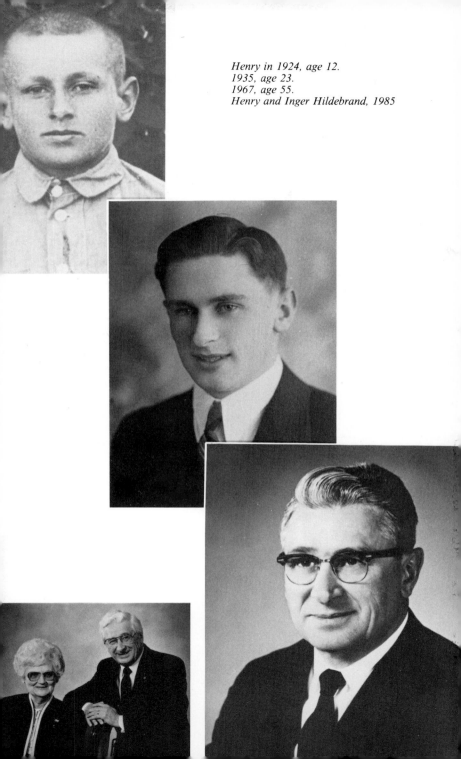

Henry in 1924, age 12.
1935, age 23.
1967, age 55.
Henry and Inger Hildebrand, 1985

Top: '45-'46 Student body.
Above: Three house dorms.
Left: Classes and dorm, Nickle House.
Below: '35-'36 Student body.

Top: Caronport
Left: Student body, '84.
Below: Dedication of Archibald Library.

THE ARCHIBALD LIBRAR
IS DEDICATED TO THE GLORY OF GO
OCTOBER 20, 1974
IN HONOUR OF
MR. A. R. ARCHIBALD
AND IN LOVING MEMORY OF
HIS LATE WIFE
WILHELMENA
THEIR COMMITMENT TO CHRIST
AND GENEROUS SUPPORT OF B.B.I. HAS

Top: Broadcast team, 1932.
Middle: Male Quartette, 1942.
Below: Radio trio and pianist.

Top: Faculty meeting, 1956-46
Middle left: Board of Directors 1960.
Middle right: My favorite spot, the study.
Lower left: Conference speakers: Dr. O. Smith, Dr. T. J. Back, Dr. C. T. Cook.
Lower right: Classroom.

Top: Freedom's Gate—to Latvia.
Middle, inset: The Peter Hildebrand family.
Lower: Inger's family, the Olaf Soylands

Upper left: Marcia and Phil Leskewich and family.
Upper right: Evelyn and Dr. Bob Moore and family.
Left: Dr. David and Jeannie Hildebrand and family.
Lower left: Paul and Corinne Hildebrand and family.
Lower right: Glen and Joanne Hildebrand.

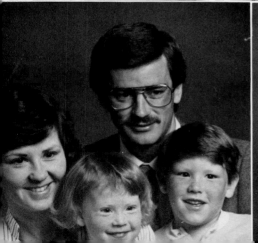

Over land and sea:
Top: With the Gauronis of Bolivia.
Center left: Jerusalem and the Dome of the Rock.
Center right: Word of Life, Germany.
Left: Crash in the Caribou Mountains.
Above: Rev and Mrs. Don Clements, Boli

Fishing, skiing, gardening, golfing.

Above: Honorary D.D. degree.
Left: Inger shares the honors.
Below: A mother's joy.

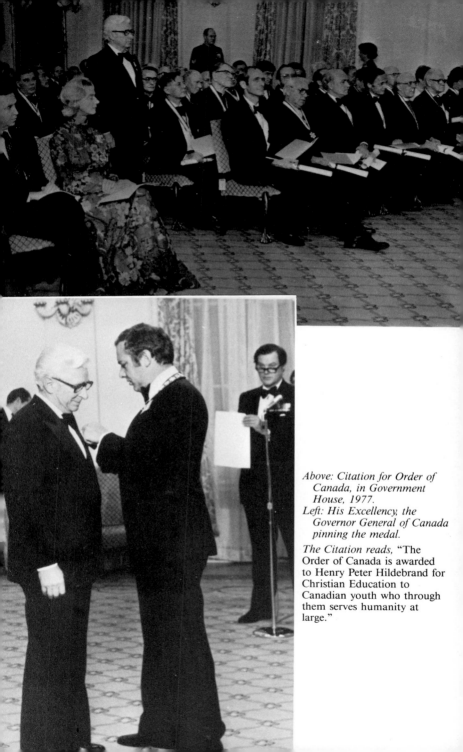

Above: Citation for Order of Canada, in Government House, 1977.
Left: His Excellency, the Governor General of Canada pinning the medal.

The Citation reads, "The Order of Canada is awarded to Henry Peter Hildebrand for Christian Education to Canadian youth who through them serves humanity at large."

Above: Assembly for Testimonial.
Left: Mr. Swenson—M. Mayor Taylor, Chairman Memory, Premier Blakeney, President Budd.
Below: Transferring BB leadership.

Above: President Henry Budd and Chancellor Henry Hildebrand in consultation.
Left: The Chapel project, a 4,000-seat auditorium with classroom space for 800. Phase I (in foreground) was dedicated April 27, 1985.
Below: The H. Alvin Memory Centre—Dining Room and Whittaker Hall Residence.

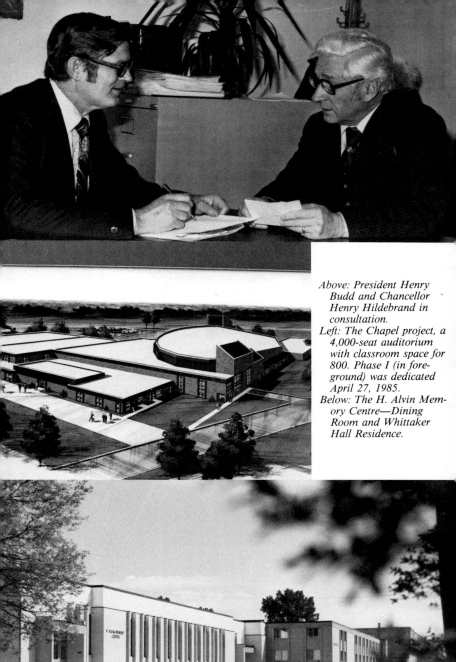

Briercrest serves people.
Above: Reimer Gymnas
um packed with conf
ence guests.
Left: Mr. John Berkma
Vice President of Ca
pus Relations, in clas
room.
Below: The BBC Senio
Chorale

when money was as rare as gold, many farmers shared what little they had. I recall how Mr. and Mrs. Ellis, of Dunkirk, Saskatchewan, (parents of Mrs. Mae Pomeroy) pressed a cream cheque into my hand saying with tears, "This is the first money we got in two weeks, we want the School to have it." It was $2.61. Truly, "Little is much when God is in it." It was much in those days, and the spirit with which it was given was even more. There is a way of giving that turns copper into gold, and this was typical.

Overall, we have few large donors and few small donors, with a solid core of supporters in between. We are thankful for all donors. After an Onward Vision dinner, when the response was meager, Mr. Barkman said, "Hildebrand, if we are not thankful for this, we don't deserve any!" Without question, BBC has been maintained at great sacrifice by many whose names may not appear in the honour rolls of human appraisal, but they will hear God's "well done" at that day.

As an encouragement to the people of God, and as an example to future Christians, the Holy Spirit in the New Testament named men and women who honoured the Lord and furthered the cause of Christ with their means. That is the purpose in identifying a few of the Lord's people who exemplify the grace of liberality today as definitely as in New Testament times. God is at work today! The donors about to be mentioned are modest people and prefer to remain anonymous, but I believe they will understand the above purpose as stated.

Dr. Stuart Boehmer introduced me to Robert McClintock of the McClintock-Pitt Foundation. As pastor of Calvary Church in Toronto, Dr. Boehmer was interested in Christian education within the church and beyond the church in Christian educational institutions. Some of his young people were attending Briercrest. During the summer, one of these young men worked for the McClintock Construction Company. Always interested in his men, Mr. McClintock noticed among the many of his workers a young man by the name of Bruce Sinclair. There was something special about this lad. He learned that Bruce with his wife, Doris, were students of Briercrest.

"And what do you plan on doing when you graduate?"

"We plan on going to India," answered Bruce.

"With what mission?"

"With the Ceylon and India General Mission."

"And which School did you say you are attending?"

"Briercrest Bible College."

That was Mr. McClintock's introduction to BBC. As pastor, Dr. Boehmer, fanned that interest. Before long a substantial donation arrived through the Calvary Church budget. The donor preferred to remain anonymous. This happened at regular intervals.

After graduation the Sinclairs went to India. Who had taken on their support? You guessed it. If only our candidates for Christian service would understand that God tests them often in the little things, how readily their support would be forthcoming. During their first furlough, I met Bruce and Doris at the Fair Havens Conference. Bruce counselled me, "Hildebrand, there are a couple of men you must meet before you return West. The McClintock-Pitt Foundation whose director is Dr. Boehmer, our former pastor at Calvary, is especially interested in special projects of Christian ministries. I know the needs at Briercrest and I'm sure they'll take on a project. And when you present a project, don't make it too modest, because they are generous."

I was interested. "We are planning on building an Administration Classroom Complex. Should I challenge them to a $100,000 share?"

"Oh, no, no," he replied, "I don't mean that big, you don't want to scare them off, but say about a $10,000 or $20,000 project."

Bruce arranged an introduction to these gentlemen. Although I had preached in Dr. Boehmer's Church and Dr. Boehmer had preached in the Caronport Chapel, neither of us had been present due to commitments away from our local ministries. On several occasions, the BBC students of Calvary Church and friends who knew us both insisted that we must meet, because Dr. Boehmer and I had so much in common. We would understand and appreciate each other. They were so right. Dr. Boehmer's dynamic ministry of the Word, his love for the Lord and His people, his business acumen and practical approach have meant so much to the cause of Christ. When Dr. Boehmer became president of Ontario Bible College, we had even more things in common. We have shared our experiences, laughed at some, and were humbled by others. Inger and I are grateful to know Dr. and Mrs. Stuart Boehmer.

Now let me go back to my introduction to Dr. Boehmer and Robert McClintock. It took place in the Foundation's office which is now the home of the Canadian office of the Africa Inland Mission. We knew at once that we belonged to each other. In the ensuing discussion I discerned that the Foundation was looking for sound investments to assist Christian ministries. They were a little disappointed with one group who were not satisfied with a 75 percent offer for a church building project. They were dickering for 100 percent support, so they did not need to bear any burden on the local level, arguing that what they could raise would be needed to get going on their work.

Dr. Boehmer looked at me quizzingly, "Hildebrand, what would you say to it?"

I felt like saying, "the ungrateful wretches," but I contained myself and said, "What an offer—75 percent!"

"Would you be satisfied with it?" The first hint of interest in Briercrest.

"Satisfied!" I replied, "if we could get an offer much less than that I would be grateful."

"How much less?"

I replied, "We would be happy for any offer." Any offer would be better than nothing. I volunteered to raise two or three or four dollars for every dollar they would invest. Seeing a happy and satisfied prospect, the gentlemen suggested perhaps 50 percent would be fair—dollar for dollar, wouldn't it? It was more than I could expect!

Our discussion ranged further about common interests in Christian work. I was impressed with what consideration, interest, and integrity Dr. Boehmer and Mr. McClintock approached their responsibility in their giving to the Lord's work. No special projects were presented or discussed for Briercrest, but we invited Dr. and Mrs. Boehmer to minister at our Spring Conference. What a favour we had of having them in our home at this conference.

We faced an expensive project, laying the new waterline. We had just obtained the source of Moose Jaw's previous water supply, five miles west of us. We also faced a heavy building project, but it would have to be delayed in order to attend to the waterline first. While we presented the waterline project to our conference guests, we stressed its urgency. This had to be cared for before we could go into a building program.

The conference guests responded well. God moved upon the whole school through the ministry of the Word. Dr. Boehmer rightly assessed that though we had the pledges, we needed cash to proceed. He discussed these questions with Mr. Bergren, our Business Manager, and encouraged him to proceed with the blueprints for the Administration/Classroom project. He requested a copy of the prints as soon as it was ready, with projected costs. "You will likely hear from us," Dr. Boehmer concluded.

Hear we did! Dr. Boehmer proposed immediate cash for the waterline. The Foundation would also go on record to provide a dollar for every dollar we could raise toward the building project. What a lift this was toward our first major building project on the Caronport campus. (Some of the details are related on pages 142-147, *Beacon on the Prairies.*)

Like Dr. and Mrs. Boehmer, Mr. and Mrs. McClintock have since visited the campus to see what God is doing. We have enjoyed excellent fellowship with them on several occasions. Margaret, Mrs. McClintock, is somewhat shy, quiet, and reticent—just like Inger. And like her, she carries a grace and charm that is so wholesome. Bob, Mr. McClintock, is more active. In fact, his modest mien hides the tremendous drive of his personality. He is gracious but pressing on. God bless you, Mr. and Mrs. McClintock.

"Henry, you must contact my brother-in-law before you leave Winnipeg tonight, I believe he will appreciate it." I knew Don Reimer as a confident, progressive businessman, president of a fast growing transportation company, Reimer Express. Contact I did, and from that moment on I count Don as my personal friend.

Soon after we had dinner together in the sparkling new dining hall at their Winnipeg headquarters. Frank, the father, and Don's two brothers, Delbert and Gerald, were also present. I was amazed at the spectrum of Christian ministries they supported and to the extent they stood by them. Since each of them was a director of a Christian school, the following conversation developed.

"We hear that BBC is adopting a policy for private ownership of staff and faculty homes."

"Yes," I replied, "and I like it."

"Isn't it better for the school to provide housing for its people and so keep better control?"

"Yes, but can we afford the luxury? How many are employed by your company?"

"About 1000," replied Delbert.

"How many married?"

"About 600-700."

"Of course, Reimer Express provides housing for all of their employees?"

"No," replied Gerald.

"And why not? By the way, what would be the cost if you provided housing for 700, say, at the low cost of $30,000 a home?"

Delbert figured, "About twenty-one million."

Gerald threw up his hands, "If we had that overhead, we'd go broke."

I answered, "That's why business does not usually provide housing at company expense? Right? Then how can we enjoy the luxury of total ownership when the businesses that support us can't afford it?"

They liked my presentation. Donald became a member of the BBC Board of Directors and the family included BBC in their generous support of Christian ministries.

"Hildebrand, you must meet Peter and Lena Dueck," said Henry Unrau, "There is a freshness about their Christian love and witness. It will do you good. They are just the kind of believers that fit BBC. They will love the school. In fact, they need the fellowship of the school, and you need them." Anyone who knows Henry Unrau, my good brother, knows it didn't take long till the Hildebrands met the Duecks. It happened this way.

Unrau arranged for Peter Dueck to stay in our home as he visited the campus. Next, Campus Crusade sponsored a trip for the Weinhauers and the Hildebrands to a seminar at their headquarters at San Bernardino. On the way we met Peter's gracious wife Lena, and discovered we were distant relatives. A true friendship was born. I hope the Duecks need us as Unrau stated, but I know we need them. We are so thankful they include BBC in their hearts. We look forward to each visit by the Duecks and are honoured to have them as guests in our home during our board meetings.

A young lady enrolled at the Maryfield Bible Camp which I was leading. Merle and Ken Moore were anxious that I meet this young lady, for she came to know the Lord at the camp. The Moores were concerned that one like her continue to grow in her faith. She must have!

Years later a gentleman by the name of Max Munday visited our campus. He just had a few minutes to look around. Look around did I say? He had only 20 percent vision, but his spiritual sight was keen. Youth Quake was in progress. He saw what God was doing and he wanted to be part of it. Before he left, I discovered he had married Gaylene, the young camper of Maryfield. He too had become a believer. From that moment Max and Gaylene Munday took to heart the regular support of a portion of the operating budget of the school. Max and Gaylene, the memory of my visit to your home will enrich my life until we see Jesus. The difficulty under which you operate, the loyal support of Gaylene and the response of your children—Jamie was but a baby then—are a constant inspiration. It must be hard, but do not allow the enemy to embitter you. From that moment of our visit, we remember you regularly before the throne of Grace. May 2 Cor. 12:9 speak gently to you.

18

Honour for Honour

For he was a good man, and full of the Holy Ghost and of faith.
Acts 11:24

Christian farmers have had such a large share in the support of the School that one farmer's vision and faith have earned for them a large place in these Memoirs.

Mr. A. R. Archibald learned to farm with a purpose. Born in Nova Scotia, he came to Saskatchewan in 1912 to begin his lifetime occupation as a farmer.

Mr. Archibald, his wife, and stepson were saved at an evangelistic meeting 30 miles south of their home. Shortly after, the Lord spoke to him about a personal issue in his life. He surrendered and with it came the joy of full assurance.

Farming in his life took on a definite purpose, for he wanted to farm on a large scale so he could give to the Lord in large ways. But exactly how this giving was to take shape was yet not clear.

While he was on a special farming venture in the Rouleau area, he met a representative of the Moody Bible Institute who was viewing land which another farmer had given in trust to their institute. Immediately Mr. Archibald caught the vision of supporting a Bible school or schools . . . but which should he choose?

About this time Mr. Archibald introduced himself to me at the close of a special evangelistic service in Mr. Whittaker's former store in Rouleau. But it was not until 1946, when Mr. Archibald called at Caronport to pick up some garage doors, that our friendship began.

He was on one of his frequent shuttles between his farms in Rouleau and Salvador. The school was just moving from the village of Briercrest to the new location at Caronport. As it happened, my wife and I were the only ones on the campus at the time he came. He knocked on our door and I opened it. There he stood—tall and strong. He looked at me and said, "Mr. Whittaker promised me there would be a man on this 'Port to help me load the doors, but I see none." I replied, "I'm not a big man but I can give you a hand." He looked at me with a twinkle in his eyes and said, "Well, we can try." Together we loaded those doors and became friends for life.

God prospered Mr. Archibald as he used 1 Samuel 2:30 as his motto for life, "For them that honour me I will honour, and they that despise me shall be lightly esteemed." He gave generously to his own church, to missions, and to BBC, one of two schools in Saskatchewan he chose to support. "Since Bible schools are doing a good job of training young men and women as preachers and missionaries, I decided to help them."

And help has come in substantial forms. His pastor estimates Mr. Archibald had given well over three million dollars to the Lord. In his own words he ascribes it all to God's goodness, "All these things God has wrought, I have merely sought to be an instrument which He could use and to be a good steward of that which He has placed in my hands. All God wants is a willing servant."

Mr. Archibald's foresight gave us a major lift in the various projects at Caronport. The Library was built in honour and memory of both Mr. and Mrs. Archibald. Mrs. Archibald, who shared her husband's toils and triumphs, went to be with the Lord in May, 1965.

Mrs. Hildebrand and I visited Mr. Archibald in an Edmonton hospital shortly before he went to be with the Lord. He was weak and weary, but strong in hope. His pastor, Rev. John Cunningham, made sure our brother Archibald had an honourable burial on January 2, 1980. At the funeral I concluded my tribute on behalf of the Briercrest Bible College:

> "We rise in deepest respect for you who have served your generation so well by the will of God, and we say, 'Thank you,' Mr. and Mrs. Archibald."[1]

In their book, *Beacon on the Prairies,* Bernard and Marjorie Palmer describe an encounter I had with Mr. Archibald that illustrates his wisdom and spirit. It is worth quoting here.

Russell Archibald didn't seem to be the sort of man who would joke about anything so serious, Hildebrand reasoned as he studied the work-seamed face of the farmer who sat across from him. He had been a friend of the school for years, ever since the day shortly after World War II when he bought some garage doors that were discarded in the remodelling of the Air Base and he came to pick them up.

Now that he thought about it, Hildebrand recalled another time when Mr. Archibald had teased him. The school president had come up to Salvador to hold some meetings and stayed with Archibald and his wife. One morning his host took him for a ride and showed him a large piece of farm land that surely must be as good as any ground in the Province.

"And how would you like to own that for the school?" he asked.

"Now that would be a tremendous lift for us."

But that was all Hildebrand heard of it.

Archibald was remembering the school regularly in his giving, however. On two occasions some years apart, he donated several thousand bushels of wheat to the school. The last such gift brought new classroom desks for the Bible school building.

This was something else, however.

"I'm planning on setting up a foundation," Archibald repeated.

"That sounds like a wonderful idea," Hildebrand told him.

"I thought you'd be in favor of it." His eyes twinkled. "I want you to get half of it for Briercrest and the Canadian Bible College in Regina is to get the other half."

Hildebrand did not know how much money was involved, but he had been with his friend enough to be aware of the fact that his holdings were sizeable.

"The Lord will bless you," the school president assured Archibald.

By this time he concluded that the wealthy farmer was serious. During the next few weeks he half expected a letter asking him to return to get the papers drawn up and signed, but the weeks became months and the press of other matters pushed it to the outer corners of his mind.

Then Hildebrand had occasion to visit Mr. Archibald in Edmonton in 1966. They visited for some time before the farmer changed the subject abruptly.

"I've still got in mind to give you that land and the machinery you'll need to farm it."

"That's fine."

His wife had died a short time before and Hildebrand suggested a memorial building. The BBC Board had already decided that they should build a high school building, a library, and a chapel as soon as the funds were available. He had mentioned them all to Mr. Archibald.

"I think the library would make a fitting memorial to my wife," he said.

Then Mr. Archibald said something that startled him.

"I've been giving a great deal of thought to this land I'm giving you and how it can best be used."

Hildebrand leaned forward slightly. He knew his friend as a careful businessman and a wise investor. A suggestion from him would be most valuable.

"I think you should use it as collateral."

Hildebrand thought about that. At first he didn't understand how the property could be used as collateral in a way to help the school. Besides, it didn't seem to fit into the plan of a memorial building.

"I don't mean that I would want to tie the property in a legal way," he explained. "When I give it to you, it will be yours to do with as your board sees fit. But I would like to see you use it as collateral. You could go to almost any bank, and, using the land as surety, borrow the money to build one of the buildings you need. Once construction is under way you can launch a drive for funds and raise the money to pay off the loan. People always give better to a project that is actually started. Then you can borrow on the land again to build another building and repeat the process. In that way you can build several new buildings with the property, instead of getting just one."

"That is an excellent idea."

Before they parted they talked at length about the transfer of the property.

"You'll be hearing from me again before long," Archibald said.

Although he had every intention of going on with his plan to give half of his holdings to Briercrest Bible College, he felt that there were some things he had to attend to first.

Mr. Hildebrand thanked him and left. He knew well enough what the elderly farmer's intentions were, but he didn't know what he could say or do to encourage him to go ahead without running the risk of being misunderstood.

So he waited.

Considering the matter from the human point of view, Hildebrand had to acknowledge that Mr. Archibald might not get to dispose of his property in the way he decided. He was approaching 80 and had been putting off making the legal disposition of his property for several years. Should he die before the necessary legal details had been taken care of, Briercrest would not get anything from his estate. But there was no choice. In a matter such as this, Mr. Archibald would have to reach the decision on his own.

In the spring of 1968 Archibald called Hildebrand by phone.

"You remember that deal I've been talking to you about?" he asked abruptly.

"Certainly." Who could forget a prospective gift of almost a quarter of a million dollars?

"Well, I'm ready to get the papers signed now. How soon can you come up?"

Mr. Hildebrand glanced at his desk calendar, but before he could speak Mr. Archibald went on.

"I haven't been feeling too well lately, and I want to get this matter cleared before I go back to Edmonton."

Hildebrand noted the day. It was Thursday and his son was graduating from the University of Regina with distinction on Friday.

"I really should be there," he said. "It's one of the big days of his life . . . and mine, too."

"Of course."

"And Saturday, Sunday and Monday I'm scheduled to speak at a youth conference in Alberta. Would Tuesday be soon enough?"

There was a trace of disappointment in Archibald's voice as he replied. "I'll be looking for you on Tuesday."

Monday evening when Mr. Hildebrand returned home from his weekend speaking engagement, his wife had some bad news for him.

"You had a phone call from the hospital in Kerrobert," she said. "They admitted Mr. Archibald this morning."

"Oh, no!" He knew that the older man had a history of heart trouble. "Is it his heart?"

She shook her head.

"They said that it's bleeding ulcers."

That was not as serious, of course, Hildebrand reasoned, but for a person Archibald's age, any ailment could eventually affect his already-weakened heart.

On Wednesday Mr. Hildebrand and Mr. Bergren drove up to Kerrobert to see Mr. Archibald. Surprisingly, he seemed to be feeling quite well for one who had just been admitted to the hospital. They had only talked for a few minutes when Mr. Archibald's eyes narrowed and he turned on his side to stare intently at the school President.

"By the way," he said, "did you bring the lawyer with you?"

Hildebrand blinked. That was the last thing he expected his friend to ask. He had only come to see his friend. He hadn't thought about bringing an attorney along.

"No, I didn't," he said. "The only one who came with me is the school's business manager, Ted Bergren. I'm sorry."

Archibald's mouth straightened.

"Why don't you talk to the matron and see if it would be all right for the lawyer to come here with you so we can get this matter taken care of while you're here? I don't like to let it go any longer."

Hildebrand went to the hospital authorities, explained Mr. Archibald's wishes and asked for permission to bring in an attorney to make out the papers.

"I see no reason why it can't be done," the supervisor said. "Mr. Archibald is making satisfactory progress. It shouldn't be harmful to him."

A phone call to Regina brought up to Kerrobert the Christian attorney Archibald had consulted previously about the matter. The following day in the ailing man's hospital room the contract was worked out, typed and signed.

In accord with what he had told Hildebrand previously, Archibald suggested in the contract that the land be used as collateral to secure loans until gifts came in to pay for a given contract. Although it was only a suggestion, the Briercrest Board determined to carry out the donor's wishes.

"We feel obligated to do as he wants us to, for one thing," Mr. Hildebrand said, "but for another, it is simply good business practice."

On the way home that night Hildebrand and Bergren talked about the gift.

"This is the biggest gift we've ever received," the school president said.

"I know. It must be at least $100,000 more than the foundation grant when we built the Bible school building."*

Hildebrand's thought went back to the gift that made the Bible school building a reality.

*We have realized almost two-million dollars from that farm!

"What a tremendous lift that $153,000 gave us," he murmured.

They drove on in silence.

"And to think how close we came to missing this gift," Bergren said.

Hildebrand was pensive.

"I wonder how much other money the Lord's work is denied every year through situations like this one? It's really disturbing, isn't it?"[2]

19

Special Events of the Year

So they read in the book of the law of God distinctly, and gave the sense, and caused them to understand the reading." Nehemiah 8:8

Secular educators regret that their setting provides almost no contact with the constituency they serve. Supported as most of them are by taxes, the leadership has not found it necessary to foster constituent interest. This may be true of some denominational schools as well.

In contrast, an interdenominational Bible college must of necessity develop a close relationship with its supporting constituency. Special events each year offer great occasions to invite parents and friends to visit the campus of BBC.

At Caronport, the Christmas and Spring Musical Festivals provide such occasions. Commencement is a wonderful day when parents and friends of the school rejoice in the achievements of young people. The Pastors' Conference ministers to Christian leaders, led by outstanding servants of God, skilled in their special fields.

An exciting event for the younger generation is our annual Youth Quake the last weekend in February. As the name indicates, it is geared to serve the youth of our land. They come from all over the continent and pack every corner of the campus. In 1984, 1578 registered! Add this to the student enrollment of over 1000, plus the campus family, and the large gymnasium is just too small, no matter how you stack them. Youth Quake has become a great ministry to the teens. They discover that they are not alone in their far-spread communities. They receive excellent Bible studies and evangelistic messages. Many decisions for the Lord are made, and they return to their churches and communities inspired to live for God. Youth Quake also introduces young people to Caronport High School and Briercrest Bible College.

But the main contact with our supporting constituency comes through the Bible-Missionary Conferences held on the first weekend of October and the last weekend in April. The spring conference begins with a Wednesday evening banquet for the grads and climaxes with Commencement on Sunday afternoon. The fall conference begins on Thursday evening and closes Sunday night. Parents of the students, their friends, and friends of the entire school family are invited to attend these conferences.

At the conferences, the school provides free meals and accommodations. Parents of students have opportunity to meet faculty members. A panel presents the life and ministry of the school, and the meeting is opened for questions. Visitors may meet each teacher in his or her classroom, where parents can discuss their student's possibilities. This discussion often includes teacher, student, and parents.

Bible conferences were featured in Briercrest before the college began, held on Mr. and Mrs. Whittaker's beautiful lawn, where we also held Sunday evening services the summer I arrived. Once the school started, the conferences became part of the school calendar.

The Bible-Missionary Conferences had proven to be an asset to all the Bible institutes on the Prairies. We saw immediately the tremendous possibility of college-constituency contacts. We eased our way into the conference program by sponsoring an opening Sunday in the fall and a closing Sunday in the spring. These soon were extended into weekends and then long weekend gatherings. It became obvious that our constituency appreciated these opportunities to visit the school. They proposed that a long weekend after the harvest would be more convenient. This also enabled us to get the school year well on the way and to be better organized. Hence, the present pattern developed.

The purpose of the Bible-Missionary conferences was clear. We endeavoured to expose our entire constituency to an excellent ministry of Bible teaching with a missionary emphasis. Some of North America's leading pastors, Bible teachers, and missionary statesmen were introduced: Dr. O. J. Smith of People's Church, Toronto; Dr. P. W. Philpott of Moody Memorial Church; later Drs. Redpath and Ian Thomas of England; Dr. Bruce Dunn of Peoria, Illinois; Dr. R. V. Bingham and G. Playfair of S.I.M.; Dr. Robert Glover of C.I.M.

(now O.M.F.); Dr. Shidler of G.M.U., and Elwyn Davies of B.C.U., etc. Missionaries are always welcome to our campus, and hardly a week goes by without having our students exposed to them.

The fall conference usually features an evangelist. Men like John R. Rice, Barry Moore, Ken Campbell, Pastor Splinter and Terry Winter, each ministering effectively at the evening sessions. Many decisions have been made, even by parents whose children were at school.

A number of our students came from non-Christian homes. They found Christ at the summer camps led by the Canadian Sunday School Mission and like organizations, and by their churches. They are concerned for their parents and loved ones. Joined by the prayers of faculty and fellow students, the soil is well prepared. Often, to the joy of sons and daughters, the parents—having seen spiritual reality in their children—come to know the Saviour too, as do brothers, sisters, and friends. Some who found Christ in this manner later enrolled in school and now serve in missions or other Christian work.

How do you measure the value of thousands of commitments by young people who resolve, by the grace of God, to be obedient to the Lord's commission at home or abroad? Even if the resolve did not result in what we call "full time service," the youths became the salt of the earth to preserve integrity and godliness in the working world.

Our people love this contact with BBC. It gives them opportunity to visit the campus and to express their thoughts about what we are doing and perhaps to suggest ways we can improve. We make it clear that suggestions are welcome. If these involve costs, we also make it clear that gifts to cover the suggestions are equally welcome! Often they respond graciously and generously. Let me illustrate.

When I arrived at Briercrest, passing an offering plate was a "no, no!" No one was to be offended. (Some tight-wads loved that attitude, but I felt a little offense would do them good, if it caused them to stop and think.)

A box was provided near the door where willing-hearted worshippers could put something in. As attendance grew, it became almost impossible for even the most willing-hearted to get to it. Later the treasurer would cozy up to the box and record what had been received. When, for the second time a thief got to the box ahead of the treasuer, it became evident, even to the most conservative, that that system would not work. Time had come for a change.

With reluctance, passing an offering plate at public services was allowed, but pledges (later called faith promises) at any public function were resisted. Some sincere folks felt that was a carnal method of raising money.

In the meanwhile, we introduced to the conference the testimonies of our grads who had been accepted for missionary work abroad. They were presented for prayerful support. At one Missionary Conference, two of our lovely young people, Edgar and Ruth Martens, who had been accepted by The Evangelical Alliance Mission for missionary work in Aruba, were somewhat embarrassed to be still at home. They testified that their outfit was ready, their support almost complete, but passage money was the problem. These are the three hurdles that faith missions ask candidates to overcome before they are sent to the field.

The difficulty was, Edgar and Ruth said, that the distances on the Prairies between interested evangelical churches were so great, that by the time they reached the next appointment, the offering received from the previous church had been used up for travelling. As far as passage money was concerned, they were not much further ahead than when they began deputation two years earlier. They were discouraged.

This challenged our conference guests. Some suggested, "Why not take offerings and faith promises while all the people are here and save the candidates many miles of travel? Besides, it will remove one of their big hurdles." This became the main issue at the following Board of Directors' meeting. The logic of the proposition was sound; no one disputed that. But the introduction of "faith promises" to Briercrest was *our* big hurdle.

This question had come up often and each time it was deferred, some hoped, laid to rest. This time the issue begged for a frank and open discussion. It was pointed out that 2 Corinthians 8 and 9 allowed for "faith promises." Some questioned this, but upon further waiting on God, the board reached a decision. The people attending the missionary conference would be given opportunity to provide passage funds for BBC grads once they were accepted by a recognized mission board or church. That decision took place in the early fifties. To this day, each BBC grad has had his or her passage to the field supplied by our Mission Conference.

The conferences have also provided a great opportunity to teach and encourage Christians giving to our constituency. Building projects have been presented time and again, and the people have responded, usually reaching the proposed amount and often exceeding it. In view of the temporary and limited construction of the war-time buildings, major building projects have been required. We faced a two-fold challenge. One by one, old buildings had to be replaced. Moreover, we had to expand to make more room for a growing student body.

Conference guests fully understand this. Our practice is to first seek God's face. Then we present a project outlining costs to our staff and faculty. As our students learn of the need, they respond with enthusiasm. Only then do we feel free to go to the general supporting constituency. Our conference guests share with us the joy of Christian giving.

Two of our frequent guest speakers, Pastor Harold Fife and Mission Director Elwyn Davies, spoke to me on one occasion while our guests were still cheering the report of an offering, "When we observe how beautifully you lead your people to Christian giving, we feel somehow that we failed God and His people by deliberately steering clear of this subject. In Christian circles in our younger days, "money" was a dirty word. Whoever mentioned it tended to defile himself. Christian giving was sort of a side issue that cared for itself. We did not realize what a large place Christian giving has in the New Testament."

"When I think of the opportunities I had in my pastoral ministry to teach this ministry and challenge especially the wealthy brethren to abound in this grace also, I feel convicted." And then, with tears in his eyes, Pastor Fife continued, "I feel I sinned against God, against faith missions and ministries who could have done so much more if they had had the support. I feel I also sinned against the potential givers, for their reward in heaven could have been so much greater, and the joy of giving was denied to them." Together we thought of Philippians 4:13-19.

Both men commended us in our venture of faith, our approach to it, and the Biblical presentations to the conference audiences. The matter is handled with good taste, and our conference guests are grateful.

We are aware that we do not succeed with every presentation. We do not resent that. Rather, we like to learn from failure too, and re-examine our presentations in the light of the Scriptures and proceed accordingly.

A by-product of the conferences is the teaching of hospitality to all of us. No hotels or motels are available to our guests. The only available accommodations are our homes and the students' homes here at school, namely, their dormitory rooms. For each conference, students in certain dormitories double up with students of other dormitories and so provide space for visitors. Most of our staff and faculty also take guests into their homes. Often we give up our own beds.

The most we ever accommodated for conference in our home was 18, but Mr. and Mrs. Whittaker hold the record for generous hospitality. At one conference, they hosted 24 guests in their three-bedroom home! At one conference, one of the guests was late for breakfast, so Mr. Whittaker went to check, for he—with others—had shared the same room. As he opened the door, the tardy missionary, Roy Martens, apologized. "I just can't find my pants! There's a pair hanging over this chair, but they are not mine."

Mr. Whittaker thought they looked familiar. With chagrin he replied, as he examined his own attire, "Sorry Roy! I arose a bit early and did not want to awaken the rest of you. While it was still dark, I must have put on the wrong pants!"

The whole conference enjoyed the joke. It helped overcome the inconveniences and hip-aches from overcrowding and shortage of mattresses. Conferences served a two-fold purpose. Our guests understood that we took our hospitality seriously. Everybody was so much more thankful to get into his own bed after the conference! In spite of it all, the people keep coming back, and in increasing numbers. Why?

The program, though flexible and subject to re-evaluation, follows the following pattern: The morning prayer meeting is addressed by a man of God known for his devotion to God. The morning session is addressed by a missionary and a Bible-teaching pastor. The afternoon sessions are divided for high school and Bible school students, with speakers to meet their respective needs. Christians in Dialogue divides the audience into small seminars, providing opportunity for all missionaries to share, and for people to get closer to the missionary of their choice. Missionary films are screened at 6:15 p.m. and the evening rally is addressed by a leading evangelist or missionary.

Music for the conferences is by the college choirs. Congregational singing is often rousing, vibrating the rafters of the Gym-Conference Hall. The testimonies and the messengers are exciting. While the presence of the Lord is felt in all the sessions, there are times when God moves upon the audience in a special way. Sometimes through rousing messages and triumphant hymns, a shout of victory is heard. At other times, God moves upon the audience quietly, speaking in His still, small voice—leading us to meditate quietly in worship and commitment.

Another asset: we have no great shopping centres on the campus nor near by. The whole conference audience stays put and gives first attention to its great ministry. In this way, even a large number become one unit, creating an atmosphere receptive to the voice of God.

In spite of a rural setting in sparsely populated Saskatchewan, attendances as a whole are excellent. When Mr. Whittaker and I first looked into what is now our chapel, but still without a horseshoe balcony and foyer, he asked, "Henry, do you think we'll ever fill this place?"

"I don't know, Mr. Whittaker," I replied, "We'll try our best."

With a twinkle in his eye he turned to me and said, "If we get this airport, I'll finally have enough room for you," remembering no doubt his statement when we organized the board. He said, "Henry, it's your duty with the faculty to get the students; it's my duty with the board to make sure we have enough room for them."

Little did either of us realize that within four years the chapel would be too small for our conference audiences, and we would have to move into the 110 by 160-foot gymnasium, which is now also too small. Nor could we have foreseen in our wildest imagination that the chapel would be overfilled by the 750 Bible school students every morning as they meet for chapel. The high school must meet separately. Nor could we have imagined that within four years of possessing the Caron Airport, we would be building to make enough room for our growing school—a building program that continues.

One year, Mr. Whittaker succeeded in getting Dr. Oswald J. Smith of People's Church in Toronto to commit himself to speak at our Fall Missionary Conference. Dr. Smith was a bit apprehensive, I learned afterwards, about promising a long weekend "out in the Boondocks." Train was the mode of travelling in those days, and Mr. Whittaker was out of the country, so it fell to my pleasure to meet Dr. Smith upon his arrival in Moose Jaw. Our farms were without electricity, hence, on the way home, we saw but a few lights. Dr. Smith wondered, "There aren't many people out here. Do you get a good enough attendance to hold a Missionary conference?" I assured him that we felt we would have a good attendance. At supper, we were discussing with Dr. Smith and Dr. Bach, another guest speaker, the difficulty of getting sufficient people together for Sunday school or services in some of our sparsely settled rural areas, especially in the winter.

"By the way," Dr. Smith asked, "what do you consider a good attendance?"

Assuming we were still thinking of a rural Sunday school, I answered, "About 50, and if its real good, perhaps 70."

Dr. Smith adjusted his collar and tie, coughed, and said, "I see. That's not very many."

Supper and Bible reading completed, we hurried to the Conference Hall. The song leader was leading about 1000 people in hearty singing. Dr. Smith got excited as I escorted him to the platform. He said again and again, "Where do all these people come from?" His response to the welcome given to him was, "Do your people live in gopher holes? We only saw a few farms all the way from Moose Jaw to Caronport!" I heard Dr. O. J. Smith on a number of other occasions, but never did I hear him speak with such fire as that night.

What Dr. Smith and most visitors to BBC do not realize is that students enroll from across the continent, and as many as 2,500 to 3,000 conference guests come from far and near. The speakers soon realize that this is God's doing.

The benefits of these conferences to the mission fields and the Christian church as a whole, as well as to the college, are difficult to measure. Missions gets a lion's share of platform time. Students are exposed to the far-flung mission fields. Guests are encouraged to renewed concern. Young people are challenged to study the Word. Faculty and staff are reminded that our main task, the goal of all our ministry, remains "world evangelism." Students are released in the spring, not with the burden of exams as the last memory, but with the shout of triumph raised in the conference.

Imagine what it does to our Board of Directors! The few who may miss the conference wonder why the others are so excited at the Monday Board meeting, the day after conference. One once wondered out loud, "These folks are so optimistic! Are they not aware that we are in a recession? Are they really with it?" He soon discovered which board member was really not with it.

As I look back, I would not want to lead a school without a Bible-Missionary Conference. Nor would I want a chairman to call a meeting of the Board of Directors without the inspiration supplied by a conference.

20

Radio: Our Introduction to the Nation

Holding forth the word of life. Philippians 2:16

"How I rejoiced when I heard the news that the Bible school was going on radio!" Mrs. Hillson told us. "During the two years when I was unable to work in the church I prayed, O God, that I might shout the message from the housetops!"

When we were able to go on radio, I realized how wonderfully God had answered that dear woman's prayer.

God answered in a unique way. Christian Service Outreach began the summer before school began. Our problem was, how to reach the little country school districts when the roads closed. Mr. Whittaker seemed always a step or two ahead of the problem and the rest of us. He saw the possibilities of radio, which had nicely come into its own in the late twenties and early thirties.

It so happened that Rev. Floyd S. Magsig, pastor of the Evangelical Church in Regina, led a Sunday School of the Air broadcast. He needed talent and so contacted us at Briercrest. We provided a speaker, male quartet, and pianist for both the morning broadcast and his Sunday services. As the closing strains of that broadcast faded, the director of a large business firm of Regina telephoned us with an attractive offer. He wanted to sponsor a weekly broadcast using BBC talent.

After serious consideration, the school declined the offer. However, the director of radio station CKCK heard of it and offered time to the school, a half-hour immediately following the Sunday School of the Air—our time, 9:00-9:30 Sunday morning. That was May, 1937.

Mr. Magsig encouraged us and announced our new broadcast, "The Young People's Hour," on his program. He invited listeners to stay tuned. Moreover, he assisted us by leading this broadcast for several months. This was very generous, so in keeping with a true spirit of a servant of Christ. Each Sunday morning we would motor 50 miles to Regina to arrive in time for last-minute preparations.

There was still the old problem to be faced in a new way. Were the roads any more dependable from Briercrest to Regina in winter? Remember, Briercrest was 17 miles off the main highway on a country road. Even today, situated on a four-lane highway, I do not know whether one could always depend on an open road in winter. The director of the radio station came up with the answer. Broadcast directly by remote control. A mike and amplifier were installed in the Whittaker home, connected to the telephone line, and presto, the problem was solved!

Solved? True, we were in business. About ten minutes before the broadcast, the technician from the radio station would contact us. This worked fine. However, one Sunday morning we could not get through to the station. The telephone line was fine, so was the amplifier, but the mike was dead. Now what? Only five minutes to nine, and we are supposed to be on the air—what tension! How helpless—except for God.

The Lord had given a double portion of know-how and practical wisdom to one of our young men, Reginald Glen, the bass of the radio quartette. Reg examined the offending mike closely.

"Have you a stove poker?" he asked. "And a good, glowing fire?" Mr. Whittaker produced both. "How about a can of meat or fruit?"

In those days, each can had a latch soldered to a metal strip to facilitate opening the can. Often a drop or two of solder remained near the latch. Glen plunged the poker into the glowing coal fire until the end was red hot. Deftly placing the mike in position, he touched a drop of solder salvaged from the can, securing a tiny, loose wire in place. Rushing to the broadcast nook, Glen plugged in the mike. It worked! We heard the studio announcer's voice over the phone, "The mike is alive. You're on the air in 30 seconds."

Radio land heard the theme song. "Good morning, dear young people! We trust you're listening . . ." Then followed a ministry of song, dialogue, and a brief message. That was close! We learned to respect sensitive equipment.

On another occasion, as I was laid aside with a strep throat, one of our men delivered the message. In fact, he did so well, I was sure I was out of a job, until the smooth flow of thought suddenly became disjointed. I heard paper rattling. Another run at the sentence was made, more rattling of paper, and then, under his breath, the speaker blurted out, "Golly, I've lost my page!" You should have heard the townsmen the following day. "Did you hear bad language on the radio? Swearing on a religious broadcast?" Embarrased we were, but also encouraged. We knew now they were listening.

Let me share another amusing incident. Reg Glen married my secretary, Miss Kathlene Parsons of Moose Jaw. Reg was known for his part in a popular radio dialogue with his sisters, "Reg and Blanche." Upon returning from their honeymoon, Reg and Kathlene visited the studio. Our regular announcer welcomed them back, congratulated them, and, on the spur of the moment, announced that Gen and Al Blager, friends of the Glens and well-liked for their singing, would sing a most appropriate song he decided to dedicate to the newlyweds.

Gen and Al shook their heads, but it was too late. The pianist was already playing the introduction. Gen and Al sang, "Are the days of long ago far sweeter than today? Has the love that once you knew, grown cold and passed away?" Well, we lived through that one as well. To the Whittakers goes the honour of turning their home into a broadcasting studio every Sunday morning.

One year later, the college acquired the Yale Hotel of Briercrest for its headquarters. It seemed significant to me that the room selected for the broadcasting studio was the room where beer was formerly sold. It was the same room where Mrs. Hillson held her Saturday night Bible classes after the closing of the hotel.

Our broadcast, known for years as The Young People's Hour, was well received in Saskatchewan. The format was simple: The theme song (written by the group to address young people), a word of greeting, hearty gospel singing, a dialogue, announcements, and a short gospel message.

After the war broke out and our young men were called to different provinces to train before they went overseas, requests came from radio managers to air the Young People's Hour over their stations. It became an important service that BBC rendered.

The Young People's Hour developed into Canada's first coast-to-coast gospel broadcast. We were on 22 stations, from Vancouver to Sidney, Nova Scotia. The mail response cared for the total cost for radio time, sponsored mostly by our prairie people.

Let me share a bit of our radio mail. A letter came from a man who suffered from leukemia—considered always fatal in those days. He knew he would not be with us much longer. Since our broadcasts had a healing ministry to his soul, he confided his deepest concern.

"I come from a Christian home, a minister's home. My parents would be shocked to hear if I told them that I was not sure if I am a Christian. It may be therefore better if I do not sign this letter. I suspect you know anyway.

"Will you please explain on Sunday's broadcast how a person can be sure he is a Christian and all is well when he dies? I will be listening on Sunday . . ."

That same week we received a letter from a husband and father in Manitoba. He wrote, "I believe we are Christians, but we are not sure. The end for my wife is approaching. The doctor says she may not be with us much longer. She is still well enough to listen. We will be listening on Sunday for a word that will give peace to our troubled hearts."

That following Sunday I spoke on 1 John 5:13. I knew that upon the words of my lips were resting anxious souls. I felt that not only the certainty of salvation for troubled hearts was at stake, but possibly the destiny of their souls. If ever I felt I stood between the living and the dead, it was that Sunday as I faced the microphone.

I prayed and preached and preached and prayed that God would quicken His Word to those hearts, "These things have I written unto you that believe on the name of the Son of God; that ye may know that ye have eternal life, and that ye may believe on the name of the Son of God." Two weeks later the husband from Manitoba wrote,

> In the midst of our sorrow we are sure that we will see our loved one in heaven. As we listened to the broadcast, we learned again that our hope of heaven is in Jesus' blood and righteousness. That the Bible says, that if we believe on Jesus, He will take us to heaven.
>
> My wife was very weak, but she was able to listen to the broadcast. She has now gone to meet her Saviour. She did so believing all was well. A deep peace came over her those closing days.
>
> Sincerely,
>
> Abraham Penner[1]
> (Father of our Dr. Lorne Penner)

"I know of three persons who have accepted the Lord Jesus Christ as their personal Saviour through your radio messages," a younger woman gratefully wrote to the Young People's Hour. "One of these is my best schoolmate. One day she came to visit me. As it was time for your broadcast to begin we sat down by the radio and listened.

As she heard the girls sing she became more interested. Then Homer Edwards sang, "Years I spent in vanity and pride." Tears began to roll down her cheeks. After this song was a message by Mr. Hildebrand.

For awhile all was quiet. Then she asked me, "Would Jesus take me to Him if I accepted Him as my Saviour?"

"He has room for everyone," I told her, "who accepts Him as personal Saviour." Then I read to her Isaiah 53:5, 6, and prayed that God would forgive her. She knew that she was a sinner and accepted the Lord Jesus. Now if somebody in her church asks for testimonies she is always the first to testify. So keep up the good work. We are praying for you.[2]

The broadcast introduced us to many, many friends that we have met over the years. While in Saskatoon, I asked the clerk in the store for a *Time* magazine. She handed it to me with these words, "Are you Mr. Hildebrand that we hear every Sunday morning?"

"Yes," I replied, "how would you know?"

"Your voice sounded so familiar."

Near Field, British Columbia, where the train cuts the figure eight through the tunnels of the mountains, I called out with excitement to my family to see the train coming out of the tunnel. Immediately two people from different parts of the country introduced themselves. They had recognized what seemed to them "that familiar brogue."

In Kelowna this summer a clerk introduced herself to my wife, "Are you Mrs. Hildebrand?" She had recognized that "brogue" when I answered a friend.

At the Grand Forks Family Conference several campers introduced themselves to us, having heard us years ago on the broadcasts.

Inger teasingly says, "Henry, you can't sin anywhere without being known!" By God's grace we shall not try.

Besides its actual ministry of the gospel, the broadcast also served to introduce our Bible college to the nation, and many young people to Briercrest. After the war, students came from almost all provinces of Canada and several American states.

In 1946 we relocated to Caronport, and our enrollment tripled. We soon faced an important decision. Were we going to operate a strong school, or a large-scale radio broadcast? Both were very important, but one or the other had to go. We did not have the strength to carry both.

Our first mandate was the ministry of the school. That was our first love. And while we had no intention of dropping the broadcasts altogether, we felt our first strength and emphasis should go to the school. The broadcast should serve as an outreach arm of the school. Having clarified that in our minds, we proceeded.

We had assumed a staggering financial load when we bought the airport. Consolidating this venture of faith became our priority. It was clear that since our support came chiefly from the Prairies, we should drop the extended outlets east and west and concentrate on the local areas.

Accordingly, we expanded our Prairie ministry, adding a Saturday night broadcast called "Light at Eventide," and a midweek broadcast called "Even Song." Mr. Homer Edwards, my associate, and I also held evangelistic campaigns for a month each night on selected radio stations—modelled after the Oscar Lowry Broadcasts. Again God used these efforts, and both radio stations and churches united to invite us for campaigns. These too we found rewarding, but again we had to choose. We believed the school should have priority. That was our mandate.

Since Rev. Homer Edwards had such a large share in the radio ministry, I have asked him to share how he was introduced to Briercrest and how God placed upon his heart one of our most successful radio ministries.

> When I think of my first association with Briercrest, I have to go back to the year 1938 when as a young farm youth in Northern Saskatchewan I would listen each Sunday morning to the 'Young People's Hour,' now known as the 'Briercrest Bible Hour.' There was no church in our community, so the morning chores attended to, we would gather as a family around the radio and listen intently to the riches of God's Word as they were brought to us by the faculty and students of the school.
>
> I liked what I heard, and as I continued to listen, an inner desire to learn more of God's Word developed within me. So in the fall of 1939 I packed my suitcase and with a very good friend, Carlton Valleau, I set out for the Briercrest Bible Institute. It was only a little over 300 miles to our destination, but it seemed as though we were going to the end of the world. And when we arrived in the darkness of the night along with a strong prairie wind we were sure it was. We consoled ourselves, however, that it was only for six months and then we would be back in the land of trees and beauty. Little did I realize that those six months were but the beginning of three years as a student and then twenty-five years as a faculty member.
>
> If anyone had told me that first night that this was where I would be for the next twenty-eight years I would have told him that he was crazy and taken the first bus home. I was a farmer at heart and to the farm I would return. But God had other plans for my life, and one evening near the end

of my third year as a student, Dr. Hildebrand spoke at our third year class prayer meeting. His text was Luke 9:62. 'No man, having put his hand to the plough, and looking back, is fit for the kingdom of God.' I knew God was speaking and I must act. At last I said, 'All right, Lord, I give myself to you, the farm, my plans, my all.' I had no idea as to what or where it would lead, but in my heart there was a deep settled assurance I was doing what God wanted me to do. Not for one moment did I think that before the year was over I might find myself back at the school as a member of the faculty.

I remember well the letter I received from Dr. Hildebrand asking me if I would consider coming to assist them. My first reaction was to quickly reply, 'No.' The second thought was to ignore the letter entirely and pretend I had never received it. And then there was a third thought; probably I should pray about it and see what the Lord would have me do.

The result was that within six weeks' time I found myself at Briercrest.

Truly the Lord was good, and one of the great wonders was that while much of my time was taken up in the classroom in the teaching ministry, I also found myself becoming occupied more and more with the tool God had used to attract me to Briercrest, namely, radio. The radio station over which the 'Young People's Hour' was being heard offered the school three to four minutes each morning, Monday to Friday, as a public service gesture. The time was 5:00 a.m.! At first we hesitated for who would be listening at such a ridiculous hour. But it was free so why not take it. To our surprise, we discovered we had not only an audience but also those who would share their gifts. Dr. Hildebrand tells of one farmer who wrote and said he had heard the program called 'Morning Meditations' from the Briercrest Bible Institute while he was milking his cows. As he listened he said to himself, 'Anyone who will get up at this time of day to be on radio deserves some help.' A few days later the school received a very sizeable gift from this gentleman; again, with new hope we pressed on, but not without some questions.

While we now had several programs going out every week, which were geared primarily to adults and young people of Bible school age, there was nothing for the children. It was true that 'Back to the Bible' from Lincoln, Nebraska, had an excellent youth program each week, but as far as we knew there was not a single broadcast in Saskatchewan for children under ten years of age. The challenge was before us, and after a great deal of prayer and discussion with the General Board of Trustees, it was decided if suitable time could be purchased we would proceed with a broadcast with the younger members of the family in mind.

We soon discovered we not only had a host of children, but almost as many grandparents, listening to what was known as the 'Children's Hour.' The campus children provided the singing, while gifted faculty members and students assisted in the general direction of the program. We tried to keep the format and the message as simple as possible, and the result was that the 'Children's Hour' was heard each Saturday morning for the next thirteen years, with scores of boys and girls coming to know Jesus Christ as their personal Saviour and as the One who alone can give real meaning to life.

I have often been asked what I consider to be the greatest contribution I made to the Briercrest Bible College during my twenty-five years of ministry there. I can't say; God keeps the books and eternity alone will tell. I do know, however, that some of my most rewarding ministry was to have a small part in the training and moulding of young people's lives, as we studied God's Word together in the classroom, who are now faithfully serving the Lord in various regions throughout the world. Another special reward was to have a young lady or a young man stop me on the streets of Caronport, or to see them stand up at a time of praise and prayer in the chapel, and say, "I was saved as a child while listening to the 'Children's Hour.' "

Much more could be said, but if I were to sum up the radio ministry from the Briercrest Bible College since its inception in 1937 I would say it has been one of trials, tears and triumphs or fears, frustrations and fruitfulness. All were needed to keep us totally dependent upon the Lord, and to Him we give all the glory.

Today, after nearly fifty years of continuous weekly broadcasts, the voice of radio is still being heard from the College as faithful men of God teach the Scriptures which alone are able to make one wise unto salvation through faith in Jesus Christ and equip him for a victorious Christian life. Pray that it will ever be so."[3]

Rev. Homer and Esther Edwards were a couple with grace and taste. They loved the Lord and the Word of God. Both were introduced to Briercrest and to us through the broadcast. Esther, with her fine Norwegian wholesomeness and wholeheartedness, and Homer, with his Irish background, lent quite a bit of spirit to our campus.

Homer was well liked by students and the supporting constituency. He served well in the classroom, on the broadcast—being in complete charge of the children's broadcasts—and in the country. He served loyally at my side and was a right hand to me, ready to stand in the breach when called upon. He was a real associate and assistant to me. If I have one regret, it is this, that we did not designate him as such, for he certainly earned the title: Assistant to the President.

After serving the Lord at Briercrest for over twenty-five years, where the Edwards gave the heart of their lives to this work, they served for a number of years in the pastoral ministry at Faith Baptist of Regina. Due to his health, the Edwards have retired to Abbotsford, B.C. At this time of writing I am looking forward to ministering at Cloverdale Baptist during a Missionary Conference that Mr. Edwards is leading. And Inger and I will be hosted in the home of Homer and

Esther Edwards, who have won our love and deepest respect.

The broadcast, now on a more limited scale, is known as "The Briercrest Bible Hour." It is Canada's longest-sustaining gospel broadcast, having ministered for 2,444 consecutive Sundays. When I transferred the leadership of the college to Dr. Henry Budd, he selected Rev. John Barkman to lead this ministry. It was an excellent choice.

Mr. Barkman and his team are committed to the same goals of spreading the Biblical message through song, testimony, and message. The broadcast is being slowly extended to Alberta and British Columbia as alumni in several areas take an active part in its support. I believe that the broadcasting ministry is effective and has a great future. As the school gathers strength, we trust that it will soon feel it can again take on the giant task of "holding forth the Word of Life" from coast to coast. This can happen if the importance of this ministry is realized, particularly by our music department. Mrs. Hillson's prayer still echoes, "O God, that I might shout the message from the housetops!"

21

Over Land and Sea

In journeyings—often. 2 Corinthians 11:26

This was an exciting ministry but also very taxing. Let me share a few highlights. The Canadian Sunday School Mission invited me to direct its ministry in Saskatchewan during the summer. Rev. D. R. Aikenhead, our first Provincial CSSM Director, became General Director of the Mission in the late thirties and needed someone to take over his duties in our province. The lot fell to me. Since the Mission's strategy was, and still is, to reach the unreached in rural Canada, this gave me a tremendous opportunity to get acquainted with many nooks and corners of Saskatchewan.

One of the great services rendered by the Mission was camping. Every child who memorized 500 selected Bible verses from the gospel of John was rewarded with a free week at a Mission camp. However, due to the severity of the depression, this great ministry had been temporarily suspended. But in the early forties, the Mission had the opportunity to purchase Arlington Beach. This venture succeeded in launching once again the great CSSM camping ministry in our province. This bold venture also encouraged us to trust God—a little later—to possess the Caron Airport for BBC's new home.

Due to the growth of both BBC and the Mission, it became obvious that each needed a year-round, full time director. Though I loved the ministry of CSSM and of the school almost equally, I discerned that my mandate was to teach the Word to young people.

Since the school was my first responsibility to God, it became obvious that in all my travelling ministry I should seek to challenge youth to study the Word of God and encourage supporters to back young people who responded positively. This I felt to be my mission, but I needed to guard against spreading my work too thin, so as to become ineffective.

As BBC grew, and the alumni went to the far reaches of the world, pressing invitations came. My ministry extended to our grads as well as to students at home. This led to some ministry overseas. But first, let me share a unique experience in my ministry in the homeland.

During mid-term break in early March, 1976, I was speaking at a prophetic conference at Williams Lake in the heart of the Caribou Mountains of British Columbia. The weather was severe for that time of the year. On Monday, March 4, my host, Ron Giesbrecht, a BBC grad and rancher, drove in 20 miles so I could get the morning plane and arrive home in time for my classes on Tuesday. Arriving at the airport in good time, we discovered that the flight had been cancelled. Sharp Wings, a local bush flying company, was engaged to fly me to Prince George to catch the afternoon flight to Edmonton and Regina. I felt a bit uneasy about the flight, but it seemed the only way out. While we were fluttering some 5000 feet in the air above the rugged mountains, I had the conviction that I should share my faith with the pilot. I was to look after God's business, and he would look after mine. The pilot responded favourably, and then it happened.

We had just come out of the wilds below, north of Quesnel, and followed the highway leading to Prince George. The motor seized! In touch with ground control, the pilot decided against an attempt to land on the highway. The traffic was too heavy. Instead, he planned to line up with a side road that led to the highway. Judging, I assume, that if a crash-landing resulted, we were at least near the highway and in reach of help.

Meanwhile I studied the terrain to locate the nearest farmer. The wind carried us too far, and we were forced to land on a small field covered with two to three feet of snow. As soon as the wheels touched, we experienced whiteout, flipped, and somersaulted. When I came to, I was hanging upside down, strapped to my seat.

Since I had only a light summer coat, and the pilot was dressed in a snowsuit, we decided I would stay with the plane while he went in search of help. I gave him directions to the nearest farmer. Soon help was on the way. Meanwhile I was shivering with the cold, and the farmer and his wife showed no little kindness to us. We escaped without so much as a scratch, though the plane was badly damaged.

The farmer agreed to take me the rest of the way to Prince George. I shared my faith with him. Arriving at the airport an hour early, I approached the counter and asked for my reservation. The man stated that it had been cancelled. I insisted that I needed it. He tried to explain why it had been cancelled, and finally blurted out, "The guy had a plane crash and may have broken his neck. So we cancelled his reservation." You can imagine the surprise when I insisted that *I* was that man. It gave me a good opportunity to share my Jesus. God had a purpose in preserving me, that I might continue to challenge young people to study the Word of God in my travels near and far.

Europe continued to beckon "to come over and help them." The invitation came from mission leaders, some of whom were our graduates. They had been our fellow workers, serving now in Europe. Europe had a natural appeal. Inger is Norwegian by birth, and all her people live in Norway. With our speaking engagements at camps and missionary conferences, we could work in a visit to Inger's beloved Norway to see her people. Hence, we have ministered in Europe on several occasions. Let me summarize that ministry.

Our first visit to Europe in 1956 was by ship as the Bergensfjord completed its maiden voyage. The purser informed me that Pastor Berg from Booklin has been given charge of the religious services on this trip. He was a fine evangelical Lutheran, and during our first Sunday morning service, some 600 attended. He preached on the new birth from John 3. For Sunday evening he had me give the message, while he summarized it in Norwegian, since most passengers were Norwegians. After that the pattern was set. He chose to lead and translate the summary of my messages. The services every afternoon and evening were well attended.

Inger remained in Norway while I flew to Frankfurt to join the John Parschauers for a tour of ministry and sight-seeing throughout western Europe. With some Europeans, I also engaged in a week's Tent Campaign that was concluded by the Janz Team the week following. It was moving to see the young respond to the invitation. That European trip concluded with a missionary conference with the Greater Europe Mission in Paris. It was a joy to encourage the missionaries in the light of the book of Acts. I returned to Norway in time for Inger's brother's wedding, then homeward bound in time for Bible school opening.

Our latest ministry in Europe was by invitation from Inter-Mission Chairman, Rev. Harvey Schultz. I was invited to minister to the missionaries at their annual conference. It was held at a Christian campground situated in the central mountain range east of Lyons in the Huguenot country of France. What a privilege to speak to them on their conference theme, "The Model Servant of Christian Leadership." I also ministered in the Evangelical Church at Blois, where our graduate, Rev. Harvey Schultz interpreted. Harvey is the Director of the French work of the Bible Christian Union. It was most interesting to see how, in the very heart of the playgrounds and castles of French kings and nobility, a faithful witness of the gospel is established.

What a delight it was to minister again at the camps of the Word of Life Quartet at Starnberg Sea near Munich. How the young men obtained the castles, with access to the sea in the heart of Germany's vacation resort, is a modern miracle of great significance. It is the centre of activity from whence the gospel spreads forth all over Germany. At the conclusion of the Senior Young People's Camp, a Christian couple went out of their way to thank me for teaching the members of the quartet the Word of God. They were so grateful that they in turn had come to Germany to lead a soul-saving ministry. With tears in their eyes they told how their oldest daughter had become a Christian at that camp, how their son and second daughter also attended and came to know the Lord. In turn, they—father and mother—had also become Christians. How rewarding!

We experienced like joy when in response to invitations from BBC graduates in South America and Mexico we were pressured to visit them and minister the Word of His grace. Moreover, they wanted us to see firsthand what God was doing in regions beyond.

First, the Henry Klassens confirmed their personal invitation extended while they visited BBC at our conference. This was followed by the Don Clements of Bolivia and Royce Barons of Mexico. Spreading these letters before the Lord, we were assured that God was in it.

How graciously the Clements welcomed us at Santa Cruz to their beloved Bolivia. A ministry to the faculty, supporting staff, and students of the Tambo New Tribes Mission School awaited me. This school serves missionary children and is supported by several missions. Mr. Lots, the director of the New Tribes Mission, and Mr. Pettinger, Principal of the one hundred students attending the school in 1979, stated that about 80 percent of its graduates were returning to the mission field to serve. That speaks well of the parents, faculty, and especially of the M.K.'s.

A highlight of Bolivia ministry was a service with the Guarani Indian believers who worked on a sugar cane plantation. These people migrate to the lowlands and return to their highland homes when the sugar cane season is over. They represent many who have been evangelized by Don and Jan Clements and their fellow missionaries. What a heart-warming experience to mingle with them in candle-lit barracks for fellowship and worship. Don interpreted so beautifully the message I shared with the people.

A week later I left for Quito, Ecuador—The Land of Eternal Spring. Henry and Pat Klassen gave us a royal welcome. Henry took me to the western lowlands and Quayquil, Ecuador's largest city, situated on the Gulf leading to the Pacific Ocean. The purpose of the Ecuadorian trip was to see the beautiful land and its greater beauty, the church in action due to the missionary witness. We saw the march for Bible Day and the rally at the Centro Cirico attended by thousands.

Next we headed up to the Highland of Colta, 11,000 feet altitude. Then we crossed over the hump of the Andes to the eastern lowlands of Mera and Shell, from whence the five martyrs launched their mission to the Aucas. A church has been born since, and the gospel witness has been extended.

Colta is the scene of Henry and Pat Klassen's main ministry. God used them to build confidence as they lived among the Quichuas, suffering and sowing the precious seed. Today there are churches all over the highlands, with thousands and thousands of Quichua Christians. Since the government encourages people to open up and settle the eastern Lowlands of the jungle—which when tamed is very productive—many Quichuas respond and take the gospel with them, establishing new churches in the far reaches of the lowland jungles.

My main purpose in going to Ecuador was to share in the GMU Annual Missionary Conference. For five days I mingled with these lovely people and their families. It was a delight to minister the Word twice a day. A fellowship evening in the Klassen home, with a house full of BBC alumni, completed my visit to Ecuador.

Then I was off to Mexico, where Royce Baron welcomed me to the biggest city in the world. The Barons introduced me to the home Bible studies which they supervise. These Bible studies lay the groundwork for new churches. Moreover, Royce did all he could to make our visit to his adopted land profitable and productive.

How refreshed we were to observe BBC alumni in their day-to-day witness, in the midst of revivals with thousands of converts, as well as in their faithful witness to the few. Inger and I thanked God and took courage.

Another mission field that impressed itself upon our hearts was Alaska. Again, invitations to serve at the Inter-Mission Conference were extended. These had been initiated by another of our grads, Leander Rempel, the Director of the work at that time of SEND International in Alaska. This trip too was frought with unique experiences. To see the great ministries emanating from their headquarters at Glenallen is a wonder and a marvel to behold. A radio station sows the seed and softens the resistance of many areas to the gospel. A medical staff and hospital serve a very large area. The Bible college, fully accredited, offers a teaching ministry to young converts and prospective pastors and missionaries. They also have fine churches in many strategic areas.

One of the highlights was our service at Copper Center, the scene of the early labours of Mr. and Mrs. Joy, the Founders of the Central Alaska Mission, now the Alaska branch of SEND International. It was a church in the natural setting of Alaska, comprised of a mixture of Native Americans, predominantly Athabascan Indians. The service was well attended. Opportunities were given during the song service to choose favorite hymns. Instead of selecting a song, one Athabascan lady in her eighties stood forth and without accompaniment sang in her own language, "When We All Get to Heaven." Her voice was not only steady, but rich, with a good ring throughout three verses. As her tones faded, we all experienced a foretaste of heaven. It was easy to speak of the Saviour after that, and the Lord sealed our ministry by saving three precious teenagers.

The Inter-Mission Conference at Victory Bible Camp operated by Arctic Missions was also a moving event. Some 200 missionaries and their families from five or six different Alaska missions gathered for spiritual refreshing. God granted it. I shared with them the ministry of the Holy Spirit according to the book of Acts. I never heard such rousing singing, outside of our own chapel at BBC! It was heart-stirring to see missionaries in true Christian fellowship. Their love and optimism, in spite of some very difficult areas of service, were inspiring. They ministered as much to me as I to them. Such a conference is no doubt God's annual provision for their need of fellowship, for many serve in isolated places with a harsh climate. Leander and Louise Rempel and Jim and Ruth Andrews took good care of me so that, notwithstanding a very busy schedule, I returned refreshed in body and soul.

After seeing with our own eyes the work of faith, labour of love, and patience of hope exercised by many missionaries, including our BBC grads; and after seeing how they hazarded their lives for the gospel's sake, faced loaded guns (sometimes asked to choose who was to go first into eternity), were beaten, stoned and yet stayed with it,

Inger and I thank God for putting us into the ministry of BBC.

What an investment in lives for eternity! We dedicate ourselves anew and afresh to God to assist in this great work with whatever time and health God gives to encourage recruits for the Lord's work. We encourage President Budd and all his associates to press ahead with the task of training young lives. Likewise, we challenge the people of God to back as never before this great work in preparing harvesters for the great mission fields over land and sea.

22

Men and Women Who Influenced Me Most

Remember those who led you, who spoke the word of God to you; and considering the result of their conduct, imitate their faith.
Hebrews 13:7 NASB

It has been said that we are products of those who have gone before, guides of those who follow, and helpers of our contemporaries.

> Edmund Hillary and his Sherpa guide, Tenzig Norgay, had completed their historic 1953 climb of Mt. Everest. It was a feat of remarkable courage and skill. As they made their descent, however, Hillary lost his footing. Instinctively, Tenzing held the line taut and kept them both from falling by digging his ax firmly into the ice. Hillary soon recovered his balance, regained a foothold, and they continued their descent. When reporters later called Tenzing a hero, he refused to take any credit. Rather, he said, "Mountain climbers always help one another." He considered it a routine part of his job.[1]

Many are the influences that have kept me from falling and helped me on the pathway to glory. Those who have been influenced by me will find it interesting and helpful to read of those who influenced me the most.

Never given to hero worship, I could study with greater profit the lives and experiences of those who had so much to teach me. When some of the finest of God's people would inadvertently draw the outer cover aside and reveal a bit of sackcloth underneath the silk (2 Kings 6:30), I was not so disappointed as to question or reject the good they had to offer. I learned early in life what Oswald Chambers cautions, "Never make a principle out of your experience. Let God be as original with other people as He is with you."[2] Share your experiences, but don't impose them on others.

We should also remember this when we read the biographies of God's men and women. Be blessed by them, but don't be burdened nor bound by them. This applies equally to the men and women who have influenced me most. I am speaking of conscious influences. Let me mention just a few.

First, my parents. Too often in my study, young people have complained that their parents are Christians but they are not all that they are supposed to be. Without excusing parental or any other failure, I ask, "Did Joseph have perfect parents?" Any one who knows the story, knows about the tensions in Jacob's household. Some of it was due to Jacob's personal failure. Did Joseph use that as an excuse to rebel at home or to sin in Egypt? Has anybody ever had perfect parents? I know of none in the Bible.

Still, the Bible teaches us to obey our parents, because we have so much to learn from them. By practice and by percept my parents taught me lessons of godliness ". . . having promise of the life that now is, and of that which is to come." They taught me where to search for wisdom to order my life in this world, and for wisdom to prepare for the life hereafter. By nurture of the Word, and by discipline according to that Word, they taught me the way of life. Their respect for God and His Word has influenced me the most. I look forward to the day when I shall be able to take them by the hand and say, "Thank you, Dad and Mom, you were a true father and mother to me."

Next in influence is my wife and family. God has favoured us with a long life together. Soon we will celebrate our golden anniversary. When your partner serves God out of the integrity and purity of her heart, you are bound to respond positively. When difficult moments come, she pours the oil of gladness into one's heart. My motor runs all the more smoothly! Her influence on the entire school has been in true Biblical feminine fashion. Few know how powerful it has been for good.

Likewise the children. God gives us children that we may teach them life's lessons, but faithful parents learn from their children the deeper lessons, if they are sensitive to God's teaching through them.

Three teachers in Winnipeg Bible College helped me greatly as I began to think through my faith logically, organize it systematically, and articulate it clearly. Rev. Simon E. Forsberg, president of the school, was a dynamic and forceful teacher. He loved sound doctrine and got us excited about that field of study. He built upon the foundation laid in our homes and churches. He remained my teacher, counselor, and friend all of his life. He reinforced the direction of my life, and made sure it would remain in line with the Word of God.

While Mr. Forsberg taught the message to be communicated, Mrs. Forsberg taught me how to communicate it. She struggled with me so I would get the language right, and then proceeded to teach me the art of public speaking. I was a slow learner—and am still learning. But Mrs. Forsberg made me realize it was not sufficient to have the subject matter well in hand. It was necessary to deliver it with enthusiasm, taste, and grace. To you Rev. and Mrs. Forsberg, my students and I say, "Thank you. We owe a lot to you."

All my life God has favoured me with excellent teachers. Some were better than others, but all were good. However, the best organized of them all in presenting the material of each lecture, point by point, was Miss Murial Taylor. Dr. Merrill Tenney of Wheaton Graduate School was her equal in organization, but she managed to get a little more heart into a lecture and was more patient with some of our questions. I had the privilege of introducing Rev. and Mrs. Simon E. Forsberg to our students on several occasions and even had Miss Taylor teach some of my classes.

In seminary, Dr. Kenneth Kantzer stands out as a man of learning and grace. Patiently he would listen to his class. He was considerate with opposing views, and always fair in answering with skill the concerns of his students. He did not hide his convictions, nor did he hesitate to declare "all the counsel of God."

Dr. Edward J. Young was a scholar who carried his knowledge of the Old Testament and the Semitic languages with humility. His opponents could not withstand his wisdom nor the spirit in which he spoke.

I also had the rare privilege of learning from Dr. Cornelius Van Til. He is one of the few Christian philosophers who could adequately defend the Christian world-view. He would trace Christianity's conflict with its foes through the ages and point out that, though Satan may intensify his attack upon the Christian faith, he has no new weapons to bring forth. All the enemy can do is to dress his attacks in modern garb. He said so emphatically, "We (they) shall overcome them all 'by the blood of the lamb, and by the word of our (their) testimony; not loving our (their) lives unto the death.' "

Of the writers I could mention many who have meant so much to me, but none have attained unto three, who in influence and direction stand second only to the Bible. They are Spurgeon, Ironside, and Morgan.

Charles Hadden Spurgeon taught me how to put the whole man, his whole personality imbued by the Spirit of God, into each message. Although Spurgeon revealed a very good understanding of the original languages, he did not burden his audiences with them. His messages were Christocentric without exception. From every text he found his way to Christ. And every audience he pointed to Christ.

Dr. Harry A. Ironside taught me how expository preaching can be interesting and exciting. He had the unique faculty of simplifying some of the deeper truths without over simplification. Many seminary students scoff at the simplicity of his writings, but it is usually those who have neither read him, heard him, nor understood the depth of his exposition. To them, depth is not equated with clarity, but rather with muddiness or bemuddledness. Read Ironside with profit and understanding. Dr. Ironside was the only one of my favorite writers whom I heard personally on several occasions.

But perhaps the writings that have most influenced me are the works of G. Campbell Morgan. He was in his mature years when I was young, and I expected to see him in action like our Master Teacher. However, World War II closed that possibility. I still have in my study 46 volumes by this man of God, and, with the exception of some of his sermons, I have read them all and studied many volumes carefully. He taught me to think and live in the light of the whole of God's revelation—to study each text in the light of the context—and the book in the light of the whole Bible.

I could mention other works and more recent writers that I love, but these three excelled in always leading me to Christ. They were at their best when they spoke of "My Beloved."

My associates have had a tremendous influence on me and the school; foremost among these is President Henry Budd. He has a unique faculty for stimulating the people of God on all levels and walks of life with the same Biblical message. As God's hand remains on him, he will be one of the foremost Bible teachers in North America.

My students influenced me much more than they realized. Not when they complained or sent delegations to see if they could improve the life of the school. Often they just wanted to be free to do their own thing. More often they were sincere and kept me abreast with the thinking of the day. They provided a text for my study of the present generation. I listened and observed. The most up-to-date screen was my study window, and the best natural performers were the students. You can see a live show almost any day or evening just by looking through my window. They were not putting on a show, they were natural actors.

My students taught me to remain young in outlook, buoyant, and optimistic. Their enthusiasm was contagious and their zeal inspiring. But it was their commitment to Christ that I love the most. Keep it up! We have a lot to learn from you.

Let me conclude by paying tribute to the many of "God's Hidden Ones" who have wrestled at the throne of God in my behalf. I am indebted to them, and they will be fully revealed and rewarded in that day when the veil will be lifted and we shall know as we are known.

23

H. Hildebrand Family Life

God setteth the solitary in families . . . Psalm 68:6.

One generation shall praise thy works to another, and shall declare thy mighty acts, Psalm 145:4. I was happy in my task largely because I was happy in my home. Both Inger and I come from solid, godly homes. The family ties are strong and for good. But by the time I was courting her, she had been away from her home in Norway for several years. I too had been away from home for several years studying for missionary work. Those first summers spent in student service found me in a new home or another home every night.

When I visited Inger she could not take me to her home which was thousands of miles across the sea, and I could not take her to my home, except on a few occasions, because it also was miles out in the country. So we would go to church, or walk the streets of Winnipeg, or sit on park benches, dreaming of a home of our own someday. So home began to have a special meaning for us.

When we married on Aug. 12, 1937, the saints at Briercrest provided a three-room suite for us. At once the touches of home made it so attractive! The second year, the school obtained the Yale Hotel, and since both fellows and gals occupied the residential area, we occupied two rooms to provide supervision. The school grew and houses for men's dormitories were obtained, opening the lower floor for our new home in the Gilroy House as it came to be called. Then when the college obtained the Royal Canadian Airforce base near

Caron, we took possession of what was then known as the Fire Hall.

We moved into the hall's open barracks. Partitions and kitchen cupboards were built by students, who gave one hour each day. So each day they messed up the place with shavings and sawdust. Patiently Inger cleaned up each evening. As I look back, that was a needless hardship. We should have insisted that the students do their work on weekends. The folks in charge of the work did not seem to catch on when gentle hints were given. But it was home and we loved it. After 24 years, the college provided a brand new house at 550 Elm Crescent. For 26 years its very walls testify to our gratitude to God for His bountiful provision. The home's colour and rugs, its furniture and pictures express our love for home sweet home.

But what is a home without children? God was so good to us! He gave two baby girls and three baby boys within the space of eighteen years. Their names: Marcia, Mrs. Phil Leskewich; Evelyn, Mrs. Bob Moore; David; Paul; and Glen. God honoured us by having our children—each in her or his turn—come to us, seeking the Saviour. After a CSSM camp meeting at Arlington Beach, Marcia, about four years old, asked her mother to lead her to the Lord. Evelyn did likewise a year later.

David snuggled up to me in my study when he was four. He too wanted to become a Christian. So did Paul, at the age of four, ask me to lead him to Christ. But Glen was led to the Lord by his brother Paul also at four.

I was away on one of my tours for the school. A guest speaker had been preaching on the second coming of Christ. Paul, nine years old, felt that Glen couldn't wait till Dad got home. That might be too late! So he turned soul-winner and took Glen into my study and led him to the Saviour, as Dad had done with him. All of our children have followed the Lord in baptism and seek to bear a good witness to their Saviour.

The schools we began to train other people's children served our own children the most. They all took their grade school, high school, and Bible school at Briercrest over a period of 33 to 34 years. Since discussion was encouraged around family meals, everyone felt free to talk—and talk they did! They must have received the "gift of talk" from their mother, for she is the quiet, listening member of the family. She must have given her "gift of talk" to them, since I kept mine.

Our family is so very human, only some of them are more so; and a few of us, perhaps too much so. Those family discussions indirectly served me very well. Like five antennas spanning 34 years, their conversation about classes, teachers, students, and general activities kept me well informed. I did not coach nor encourage our children for such a purpose. They just felt free to talk about things that were of interest to them, and since life on the campus was of interest to me, I needed no official briefing. I just kept my eyes and my ears open, and I saw and heard all that was profitable in leading a school.

Neither Inger nor I pretended anything but what we were before our children: they knew that we understood them, felt with them, and encouraged them to turn their lives over to Jesus, who alone is worthy of our fullest trust. Glen gave me what I felt was a fine compliment. "Dad, you are at home exactly what you are in chapel before the students. We all love you for it." They appreciated that we prayed for them regularly, and, that in God's time, He would lead a Christian mate into their lives.

God answered that prayer, and everyone of our children found a Christian mate. All of them married school mates of our own campus. Marcia married Phil Leskewich, who is now Divisional Manager of Mid-Continental of Calgary, a division of Reimer Express. They worshipped at Grant Memorial Baptist Church were Phil served his term as Chairman of the Board. They have three daughters; Donna, Sandra and Rhonda. Donna graduated from BBC in 1982 and is in full-time Christian work with Campus Life in Winnipeg. Sandra is studying at BBC. Rhonda hopes to join her in a year.

Evelyn married Dr. Robert Moore, whose practice is in Lakefield, Ontario. They worship in their local First Baptist Church. They have three children; Paul, Daniel and Rebecca. Paul is completing his senior high school year.

David married Jean Fuller. He is an ordained minister of the Christian and Missionary Alliance. He completed his doctoral studies at the University of Toronto and is Associate Dean—Education at BBC. They have three active sons; Robert, Timothy and Jonathan.

Paul married Corinne Armstrong. He completed his B.Ed. and is now teaching in Usher High School in Regina. They worship at Faith Baptist Church, and he serves the church as moderator. They have two children, Tyler and Dawn.

Glen married Joanne Heinrichs. Like our other children, he completed studies at BBC, then continued at Trinity Western for his B.A. and at Simon Frazer for his B.Ed. He teaches at Abbotsford Junior High. They worship at Seven Oaks Christian and Missionary Alliance Church and are active in Bible studies and in a musical ministry. He has been representing the BBC Alumni in the Frazer Valley. For healthy children and grandchildren who know the Lord, we give our thanks, praying that each may be kept in His way.

Travels in the interest of the school were plenty, although I always felt that the time at home was the more profitable. Still the college had to be represented out in the field, and it often fell to my lot to log my share. As the broadcasts extended across the nation and the school began to be known, invitations came for conference ministries farther afield. As faculty members, we took our turns. On one occasion, due to conditions beyond our control, a member of the faculty was unable to spell me off as planned. So my travels in Central Canada extended for three months.

Desperately lonesome were both of us! It was especially difficult for Inger to manage the children and the affairs of the home all by herself. But we accepted this as from a Higher Hand and did it for His sake and the ministry of the school. If Inger had not so willingly served in this capacity, we could not have escaped serious consequences to the family. Since she shared the burdens without bitterness, the family was led to do likewise.

Inger had earned my total trust that she would manage the household well. I dread to think what might have happened to our children if she had not accepted full responsibility. She was a good disciplinarian, and dealt with each case promptly. Whenever possible, right on the spot.

Moreover, during my frequent absences, she was my most reliable listening post on our campus. I was well briefed about the atmosphere and state of the School. This prevented me from blundering, not aware of what was taking place and what was needed. We always looked forward to fall and winter, largely because we entered into our major ministry—classes with students. But also, we could be mostly home together as a family. I often wonder whether, as a result, we unconsciously developed a love for fall and considered it the most beautiful season of the year? We loved Saskatchewan's winters, because we were home those days.

How grateful we are to the Board of Directors that upon our retirement they voted that the college would pay for Inger's expenses whenever we made a trip for the school. With the family on their own, this is part of our reward, to be able to travel together. Even then, we want to use this privilege judiciously. Frankly, no matter how exciting the prospects of a trip and how well it turns out, the best part of any trip is still—the way home.

It is obvious to the reader that both Inger and I love family life. It is so natural, unfettered, and free. God meant it to be so. Both of us came from well-disciplined homes, and we agreed that it would be a must in our home. Of the two, Inger is the better disciplinarian—always consistent. I still enjoy the debates with our family around the table. I often smile at the memory of them. Our girls and our boys felt free to debate issues and how the school should be run. At times the discussions would become rather spirited! Mother always insisted that even in the excitement of discussion and debate, the children must respect their Dad and speak respectfully to him. It was hard for them to think of that when excitement reached fever pitch. Our silent listener would speak up, "Paul—or whoever—remember you are speaking to your Father." No wonder I won most of the debates, since Mother was the official referee!

One day Paul, turning 14 or 15, came through the front door, plunked his books on the table, and in an aggravated tone rasped out the following, "That's what I say! This campus is too restrictive for campus kids. We're under these rules all our life!"

He was due at one of his class activities and I was busy. I felt the time wasn't propitious to take up the challenge. I waited until both he and I had the time to discuss the matter. So one evening while he was in his room studying (he was well disciplined in this), I stopped in and asked what he meant by saying that the campus was too restrictive.

"Well isn't it?" he answered.

I asked, "In which way? Give me some specifics."

He fumbled a bit, and then mentioned that he wasn't allowed to go to Moose Jaw on Thursday night to watch a hockey game. I explained that the campus had nothing to do with it. For example some campus kids do attend.

"Then why can't I?"

"Are you satisfied with the same grades they make in school?"

"No," he replied.

"That's why I insist that you study on Thursdays. The campus has nothing to do with it. It is your Dad that insists on it."

I asked if he had any other examples where the campus rules were too restrictive. He couldn't think of any but he felt sure there were. I suggested that if he thought of any he should tell me.

Nothing was ever said about it again. About three months later, on a beautiful May holiday, the boys were romping on our lawn. Our windows were open. Suddenly I heard a voice that sounded so familiar, lecturing his own campus buddies. "Fellows, don't blame the campus rules for it." I looked out the window and saw about eight of them in a circle in the shade. Paul continued, "It's not the campus rules, it's your Dads who are responsible for many of the rules. Blame them for it. It's not the campus' fault, it's your Dad's." I observed that the lesson had been well learned, so I never referred to it again. Nor did he.

As in my father's house, family worship was the practice of the day. During my frequent absences, Mother dutifully took over. Here the family learned in a special way to face the stress and temptations of life together and so look to God for aid through the day. Truly, "In the fear of the Lord is strong confidence: and his children shall have a place of refuge" (Proverbs 14:26). I will let David describe the family devotions in his Father's home.

Family Devotions

Family Bible reading and prayer in our home was usually around the table. Always someone would ask the blessing before meals, and also before coffee (somehow watermelon didn't count!). Family devotions were twice a day—after breakfast and after supper, except on Sunday, when they followed the noon meal. One might per chance skip breakfast, but you needed to be up and at the table for Bible reading and prayer. This was adhered to regularly, though not without struggle, for gym or skating were right after supper, and so were class program practices. These activities would begin at 6:35 or 6:40, and Dad regularly didn't get home from work until 6:20 or 6:30. While one could be a few minutes late for skating without difficulty, it was another thing if you were the conductor at the class practice and needed to have everything set up early! More than once supper devotions were immediately upon Dad's arrival at the table and before my departure. Still the family regularly ate every dinner and supper meal all together. When Dad was away, as was often the case, family devotions continued as usual, with Mom in charge.

One of us would read, often in Scripture Union's *Junior Notes* (later *Daily Bread*), and another would pray. The time spent was fairly brief, at least we realized that was the case as we grew older. It was to an invitation at the end of breakfast devotions that I responded, albeit somewhat later in the morning, and knelt to receive Christ. Once in awhile there were special needs within the family circle—the system was in place for bringing these needs to God as a family. Prayer was always made for all members of the family, whether present or absent.

In my younger years I can remember that devotions sometimes included memorization (especially Psalm 103). Then as we grew up, singing became a regular addition to our Sunday dinner devotions. Often there was four-part harmony, and often the grandchildren got their choice. If there is ever a touching moment in our family circle, it's usually during the singing that follows right after the prayer in which each of us has been mentioned by name. Mom made Sunday dinner very special for us—we still drive for miles to make it home for that. Our time together in devotion to God was always a fitting close to the meal.

How well I remember coming home one weekend after a particularly disturbing class. It was at the beginning of my university days. I realized with thanks and tears what a difference there was between one pagan professor and a faithful father. Home set a good pattern and, together with Jeannie, I seek to follow this pattern in my own home.

Like my friends, my family has been good to me, much better than I deserve. They have been a blessing and an inspiration to both Inger and me. Our family gatherings mean so much to us. Perhaps Jeannie, our daughter-in-law, can give you a more objective description of these.

Family Gatherings

We ring the doorbell and walk in—we're home for a family gathering. Even though our family lives close by, both Dad and Mom come to the door making us feel special and wanted. Dad's greeting is invariably the same; a hearty "welcome here," while Mom's face is wreathed in smiles. Her greatest joy is to have her children all home. Mom looks relaxed and is beautifully dressed, but her apron, the heavenly smells, and the spotless house all testify to the many hours she has spent preparing for this time.

One by one the families arrive. While the adults comment on a new outfit or begin joshing about lost (or gained) pounds or emerging grey hairs, the grandchildren head straight for the cupboard to check out the supply of Gramma's special chocolate chip cookies.

Hildebrand family gatherings inevitably include food. While some families might lounge together in jeans with a sandwich, our family likes to dress up to complement the extended table, gracefully set with silver, china, and candles. And what meals we have! Beef and Yorkshire pudding on a Sunday, turkey for Christmas. As the several vegetables and salads are passed, two comments can be expected: Glen or David will say there is not enough room on his plate; and Dad will urge everyone to eat plenty of jello salad so he won't have to eat leftovers for a week! Highlights of each meal are the homemade favorites—Mom's grape juice, buns, apple pie or the Norwegian flötkake. The conversation is lively during the meal. Paul, interested in politics and history, might have a new theory to try out on the family, or some phrase might bring back an amusing incident from the past and the reminiscing will begin. Because we are not all together often, the conversation spills over as we try to catch up on each other's lives. Though his children are interested to find out about Dad's travels, an outsider might be surprised at the short space of time in conversation given to this until they realize that this has always been their dad's way of life and is neither novel nor surprising to them.

After dessert, there is devotions. Usually a grandchild reads the Scriptures and Grandpa prays. As he mentions each by name it seems, to me, almost like a small commissioning service that sends us on our way with new spiritual encouragement and a sense of continued parental support. The meal ends with singing. Especially in later years, some tears might choke up this or that one as the realization dawns that these special gatherings might someday come to an end. One memorable meal, Marcia choked up and one after another the family followed until Dad was left to bravely finish the song alone—and even his voive wavered. That day tears gave way to spontaneous laughter.

In the afternoon, there might be a football match on TV, or a game to play (crokinole is a favorite at Christmas), but the usual gathering finds the children romping in the basement while all the adults sit in the living room continuing the dinner conversation.

All too soon it's evening—time for a light supper, and then time to say goodbye. We leave with beautiful memories and a bag of homemade buns.

Marcia will describe how valuable were the opportunities of studying on this campus to her as they now are to her children.

Educational Opportunities

As campus kids at Caronport, we had tremendous opportunities and advantages.

When I think back, I have very happy memories of my life as a campus kid. Now, as a parent, I realize more than ever how truly fortunate I was to have the fellowship of Christian young people, the godly atmosphere, and the example of teachers who have had a profound influence upon my life.

We had access to all campus facilities, sports, and academic life at little or no cost and had opportunity to learn skills and disciplines that have been a benefit to me over the years.

A special highlight and blessing of living at Caronport was to be exposed to truly fine music, both sacred and classical, and to develop an appreciation and enjoyment of it. We had opportunity to learn music skills and to participate in choirs of fine calibre under good leadership.

Often during the course of the winter months we were privileged to sit under the ministry of men of God who were giants of the faith. As a campus kid, I would often have opportunity to meet these great men and women of God in our home on a less formal basis and could observe their close walk with their Lord.

Having the privilege of absorbing God's word under the tutorage of Christian professors had a tremendous influence on my life. For me, the highest privilege of all was to sit under the beautiful teaching ministry of my father. Believe me, I had a great deal of incentive to achieve academically! Also to ensure that my walk with the Lord was in line with the Christian principles taught by my esteemed professor.

Having the opportunity to learn God's word and having fine Christian examples from which to pattern my life has helped me to develop a Christian philosophy for my life and, as well, to enable me in the training of our children.

The choice of a life mate is of great importance to any young person, especially so for a Christian. What better place to "look" than a campus where most of the young men are Christians? For me that was right at home on campus. God was good in bringing into my life a young man who had the same commitment as I and who loved the Lord. We have been married now for 25 years, and I continue to thank God for leading Phil to Briercrest and then leading us together.

God has been good to Phil and me and has given us three daughters. How thankful we are that now our children have opportunity to attend our school and also to have the privilege of being influenced by godly Christian grandparents whom they love dearly living right on the campus. Our eldest daughter graduated two years ago and now our second daughter is attending. Our youngest daughter hopes to enroll at Briercrest this next fall.

I have much to be grateful for in being brought up in a loving Christian home under such wonderful parents whose influence and example were very evident in our home and upon my life. Because of their call, I was privileged to live in a Christian community right on campus with its many advantages and blessings, for which I will always be grateful.

"How do your children feel about the pressure of "fish-bowl" living on campus?" I am sometimes asked. I believe they have, as a whole, positive feelings about it. We never tried to warn them of certain "No, no's," because they were children of the President. Rather, we tried to instill the Lordship of Christ as their guide. Perhaps I had better let Glen express it.

Growing up as the President's Son

What was it like being the President's son growing up at Caronport? This is a question I have often heard from my friends and from others I have met. As I look back at my twenty-three odd years at Caronport I can't help but look at them with appreciation. Although my father was the president of Briercrest Bible College, for some reason that concept was never really prevalent in my thinking. Oh I knew the position my father held, and I suppose others did as well, but it never seemed to matter to me nor to my friends.

The upbringing I had from both my father and mother never entertained that kind of thinking. I believe that was largely due to the attitude my parents had in the beginning of Briercrest Bible College and maintained while I was growing up. An article written by Dr. Henry Budd in the September issue of the *Briercrest Echo* states: "If you aim to be a leader, you will be frustrated, because no one wants to follow; if you aim to serve, you will be needed." Matt. 20:28, states that Jesus came "not to be served but to serve." It was with this attitude I know that my father began the work at Briercrest and the same attitude was shared by my mother that blessed the work throughout their lives. This was the attitude I grew up under. My parents never thought I was anything above average, but, at the same time, they never thought that I was less than average. With that type of guidance and instruction at home it never crossed my mind as I was growing up that I should expect certain privileges or recognition. I can honestly say that I cannot recall being expected to be better than any normal youngster growing up in that environment. I'm sure there were those that felt I was expected to "perform" better because of my father's position, but to their credit, and to that of all the staff and faculty at Briercrest, I never felt that pressure.

That attitude also seemed to have contributed to the relationships I had with friends while growing up on campus. To my knowledge I was never treated in any way "special," or looked down upon by my friends. We played together, learned together, fought together, and shared together all in a way friends would. I could see this because my friends never treated me differently than they treated each other. My being the President's son was never mentioned. It was simply immaterial, unimportant, in our attitude as kids.

The same happened at school from elementary on through to Bible school. I never realized any difference in the way I was treated from my classmates. I knew that if there was trouble at school of my own making, Dad would support the teacher. I would likely pay double for any transgression. Knowing this, I expected no different treatment, and to my knowledge never got it. I enjoyed my schooling and the many teachers I had.

When my wife, Joanne, and I were beginning to date, my parents' position was never an issue. She mentions that some of the other girls in the dorm would ask about it, but she had never really given it thought. As we were becoming seriously interested in each other, it is a credit to the attitude of my parents that Joanne saw no sign that I felt in any way superior to any other individual on campus. To her I was simply someone she had met and was beginning to become interested in.

What was it like being the President's son at Caronport? I could probably ask any of you who have had the privilage of being raised by committed Christian parents, who loved the Lord and who loved each other, and your answer would likely have been as mine. It was special; special to me.

Our children learned to accept hospitality early in life. For years the Hildebrand home was the guest room for visiting missionaries and speakers. Many a time our children were rooted out of their bedrooms to make way for guests. They did not exactly shout for joy, still they responded and profited by it. In the home and around the table these men and women of God were an inspiration to all in our household. They enriched our lives. Our son, Paul, expresses it so profitably.

I Remember

The other day, my five-year-old son, Tyler, slipped into our crowded living room. It was full of adults who had gathered for our regular home Bible study. Our turn had come to host the study. As the study progressed, Tyler sat as quietly as he could. He knew that if he became noisy or distracting, he would be sent out of the room. But it is such a pleasure for a "little guy" to pretend that he is an adult, to sit with adults, even to participate in discussion every once in a while, as considerate friends included him in conversation. Nothing was going to jeopardize this chance!

As I observed, my mind went back to my childhood when I relished such opportunities to "be an adult" in Mom and Dad's living room. As a youngster, it was enough just to be there. As I grew older and began to follow the discussion as it went back and forth, I wanted to be there because it was fascinating.

Missionaries, preachers, politicians, and businessmen from many parts of the world passed through that living room. Ideas and arguments were bantered back and forth, covering a variety of topics. World problems were often discussed from perspectives of people who had been there or who had been involved.

I loved it. As I matured, I was allowed to enter the conversation, then to ask questions, then to timidly test my ideas, then to defend my ideas. It was an experience that has affected my life and interests. Mom and Dad's hospitality played a part in developing a boy's thinking process and self confidence. That boy is grateful.

Fifteen years later, I was to sit in a diplomatic reception at NATO headquarters in Brussels as a Canadian Teachers' Federation delegate. I enjoyed every minute of this opportunity to interact with diplomats. It was almost like an extension of my childhood experiences.

Today, I am a teacher of Social Studies in a Regina Collegiate. Every day I get to discuss local, Canadian, and world problems with high school students. Hopefully, I am imparting to them the same enthusiasm that Mom and Dad had for the world in which we live. All of its problems and complexities are challenges which we in our society can do our part to overcome, with the help of God."[6]

No matter how limited the finances, we planned to set time aside for a vacation or picnic outings. One morning, the lunch was packed and in the car trunk. The children—three of them—were excited and already in the car. Inger stepped in, and I closed the door, went around to get in, when suddenly a car drove up. A fellow got out and with a sigh of relief shouted, "Hm! . . . am I glad I caught you home! I drove miles to see you, and I was just hoping you would be home."

I could hear three other sighs through the open window of the car, "Oh no! we've had it." We finally ate the picnic lunch at our kitchen table. Lesson learned: Next time get away *before* the phone rings or somebody catches you still at home and keeps you occupied for the better part of the day.

As ministry pressures mounted, holidays were often planned in conjunction with speaking engagements at camps or Bible conferences held at Banff and Jasper. It was not the same as when Dad was completely free, but it was a pleasant change. When propitious to do so, we would remain the week after and enjoy ourselves to the full.

The importance and security of a caring family is obvious from the testimonies above. It took a devoted wife and willing children to make it possible for me to lead BBC in difficult times.

24

Family Health and Strength

For my strength is made perfect in weakness. 2 Corinthians 12:9.

J. Oswald Sanders informs us that when Robert Murray McCheyne, the saintly young Scottish minister, lay dying at the age of 29, he turned to a friend who was sitting with him and said, "God gave me a message to deliver and a horse to ride. Alas, I have killed the horse and now I cannot deliver the message."[1]

Both spiritual and physical health are important to the Christian ministry. John wrote to the well-beloved elder, Gaius, saying, "Beloved, I wish above all things that thou mayest prosper and be in health, even as thy soul prospers" (3 John 2).

How do you handle this issue when you are not naturally robust? When the question of health is ever before you? When it seems that it is only a matter of a day or so and your strength is gone? Should you pamper the body? Play it easy? Look only for soft places and easy tasks?

The answer is simple. Work all the harder at it. Not in thoughtless abandoned of health, but in disciplining your body as yourself, by rationing your strength to accomplish the task with God's help. Let me illustrate.

My people tell me that I was a sickly child. I was susceptible to all the childhood diseases and had difficulty in shaking them. When pestilence stalked through our area with the Revolution, I escaped the dread typhus fever, but cholera got me. Weakened, I succumbed to rheumatic fever. Slowly recovering from it, my nerves, already frayed from the frightening revolution, gave way to a bout with St. Vitus Dance. Sound familiar—an old man talking about his aches and pains? But read on. I have a purpose for you.

Before I was a year old, I'm told, I managed to grab a fork at the table and poked it into my left eye, scarring the tissue covering the pupil. Learning to swim, we boys as a group loved to dive until we would dare venture to dive off the bridge. That was the heroic thing to do. Whatever I did wrong, on one occasion, as I hit the water, I split an eardrum. I also contracted trachoma, a contagious inflammation about the eyes. This had to be treated with blue-stone and delayed our emigration to Canada by a year.

Years later, the Saskatchewan T.B. vans came to our school to take x-rays—a preventative measure to curb this scourge. They discovered scars in my lung. As they examined me carefully, they asked when I had suffered from tuberculosis? What contacts I had with the disease? I recalled that while I was still very young, my parents had a close relative in our home who suffered and eventually died from T.B. Hospitals were not available immediately after the Revolution and since our cousin had lost his parents, my folks took him into our home. The examining specialists here in Canada deducted that I must have contracted T.B. but somehow, unknown to us, God healed me. This, however, might explain why I was so weak and sickly those early years.

All this has left me with an irregular heartbeat that worries the heart specialist, a blurred vision on my left eye that makes it difficult to judge distance, impaired hearing on my right ear—which a hearing aid can hardly correct, a contracted esophagus which I have to stretch periodically with a bougie so I can swallow food, and a nervous stomach that needs constant consideration. But here I am at 74, enjoying good health!

Over against that is Inger, my mate, who has been exceptionally well. She has not needed hospital care except to give birth to our five children. Our girls are still laughing about the time their mother told them, that on our first date, I inquired about the state of her health. When Dr. Goertzen, a close friend, heard about it he felt it had been a wise consideration. Inger bravely took my welfare upon her heart and determined to keep this body of mine functioning and fit to do the work with its heavy duties that God had entrusted to us. And with God's help we succeeded.

How did God so teach us, that in spite of so many limitations, I hardly missed a day at work? First, I learned to accept limitations.

They faithfully served as a yellow light—a warning light. It's time to stop and take a breather, physically—spiritually. I visited a robust friend once who was laid aside with little hope of recovering sufficiently to do any meaningful active service. He had been so healthy, so strong. I asked him what had invalided him. I shall never forget this answer, spoken in a weak voice that had been so vibrant, "Henry, I went through too many red lights, thinking I could get away with it, that's all. Through too many red lights, and I got caught. God has forgiven me, but my body hasn't."

Second, accept your limitations, either to correct them or at least make them serve you. Learn to do not just what you like, but to like what has to be done (Phil. 4:11). For me it meant guarding my diet. This was not easy when months on end were spent in different homes. Most hostesses, however, served good, healthful meals that with a little selection and a lot of discipline served me well.

Exercise regularly. With determination and discipline this too was possible, even away from home. One exercise or another was usually available. Fortunately my hobbies served me well too. I like swimming, golfing, fishing, and gardening. I relax completely listening to good music over the stereo or when attending an occasional symphonic event. I love to hear our student choirs and musical teams. And I like reading for pleasure. I also enjoy active games, watching athletes display their skills in competitive sports. I much prefer watching a hockey game to a shuffleboard drag. I do not find the latter too relaxing.

When possible we enjoyed holidays with our children, but more often we had our holidays at camps or Bible conferences. When teaching is a delight and mingling with people is an inspiration, camp life can be so rewarding and refreshing.

Moreover, God has been so good to me that till this day I do not know what a headache means. He also gives his beloved sleep. Here, in Canada, I can recall only a few nights when sleep was gone, and even then I dreamed off at times. No matter how difficult the problem or how impossible the solution seemed in the evening, God gave to His child the needed rest. At times the more difficult the situation the better the sleep. In the morning, well rested and refreshed, God usually met me with the most appropriate Word. Assured of His help, I could face the day with confidence that all things were working together for good and they did (Romans 8:28). With gratitude in my heart and spring in my step, I went to greet my students in chapel.

My purpose was to keep soul and body fit for the task. God

honoured the effort and I could carry the average load of work without interruption, and hardly ever missed a class due to sickness. Hardly ever, except when I broke my ankle playing hockey! It took a little while to knit; in fact, it had to be reset. While convalescing in the hospital I received a card of sympathy from one of my preacher friends. He wrote, "Now that you are cracked up at both ends, whatever can we say to our friends who never had a doubt about the state of the upper end?" The ankle healed and I was back in the classroom, having learned a good lesson. Since we did not have nor could we afford replacements, was it really right for me to engage in such youthful sport? Was it not about time to act my age?

Several young men in radio land heard the report about my ankle on our broadcast and took heart. Said they, "That school is human! Its president plays hockey. I want to enroll there." They did, and told me so when they studied with us. Many of our students have taken heart because their president is so human. But not all responded so. On one occasion one student lectured me, "We know you are so human with human weaknesses, but let's not brag about it." That too was a learning lesson for me.

Every home blessed with children knows the tests that come when their own become sick, the fever rages, and the best of medical help has been sought. But you keep vigil by the bedside, feeling so helpless. It is then we know that the Great Physician is with us, the Sympathizing Jesus. Sometimes He pitches a burden upon our hearts too heavy to bear. So He says, "Will you come to me with your burden? I will carry it for you and give you rest."

David had been ailing for some time. He was susceptible to flu and colds. The glands about his neck were swollen. Our family doctor kept an eye on it. When the swelling did not subside, a biopsy was taken. I was engaged in a weekend Bible conference when Inger received the report from the doctor. On the way home, David, not 12 years old, noticed that Mother was heavy of heart. He suspected that the diagnosis was serious, and it was. Inger phoned Saturday night after the evening service. The doctor diagnosed David's trouble as Hodgkin's disease—considered fatal in children 30 years ago. David was to be informed by me when I got home.

I was staying at the Irvin and Ethel Rodin home in Unity where they shepherded the flock. They were very gracious in their ministry of comfort. So God enabled me to complete the services and return home by night train to Saskatoon and by bus to Moose Jaw. When word of David's illness got around before I left Unity, some well-meaning folks tried to counsel me, insisting that when I got home I would tell David the whole truth. A Christian Father must not lie to his boy.

I, too, meant to remain true to my boy. He was still so young. How much would I say to him? On the way home I sought the face of my Heavenly Father. In my Bible reading I had come to Genesis 22—the story of Abraham and his son Isaac. Isaac, about David's age, knew that his father was heavy hearted as the two trudged up Mt. Moriah. Isaac broke the silence, "My Father . . . behold the fire and the wood: but where is the lamb for a burnt offering?"

Abraham answered, "My son, God will provide himself a lamb for a burnt offering." Note the comment, "So they went both of them together."

There was my answer to the questions that David was bound to ask, for his mother had told him, "Father will explain when he comes home."

Abraham was true to his son, but not brutal. At so young an age, Isaac could not possibly have understood if his father had said something like this. "Son, you will be the lamb and I will plunge my knife into your bosom, and you will be the burnt offering. God has asked me to do so, and I cannot be disobedient to God."

Abraham said nothing of the kind. He simply answered, "God will provide himself a lamb." His young son was satisfied with that answer. Abraham's example became my cue. Inger met me at the bus depot in Moose Jaw. On the way home we discussed how God had met me with the story of Abraham and Isaac. She warned me that David would be persistent in his questions. He was. But God enabled me to answer all his questions wisely and to his satisfaction. I did not mention the name of the disease, for he would at once go to the dictionary and find the blunt facts. He accepted the fact that his life was in Higher Hands—that God was gracious to him. I told him that the doctors recommended deep x-rays to arrest his disease, and that the treatments would be unpleasant and may have to be repeated. He responded favourably, accepted the explanation, and submitted to the treatment with its side effects. But he also trusted God to undertake and do what was best. God did.

Furthermore, we availed ourselves of the avenue of prayer with the people of God who volunteered to meet with us at the Throne of Grace on David's behalf. God also met us personally. Every parent in similar conditions knows how keenly the searchings of God are felt and how deep the waters can get. But God was there and sustained us.

A question that frequently came up at the outset was, "If at the most our boy has only two years left, why burden him with school work and music lessons, etc.?" But God met us in that concern as well. The doctors advised us not to push the lad, to let him take his own speed. He dropped out of strenuous sports, because David could not keep up and he did not like to be left too far behind. But he continued with his schooling and music lessons. By the hymns he chose to play on his own we discerned the mood of his life.

As for ourselves as parents, God undertook in the following way. In our Bible reading we had come to Ephesians 2. A little earlier I had heard the Rev. L. E. Maxwell of Three Hills speak from this chapter at the Red Rock Bible Camp Memorial Service for a young lady who had lost her life at the camp. Now as we read Ephesians 2 it all came back to me, and I shared with Inger how Mr. Maxwell had pointed out in the light of Ephesians 2 that God has a plan for everyone of His children—an immediate plan for this life in preparation for an ultimate plan in glory, where He will show through His children in the ages to come the exceeding riches of His grace.

It was clear to us that although we might have David only a short time, his life and service would be completed in glory. You can hardly imagine with what comfort and practical approach this gripped us. There will be no incomplete lives in glory—Hallelujah! Moreover, if we were to have David only at the most two years or so to prepare him for his ministry in glory, then Dear Lord, help us to redeem every day so that he will have the best possible preparation. At the same time we and David followed the advice of the physicians.

We learned in a new way what every Christian parent knows. Our children are given that we might prepare them for eternity, and the best way to prepare them for this life is to fit them for eternity. How true, as we reflect upon his condition well nigh 30 years later. God graciously healed that boy. David continued with his music lessons. Today he honours the Lord by leading God's people in worship. He continued with his studies until today he has completed his Ph.D. in the Old Testament at Toronto University and is teaching God's precious Word to many of your sons and daughters at BBC. Can you imagine how guilty we would now feel if we had withdrawn him from school and pampered him? Truly the best way to prepare our children for this life is to fit them for eternity.

One heartbreak from which God has hitherto spared us is to follow a hearse bearing one of our immediate family. As a minister I have been called often to lead a funeral procession, and our minds and hearts are also with the loved ones who follow. If the Lord tarries, we will likely be called upon sooner or later to share this sadness, and we believe that His grace will be sufficient in that hour too.

As we passed through life's joys and sorrows, the importance of security became so clear—the blessed security of a caring family and a caring family of God.

25

Convictions, Characteristics, Conduct

Take heed unto thyself, and unto the doctrine; continue in them: for in doing this thou shalt both save thyself, and them that hear thee. 1 Timothy 4:16.

God preserved me from error through studying His Word and a commitment to obedience by the power of the Holy Spirit. I soon discerned that sound doctrine and a spiritual life go hand in hand. Nor is it necessary to choose between a clear head and a warm heart. Neither must we divorce sound Christian thinking from humble Christian service. Sound convictions produce sound conduct.

In Paul's day, the sum and substance of good theology was Jesus Christ. Finding Christ to be all in all was the high point of Paul's teaching, while the love of Christ moved him to proclaim that "God was in Christ, reconciling the world to himself" (2 Cor. 5:19).

Unaided by the grace of God, man's soul is vile. But in grace, man is capable of boundless possibilities. In my younger day we were horrified when missionaries would report how pagans threw away their babies. Now we are witnessing enlightened pagans murdering their babies! Instead of horrified citizens rising in protest, leading murderers brazenly seek justification in our courts. Dare anyone call this evolution of evil progress?

All men are in need of redemption from the bondage of sin and from condemnation of the justice of God. The Bible clearly teaches the sovereignty of God and the responsibility of man. Both truths are spiritual because they are Biblical, and I teach both. Every truth becomes a trust. If a doctrine leaves me cold and indifferent, either it is not true or I do not understand it. Hence the truth of redemption calls for the redeemed to share this gospel of hope with all mankind. In the light of our blessed hope and our accountability to God, I seek to order my steps.

Time has brought a clearer and fuller development of these convictions, with a much more mature appreciation of them, but change—never! In John 3:16 I found conversion, and in John 3:16 I find renewal.

This precious gospel of our hope in Christ gives me an optimism that I pray will lead to an optimum effort. When a person is rightly related to God through Christ, there is bound to be joy and "the joy of the Lord is your strength." True, there is an enthusiasm that is worked up by the flesh. (Remember when Peter swung at Malchus, the High Priest's servant?) There is also an enthusiasm borne of the Holy Ghost through the Scriptures (when Peter stood forth on the day of Pentecost and preached the historic, crucified, resurrected and exalted Christ).

Such optimism is contagious. Young people, especially teenagers, respond to it. To this day I am grateful that God has given me favour with young people. They have been and continue to be so respectful and kind to me, and responsive to the teaching of the Word of God.

Although God has used me to prepare and gather large crowds of people and of young people for other speakers, I have never been able to draw large crowds as a speaker. But given the environment of a Christian camp or a campus, where you get to know young people and be known by them, God has given me their confidence and love, which I have sought to use to lead them into the Word and closer to our Lord. You cannot be among young people and not feel the throb of enthusiasm. And with true optimism goes a genuine humility.

> Humility is not having an inferiority complex— . . . I went through the pain of thinking that in order to be spiritual, I had to be a worm. Authentic Biblical humility is seeing myself as God sees me and knowing I can do all things through Christ which strengtheneth me.[1]

When our sense of worth is tied to achievement, it is not of the Spirit of God. Such self-worth will make you proud, or frustrated and defeated. Our sense of worth must be anchored in God's love and acceptance. From that position we can go forth with a holy drive and ambition to serve the Lord. True, it has been said that ambition is "the last infirmity of noble minds." And Shakespeare makes Wolsey express a profound truth: "Cromwell, I charge thee, fling away ambition, by that sin fell the angels; how can man then, the image of his Maker, hope to profit by't?" Still Oswald Sanders points out, "that there is an ambition that warrants these strictures. . . , there are ambitions that are noble and worthy and so to be cherished." When 1 Timothy 3:1 and Jeremiah 45:5, "are held in constant tension by one who desires to be effective in the service of God and realize the highest potential of his life, there need be little fear of the outcome of that ambition."[2]

"Be ye followers of me, even as I also am of Christ" (1 Corinthians 11:1). This must be very humbling and challenging. One trembles in the face of such a lesson. But I want to be a learner in that course, because young people have a tendency to follow those who are before them.

Continuity is another characteristic that attracted me. The Lord has His starters, relievers, and stayers—some sprinters, some milers, and some marathoners. I was no natural sprinter, nor miler, but God gave me strength to endure. I could not outrun others or outlift them, but I could hold my own in the long run. Both Inger and I are by nature stayers.

From our conversion and commitment to our Lord, we have experienced His sustaining strength in every area of life. When invitations to other fields or areas of service came, we could hardly take them seriously. We did spread them before the Lord, but the cloud was not lifting to lead us elsewhere. We were grateful for it, for we loved our work and we loved our people. Only on one occasion did we seriously consider the invitation to lead the CSSM work in our province. Since I was saved through the Mission, I felt its pull. I even resigned from BBC to accept the invitation from CSSM, but Mr. Whittaker, chairman of our board, pled with me to reconsider. We waited on God and observed that the cloud was not lifting. We had perfect peace in staying with BBC.

I have often been asked, "How did you consolidate and invigorate an institution after the romance hardened into a day-to-day task?" It was not achieved by working more feverishly, but by keeping our eyes on the Lord. By dwelling in fellowship with Him from day to day, we sought His face in the Word. That is perennially fresh and invigorating. Our conference speakers challenged and refreshed us as much as they did the students and guests. Refresher courses and summer school helped to replenish the springs of living water (John 4:14), so that each morning I could go to my task thanking God for counting me faithful to entrust this ministry to me.

And so we stayed put, progressing in the Lord. We prayed for men and women to join us who would make this also their life ministry. God answered that prayer and BBC holds the record in the AABC for a continuity of faculty and staff. For this we are grateful to God, realizing that permanence is God's promise for the future (Hebrews 11:8-10).

Conduct is the product of characteristics that develop from convictions. From convictions spring principles and policies. It was said of C. H. Spurgeon that he possessed the mystic combination of the Word of God and the words of someone who is wise therein. He was a veritable "Mr. Valiant for Truth." That has been my prayer for myself, "speaking the truth in love" (Ephesians 4:15).

A shady ministry is not due to lack of genius or education, but to an ineffective spiritual experience in a person's relationship with his Maker. A tendency then is to seek to cover a lack of spirituality with intellectual professionalism. I have often warned myself and my students against a pretense of spirituality. "If we are, we need not pretend; if we pretend, we are not; when you are true, you will tell the truth and when you tell the truth you never need to remember what you said."[3]

My understanding of people has not been learned so much from books as from the one Book, the Bible, and by spending time in the clinic of personal discourses with people. The failings of great men but confirms the Scripture that says, "For thou hast made him (man) a little lower than the angels" (Psalm 8:5). Faults of heroes never surprised me, though often they disappointed me. Instead of stumbling over them, they caused me to lift my eyes higher to behold the Christ.

Christ is the Model of servant-leadership. His flawless life makes Him a perfect pattern. We are transparent before Him, but He does not see through us to condemn or to condone, but to supply that grace needed to be transformed into His image. "He sees us ruined by the fall, Yet loves us notwithstanding all." So then, before God we are transparent, and we seek to be likewise before our fellow men, as much as is possible and profitable.

That applies first to my personal life. Inger was with me for a week's ministry in South Dakota. It had been a heavy week, so we decided to book into a hotel at St. Pierre to spend a day relaxing and reading. One of our students drove by just as we were going into the hotel. He knew it was me, but he wasn't so sure about Inger. He parked his car, rushed into the hotel, meeting us as we checked in. He seemed to be so relieved to know that the lady with me was Inger! When she is not with me, and I stay in a public place, I always ask at the desk or of the bellboy if there is a Gideon Bible in the room. It helps to create a protective atmosphere, and God does preserve.

In my personal life as in my public responsibility I always sought to be open. Not for a moment did I think I could meet everyone's expectations of me, but I sought to be true and open before God and men. When in need financially or otherwise, I took our students into confidence for prayer. They then rejoiced with me when God answered prayer. On one occasion we were in need of $20,000 before the end of the month. I shared this with my class of pastoral students. They took me seriously. But I can still hear their laughter of incredibility when I suggested that it might be in the pocket book or bank account of one of them. After all, most of them were broke. But sure enough, a week later a student came with a $20,000 cheque, requesting that it be confidential. I honoured his request, but how I would love to have informed them that their laughter was a bit like Sarah's behind the tent door. Time and again, when it was appropriate to inform them, the students and supporters rejoiced with me and praised Jehovah-Jireh. God will supply.

One day I sat down and figured that to take on the leadership of our high school, our principal had taken a 60 to 70 percent cut in his wages. The sacrifice of my associates became very heavy upon my heart. I asked before God if there was anything I could do in return for their commitment to God and His work. Paul had spoken of that principle in Romans 15:27. "It hath pleased them verily; and their debtors they are. For if the Gentiles have been made partakers of their spiritual things, their duty is also to minister unto them in carnal things." I felt the converse is true. So it was placed upon my heart to remember the faculty and staff and their mates and children regularly in prayer, mentioning each by name. This I extended to our Board of Directors with their families and to many of our supporters. We share aspirations and apprehensions as one great family, and so mutually serve the Lord our God.

In this chapter I have drawn the veil aside to let you see how the grace of God operates and enables the least of His servants in His vineyards. "I (truly) thank Christ Jesus our Lord, who hath enabled me, for that He counted me faithful, putting me into the ministry." His grace has been exceeding abundant by saving and selecting one least qualified, except for the fact that Christ Jesus came to save sinners. He demonstrated His mercy in me as an encouragement to all of you who are also conscious of your limitations and in need of His grace (1 Timothy 1:12-17).

26

Enlarge the Place of Thy Tent

Enlarge the place of thy tent, and let them stretch forth the curtains of thine habitations; spare not . . . Isaiah 54:2

From the early beginnings of Bible school classes, we have barely been able to build fast enough and large enough to accommodate the students pressing for entrance. That sounds so simple, but it is very costly. What was said of the man who did not take the time to plan adequately and count the cost has been in another sense so true of us. "This man began to build, and was not able to finish" (Luke 14:28-30). We have been involved continually in building since we began, and building is expensive at all times.

It has been said that even if a pastor survives a major church building program, he and his people are so exhausted that he has to resign. Major building ventures tax the endurance of the people involved. I found it very interesting to read that even the great Charles Haddon Spurgeon did not altogether escape the tension. Early in his Park Street ministry in London it became obvious that a large house of worship was needed. The church was so crowded and ventilation so poor that one Sunday morning the worshippers found the windows smashed. The church board offered a reward to anyone who could help to find the culprit, but he was never found. Some suspected that the pastor could have received the reward! Still, many remained convinced that it was folly to erect a new, larger structure.

Spurgeon commented tersely on this point, "Build or I resign; either erect the Tabernacle or I become an evangelist."

> A building committee of thirty was appointed in June, 1856. Lorimer states that, at their first private meeting, Spurgeon exclaimed, "I hear some of you are doubtful; if so go through that door and stay there." At a later meeting he repeated the statement. Twelve went out. Said he, "Any more?" Three more departed, and with seven he marched to victory.[1]

To Richard E. Day this sounded like a tall story, but he also admits that there may be some truth in it.

> Three years later in February, sixty-two separate plans and one model were submitted by the architect . . . The cornerstone was laid in August 16. The money on hand was far short of the needs. But they moved forward.[2]

True in detail or not, the story pictures the strains that a heavy building effort creates. What of continuous building? The more I reflect upon it, the more evident becomes the marvelous grace of God. Over the fifty years we have faced tense moments—very difficult moments, moments that we had serious doubts if BBC could survive the pressure. But to this day I am not aware that any person in the organization resigned because of constant building. Moreover, God has seen us through the most difficult times and showered His grace in increasing measure. That this work is a miracle of God is most obvious to those who are closest and totally involved in it. Let me share this difficult yet triumphant part of the story.

We began in a small, five-room, rented house in Briercrest. It served as classrooms, kitchen, dining hall, dormitory and meeting place of the local assembly for their Wednesday evening Bible studies. Empty buildings in town were rented as the enrollment increased. In 1938 we obtained the vacant hotel which became headquarters, classrooms, and main dormitory for BBC. We purchased more houses, moved in a larger house from the country, and rented every vacant space in the village. Mr. Whittaker, our board chairman, spearheaded this drive for space, climaxing in the purchase of our present site in 1946, the Caron Airport. He felt, as someone put it, "Now we have enough room till Kingdom come!" It took four years to consolidate this venture, but by 1950 we began to build again.

The Rev. L. E. Maxwell and his associates at Three Hills in their continuous building have been a great inspiration to us. When on one occasion a mild tornado knocked down the walls of a new structure, they sought the face of God, picked up the pieces; started over and finished the structure. Thank you, Three Hills, for your noble commitment to the task.

Rebuilding and refurbishing the old Air Force structures and putting up new buildings was taken in stride until 1976 when major steps were taken by the BBC Board to meet the increasing demand for more space. God had prepared the heart of a good man and a well-to-do land owner for this task (Acts 4:36-37).

Mr. Russell Archibald had studied our set-up very well. He believed we were in for a very big job. Soon we would face the double burden of having to replace temporary Air Force buildings while having to build faster to provide the needed room. He was led to give us the better share of his beautiful farmland with the following counsel: "There will be no strings attached to these sections of land. You may feel free to sell them and use the money to build one major building. However, if you are wise, you may keep the land and use it as collateral for many building projects that you face. Each time you build, you go to the bank and arrange for the finances. Then obtain the best building contract. Then go to the Christian public for support. If you handle this right, they will back each project. In this way you will be able to rebuild the greater part of your airport buildings. Then sell the land at the most appropriate time to achieve your purpose."

We followed his advice and achieved his designs. As a result we were able to build the high school classrooms. We built Whittaker Hall in memory of Mr. and Mrs. Sinclair Whittaker and the library in honour of Mr. and Mrs. Russell Archibald. This was but the beginning of this strategy.

With the pressure of increased enrollment, the Board of Directors felt we should take greater strides in building projects. They launched Operation Vision in 1976. The aim was to raise $1,500,000 in three years. The people of God responded. We renovated some of the better buildings and added to our ladies' residence, Hillson Hall, named after Mrs. Walter Hillson who began the home Bible studies in Briercrest. We also built Clements Hall, our guest rooms, and three fourplexes—suites for our staff.

Interest in the campus development program was in high gear as we successfully completed Operation Vision. Hence, Onward Vision was immediately launched, aimed at raising $3,000,000 in four years. As Mr. Archibald had predicted, the Christians responded again with even greater enthusiasm. Our water supply was greatly increased and the sewage disposal doubled. A home economics classroom and music room were built for the high school. A ladies' residence, Glen Manor; and two male residences were built—Fender Hall and Brygmann Hall. The free-standing structure of the large gymnasium was restored to its required strength and a new floor was laid. But our largest and most challenging venture was building the H. Alvin Memory Centre—a multi-purpose structure to house the kitchen, dining hall, student-centre complete with lounge, smaller halls for special dinner occasions, project and committee rooms.

Just before Mr. Archibald was promoted to higher service, Inger and I visited him, and he felt the time had come to sell the farm. We did so in 1982-83. We completed our payments on the building projects with about $1,000,000 remaining for the greatest building venture that is now upon us.

Onward Vision Jubilee was launched in the spring of 1984. It is so named in keeping with the jubilee year of BBC that is fast approaching—1985-86. It will take all of our combined efforts to guide this project to a like successful conclusion. Again it is a four-year project designed to raise about $6,000,000 to build the chapel-classroom complex.

The project is divided into two phases. Phase I is under construction, now designed to be completed by April, 1985, in time for dedication at our spring conference and commencement exercises. The cost is estimated to be about $1,500,000. This phase will provide additional classrooms, a library extension, music rooms, a media centre, and a book store, plus some office space. Phase I will be named in honour of Rev. and Mrs. Orville Swenson, an honour well deserved.

Phase II, the Lord willing, will be the much needed chapel or conference hall to provide classroom space for an additional seven- to eight-hundred students, and a hall or chapel seating over 3,000. This is a must. We have now nearly 800 students enrolled in the college. With the completion of Phase I we have room for a little over 500. This is a crowded situation and calls for very early morning and late evening classes to provide room for our students. At this writing, about $2,000,000 has been committed by Christian friends to Phase II. The Board of Directors would like to become responsible to raise another $1,300,000. The decision was, that when we reach $2,000,000 in cash and another $1,000,000 in faith promises, we shall proceed with Phase II. It is hoped that we will be ready to begin building by the fall of 1986—the climax of our Jubilee year.

As the Apostle Paul prayerfully presented the need of the Jerusalem saints to the Gentile churches, we have sought to follow that pattern over the years. Each project was developed in prayer and presented to the Board of Directors for evaluation and refinement. Then it was set forth in literature. The projects were presented to the faculty and staff, then to the students, so they were all informed and enlisted for prayer and support. Then we presented the project at our Spring Conference to our guests. (At the Fall Conference the responsibility of Missions is presented.) Thereafter, we presented our need to different constituencies during fundraising banquets. We have about fifty of these throughout Canada. These more frequently have turned out to be actually *friendraising* occasions. This was followed by personal visits to prospective donors.

Backed by the best possible accounting of funds by our administration, and closely scrutinized and confirmed by a reputable accounting firm, these donations were directed as designated. This is designed to provide an honest record, not only in the sight of the Lord, but also in the sight of men (2 Corinthians 8:19-23).

I cannot close this chapter without acknowledging once more the faithfulness of God and the generosity of God's people. They have given, often beyond their means in difficult times (2 Corinthians 8:1-6). For this we say thank you. Your reward will be great in glory.

27

Strengthen Thy Stakes

Enlarge the place of thy tent, and let them stretch forth the curtains of thine habitations: spare not, lengthen thy cords, *and strengthen thy stakes.* Isaiah 54:2.

After hearing Spurgeon preach his first Water Beach anniversary sermon, Cornelius Elven said to the young pastor, "Lad, study hard; keep abreast your foremost Christians; for if they outstrip you in knowledge of Scripture, or power to edify, they will be dissatisfied with your ministry." Spurgeon responsed, "That spur was useful."[1]

The apostle Paul exhorted young Timothy saying, "Till I come, give attendance to reading, to exhortation, to doctrine. Meditate upon these things; give thyself wholly to them; that thy profiting may appear to all" (1 Timothy 4:13, 15).

Since God had entrusted this great ministry to me, I meant to give my best to it and serve my generation by the will of God. I felt so limited in so many ways, but when university undergraduates began to enroll, I felt strongly my need for further training. I had been conscious of this from the outset, but each opening or scholarship for further studies meant quitting the ministry to which God had called me. It was this that made the invitation of the CSSM to settle in Saskatoon so appealing. The understanding was that I could take the winter months off to study in a university city. But when I went to the Lord about it, after Mr. Whittaker's plea on behalf of the Board, this was not to be, and I cast anchor at Briercrest, fully persuaded that BBC was my life.

But longevity of service demands a price. To remain buoyant healthy, and vigorous, there must be a regular quiet time with God to assure a perennial flow of fresh water from the everlasting springs. Another key to freshness was the stimulation of our semi-annual Bible-Missionary Conferences. Wide and continuous reading of the best of literature also builds a reserve from which to draw. One must read up-to-date periodicals and journals to keep relevant.

The experiences of life, when properly filtered, also prove to be a training by the hand of God. A teachable pupil learns from these lessons to become stronger, yet more tender and sympathetic. In my younger days it was often argued that the twelve Apostles were humble fishermen who bumbled their way to success by the power of the Holy Spirit. Why should we be concerned about formal training? All we need do is trust the Lord. The Apostles had no formal education, except what they received while in company with Jesus, it was affirmed.

But that's it! They were in company with Jesus. That was the key to their effective ministry. I believe we do the Apostles as well as our Lord an injustice if we accept the first part of the evaluation of the Sanhedrin recorded in Acts 4:13: "Now when they saw the boldness (confidence) of Peter and John, and perceived that they were unlearned and ignorant men . . ."

The rulers were wrong. By any measure of education, the apostles were among the best prepared for their mission. The quality of a school is judged first by the quality of the faculty. Did Plato have a better teacher than Peter? Next, there was in-depth and extended discipline. Has any Ph.D. today a more comprehensive training than Jesus' disciples? They were in company with Jesus about 40 months, day and night. What about the field training, supervised personally by their Master? Even the Sanhedrin began to rethink their evaluation, they "began to recognize them as having been with Jesus" (NASB). Training with Jesus is quality preparation—make no mistake about it.

The need for further training for the senior faculty I shared with our board. The increasing enrollment made it obvious that we needed to enlarge the place of our tent and to stretch forth the curtains of our habitation. It seemed not so obvious that we needed to "strengthen thy (our) stakes." After all, students kept coming. Yes, the young people continued to come—that was good. But we were determined to serve them well and meet their needs. They were asking questions. The Bible had the answers, that we knew, but some of these answers we did not know. In time this would not only create a problem for the faculty but present a real difficulty for the BBC Board of Directors.

"You may have a very difficult decision to make," said I, as I presented to our board the need for further formal training for our faculty. "One day you may have to come to some of us and say, Sorry, you have carried the burden of pioneer work, but these times demand. . . ." They assured me that they would never feel that way, but, "What do you have in mind?" they asked.

I outlined a program of inservice training available to us through summer schools at Winona Lake School of Theology in Indiana. Also, study programs at Wheaton College in Illinois. Since we had served our school for many years at minimum allowances, the school would have to foot the bill. The board agreed, and such training became available, first to the senior members of the college, including yours truly. The policy provided service to complete our undergraduate studies and to proceed to a Master's level in each major area of teaching. The purpose was to "serve our generation of students by the will of God."

From this original policy the college has developed an inservice training program for its faculty leading, when required, to a Ph.D. in the area of a teacher's particular teaching ministry. A like policy has been developed for our tradespeople who desire opportunity to acquire their journeyman's license. Several have done so. Our experience proved that a skillful person of integrity and loyalty to the college merits such an opportunity. Moreover, the school gains by having well-prepared people serving the students.

Now I believed that our students earned a respected degree upon the completion of their courses. We applied to our provincial government that has the power to give a university or college authority to grant degrees. Hitherto this sacred rite had been reserved for the university, and they meant to keep it that way.

It was, therefore, natural that they would resist our application for authority to grant degrees. And they did! They felt it was an intrusion into their field, without supervision or control by them. We were asked to defend our application at the Government's Private Bills Committee. I found that to be an exciting experience. I had appeared before similar committees on other BBC business and found them responsive to clear, concise, logical presentations.

As I studied the 30-member committee, I could not help but smile. I had had previous and pleasant contacts with so many of them. The Chairman was a devout Lutheran and a teacher by profession. He enjoyed speaking to our students in chapel. The government lawyer had been a student at our school. The member of the Legislative Assembly who sponsored our bill was also our alumnus, and the lawyer in defense of our bill had married a BBC student. It seemed as though we had stacked the meeting, yet all unknown to us.

Although two members of the committee representing the university presented their arguments against extending degree-granting authority to us, the debate shifted in our favour. When they appealed to the Education Minister of the previous government, who was also a member of this committee, he spoke up in our defense.

In all his experience with BBC, as Minister of Education, he declared that our quality of education equalled or exceeded what was offered by the Department of Education. He proceeded, "If it's in order, Mr. Chairman, I move that we grant authority to BBC to grant degrees in keeping with the philosophy, role, goals and courses of that college." The motion was seconded and all voted in favour, except for two, who abstained from voting against it. Bill 03 received a third reading and became law on April 5, 1974. And so BBC became the first educational institution independent of the University of Saskatchewan to receive this authority in our province.

Coached by Dr. Boehmer of Ontario Bible College and Dr. Hanna, then President of Winnipeg Bible College, the preamble to the application was so precisely stated that it included the granting of graduate degrees as well. We accepted it all as another favour from God.

In the meanwhile, we felt we were ready to make application to the American Association of Bible Colleges for accreditation. Our purpose was two-fold. First, we had so much to learn from this fine organization which had pioneered the ministry of Bible colleges and had gained years of experience. Second, our students were doing credible work to meet the entrance requirements to all well-known evangelical seminaries, without losing credits in their transfers.

After rigorous self-examination and correcting some weaknesses, and after several visitations of the examining teams, we received first-applicant status, then candidate status, and finally full accreditation status in October, 1977. Our president, Henry Budd, has since been elected to the Executive Board of the Association. In the fall of 1984 he was chosen to be its secretary. We have learned a good deal from the schools in this fellowship. They have contributed so much to us and our students. Now we are grateful that we can also serve them.

To avoid confusion our new name, Briercrest Bible College, has been used throughout these memoirs, though for its first years the school was known as Briercrest Bible Institute. Occasionally a contributing writer used the original name.

Because of the connotation on the Canadian scene, President Budd proposed the new name to the Board of Directors, and it was adopted on April 27, 1981, thus BBI became BBC. The name became official on July 1, 1982. The timing was right, and the college family accepted and appreciated the new name.

It remains the task of our present administration to obtain like transfer of credits for our students to Canadian educational institutions as we have obtained in American schools. This is not going to be easy! We must remain true to the role and goals of our college while doing so. A number of universities are already recognizing the quality education given by accredited Bible colleges and are offering excellent transfer credits. Some even send their registrars to us to enroll our students. Negotiations continue with the universities in the province of Saskatchewan. We believe in time the humanistic opposition of a few will have to give way in the interest of quality education. We believe God will undertake in this area as well.

More recently we began offering summer graduate studies. This gave a number of us the opportunity to proceed with our studies without giving up our regular ministry. We felt there were many fine servants of God in like situations, especially on the Prairies. The enrollments of the past summers have proven that assessment correct. BBC is offering an excellent ministry, thereby making it possible for many pastors and Bible school faculties to enhance their ministry and thereby glorify God.

It is very humbling to reflect upon God's leading and undertaking in the ministry of BBC. He has enlarged our tent, stretched out our curtains, and enabled us to strengthen our stakes. It is an ongoing ministry that we pray will increase in wisdom, stature, and in favour with God and man (Luke 2:52). Again, we say, thank you to our heavenly Father.

28

Our Supporting Staff

And I intreat thee also, true yokefellow, help those women which laboured with me in the gospel, with Clement also, and with other my fellowlabourers, whose names are in the book of life. Philippians 4:3

In the early days the great organs in European churches required a musical apprentice to pump the bellows as the Maestro performed. After a great performance one day, the bellows boy, hearing the tremendous response of the large audience, said to the Maestro, "We had a great concert tonight!"

"What do you mean we?" replied the Maestro. "*I* had a great performance tonight."

The story goes on to tell that at the next concert, the Maestro was introduced, accepted the applause, and sat down to play. But no sound came forth. The apprentice refused to pump the bellows until humbly requested to do so.

The lesson is clear: without a supporting staff there can be no performance. This is even more so in our mechanical, electronic age. How much we owe to these unsung heroes who work behind the scenes only eternity will reveal. Paul implied this when he spoke of his unnamed fellow-labourers "whose names are in the book of life." The unnamed supporters abound in our story, but there are some who have worked hard enough and long enough to be named in these *Memoirs.*

Let me first mention the women of our campus who, behind the scenes, have "laboured with us in the gospel." Many of our wives may not have been as directly involved as their husbands, but they served just as definitely, often at great sacrifice.

During the regular school season there are no public accommodations on the campus. The college has to go to request of its staff free accommodation for guests during public functions, such as the two major conferences each year, Youth Quake, Pastoral Conferences, Seminars, Board Meetings, Musicals, Commencement Exercises, and banquets. The list of special functions goes on.

Our faculty and staff have been unusually responsible to provide generous hospitality. But the burden is borne mainly by those "whose wives don't work." Although hospitality is extended with joy, the wives face difficulties. Hospitality is costly, especially for those who have only a "single-allowance income." Without such warm response, the work of the college would be severely curtailed. In fact, could it function without it? While our ladies so involved consider hospitality a ministry of love, and the Lord surely takes note, I felt that special recognition should be given.

Many contribute service in our offices, dining halls, and lunch counter, without whose ministry the college could not operate either. In the earlier days, Mr. Whittaker stressed that the school could not afford too many married men, so we recruited single men. We also engaged single ladies. But Mr. Whittaker had no answer as to how we could keep them single! It soon became apparent that in choosing a single secretary, we were choosing a wife for one of my single associates. Let me illustrate.

Kay Parsens, became Mrs. R. Glen; Clara Kualnes—Mrs. O. Swenson; Esther Hanson soon became Mrs. H. Edwards; Joy Brown—Mrs. O. Bygmann; Isabel Mann—Mrs. H. Shauf. A little later, Dorothy Schultz took the name Mrs. L. Reed. With Prince Charming in the wings, believe you me, I had no difficulty obtaining secretaries, etc., in those days. I still smile when I recall how neatly one applicant stated that she felt she was called to join our work. In all sincerity, they all have made excellent wives of my associates and worthy mothers of their children—a perfect fit for our campus.

Our treasurers have been faithful in their accounting, keeping accurate records of finances entrusted to us. They have rendered incalculable service to the cause of Christ. The integrity characterizing Mr. O. Brygmann, our first official treasurer, was followed by Ron Reynolds and now by Larry Hamm.

Our business manager operated on the principle that a good deal was achieved when both parties involved were equally well served. This made our college credible and respected in the business world.

Mr. John Ward followed this pattern set by Mr. Ted Bergren, and it is still in force.

Werner and Celia Schroeder have also given nearly 30 years of faithful service to the work. The Schroeder's joined us shortly after graduation from BBC. They have served in different capacities in our office with integrity and scrupulous accuracy. Werner is our Personnel Administrator and Celia an Accounting Clerk.

In view of our rural setting, we needed a general country store to serve the campus. We did not believe that it should be a financial liability to be subsidized by donations. Nor did we think of it primarily as a money maker at the expense of the school family. Like all auxiliary departments, the store was to serve the constituency honourably, financing its own function.

Mr. Arthur Sundbo, with his experience in operating a country store, stepped into our need. How sacrificially and loyally he served the Lord in this department! Arthur went out of his way again and again to serve. As the school grew, he became our purchasing agent, while Peter Wollf joined our staff to take charge of our store. Since Mr. Sundbo's retirement, Mr. Wollf has taken on double duty as purchasing agent of the college and manager of the store. Lately he has earned the trust of our President to become manager of all auxiliary services.

Building, maintenance, and repair are continually upon us. Again, because of the rural setting and growth of the school, we needed a foreman, carpenter, plumber, mechanic and electrician, etc. How God provided skilled men committed to this task was a constant marvel to me. As foreman and carpenter, Mr. Oscar Eliason made a unique contribution to this cause. Although Oscar has officially retired, it seems that as long as we have high school boys in our dorms, Mr. Repairman will be called upon often.

Mr. Lenard From likewise serves the college well. The entire department is now led by the energetic and enthusiastic Mr. Norman Klassen. Norm is superintendent of the entire campus buildings. Art Kroeker has also been led to the campus to give his life to this task. Art has the unusual quality of a skillful carpenter who does his work with speed. The burden of plumbing has been carried diligently by Gordon Diggins. Lillian, Mrs. Diggins, has rendered excellent service as Alumni Secretary for years. She now serves equally well in another department. Gordon has been more recently joined by Hugo Bach.

Our electrician and furnace engineer for years has been Herbert Shauf. I have never heard Mr. Shauf complain at any hour of the day or night when his services were needed. Although now retired, he is still frequently called upon to serve. Dale Bergren is now our electrician. Kurt Rempel is skilled with heavy machinery. He and Joan, his wife, serve us well, as do Harold and Gertrude McKay.

Mechanical work on the campus is attended to by Mr. Irvin Rodin. Ethel, his wife, has often entertained us profitably with her folksy, down-to-earth poetry during campus family functions.

To the credit of these men, they continued to study and develop their skills to meet government requirements for their trades.

Space would fail me to mention all of our people who have rendered faithful service. We needed a bus depot at the gate by the four-lane Trans-Canada Highway. A service station and a lunch counter provided the answer. Osbjorne Amundsen, with his experience in garages, served the public well. So did George Janzen, and now Royden Taylor.

The wives and families of the men in all of these departments made it possible for their men to serve so wholeheartedly. Many of the wives stand in their own right actively engaged in productive ministries.

For years we had an infirmary staffed with qualified nurses to serve our students, but we needed a doctor with a clinic on the growing campus. God provided this need too. He sent Dr. and Mrs. Lorne Penner with their family to us. Health reasons did not permit the Penners to return as missionaries to Eritrea, so they became medical missionaries to the Caronport campus, serving the surrounding community as well.

During the difficult period in the life of the school, when it was almost impossible to get certain qualified teachers and workers, God met me with His promise through David to Solomon in 1 Chronicles 28:21, ". . . and there shall be with thee for all manner of workmanship every willing skilful man, for any manner of service . . ." I came upon this passage one morning in my devotional reading at a most critical time. I claimed the promise from that moment on. Every decade that has rolled by since has confirmed this wonderful promise. I recommend it to every Christian servant-leader.

29

Our Students, Our Love

And the things that thou has heard of me among many witnesses, the same commit thou to faithful men, who shall be able to teach others also. 2 Timothy 2:2

Our students have been so open with me. At times this has led to real soul-searching, at other times it has been quite amusing.

David, a grade eleven student came into my office about 11:45 one morning to share his concern. His demerits were accumulating so fast that he felt, unless someone with influence spoke up for him, he might be graduating before Christmas! At that time we still had the merit-demerit system.

It wasn't that he was worse than other boys, but the deans were keeping a sharp eye on him, and he seemed to always get caught while others got away with it. Just then the first bell rang for dinner. I did not want him to be late and gain another 5 d's. I advised him to speak to his counsellor who, I assured him, would understand him, because I knew we had been praying together for the boys.

He did not think the counsellor would understand. "Mind you," he said, "we all respect him. He is strict, he is more strict with himself than he is with us. That man is righteous, so righteous, I don't think he ever sins. No, he wouldn't understand me."

"You don't want to see him because, he wouldn't understand you, because that man never sins? Is that about it?" I asked. I continued, "If you think he would not understand you, because he never sins, then why are you coming to me? Why are you knocking at my door?"

He drew back, a bit embarrassed, for the conversation had taken a strange twist. After all, he was there seeking to enroll my help. He nobly endeavoured to recover. “No, no, Mr. Hildebrand! I don’t mean to suggest for a moment that you do sin, but you are the kind of a person who *might.*”

I sought to reassure him, and we closed our conversation with prayer. As soon as he left, I said to myself, “David, you are so right. You read me accurately, but for the grace of God.” Isn’t that all our story? “*But for the grace of God!*” Our students identify with that and take heart.

As mentioned earlier, I never could take young people by storm. I would make a poor youth rally speaker, who must grab his audience the first and only night he has. My opportunity came in the atmosphere of a week-long camp, where we grew closer to each other. Young people sensed that I understood their aspirations as well as apprehensions. They would warm up more to me in a campus setting for a semester or two. In confidence we could share our mutual concerns. We could lead them step by step into the Word and therefore closer to Jesus.

It is a miscalculation when some leaders count each student as a financial liability. Boldly it is stated that the education of each student costs so-and-so-much per semester. While that may be true, it is only one side of the coin. Each student is also a financial asset. Have you noticed that the colleges that have good enrollments are in less difficulty financially? The problem may be capital expenditure to make more room, but the operating budget is usually healthier. Why?

There are good reasons. Every student brings with him or her a whole new group of potential prayer supporters. The student’s parents become more interested in the school and how it develops. So are his church, his relatives, and friends. It is up to the school to wisely maximize this potential for prayer and support. Introduced to the school through a student, some of these new acquaintances remain friends of the work for life. Farther down the road, they hold tremendous potential for student recruitment and financial support. We have well over 200 second generation students in our present enrollment, students whose parents attended the school. In fact, the third generation is beginning to show up, student’s whose parents and grandparents attended. By now, our alumni is providing almost half of our total donations. Such loyalty and support is the envy of many of our sister schools.

A more mature student whom the Lord had redeemed from a difficult life consulted with me frequently about hang-ups that were still disturbing him. Conscious that he might be using too much of my time, he sheepishly apologized as he approached me with a grin, "Of course, Hildebrand, you and your people should not forget, that we students are your bread and butter." Both of us smiled, and I appreciated his insight. It is true, but our students aren't only our "bread and butter," they are our labour of love, our very life. This viewpoint must motivate our service.

With the coming of our own children I became more and more conscious of parental concerns and hopes. There were occasions when parents would trust their newest-born child to my arms. I learned that their future—parents and child—lay in that moment. Frequently we would pray briefly for God's grace upon the precious little one. When 17 or 18 years later those same parents would entrust that same youngster to our care for studies, I became aware of parental influence, and of our mutual concern. The young person could not possibly remember that first encounter, but the parents did.

And so the students came from families and communities that God enabled us to reach and encourage over the years. In an earlier chapter I mentioned the William Fulmore family who have had one of their children, grandchildren, great-grandchildren, or near relatives enrolled throughout our fifty years. Then there is the Rev. John Nickel family of Main Centre, Saskatchewan. John was a gracious servant of God as bishop of the Mennonite Conference Church and pastor of the local church. Thirty of his grandchildren and great grandchildren have attended BBC over the years—if in-laws are included, the number rises to about forty! The Gerald Frostad family of Kincaid sent all of their eight children to study with us, as both parents had before them. But the record for most children enrolled at BBC is held by Mr. and Mrs. William Baron of Fenwood, Saskatchewan. Nine of their ten children attended Briercrest. The very small village of Gouldtown and its community have sent thirty-three students over the years. And so the students continue to come from near and far. There is no explantion to this but—"a movement of God."

I have given just a few pictures of student interest among our constituencies, that grew out of interest fostered by parents and grandparents. We welcomed them to our campus, our dormitories, and our classrooms. To this day a classroom of eager students is my first love. I sought to make them understand right at the outset the worth of each student because of Calvary. How precious each young person is in the sight of God!

As long as I possibly could, I sought to maintain an open door for spiritual counselling or for mutual school concerns. As the work grew, this responsibility was shared with counsellors and faculty. But I wanted to keep in touch with student life, so I arranged for weekly meetings with the student representatives.

There is merit in listening to the students. Through it you sense their needs and concerns, their ideas of how the school could be improved. However, if the ideas cost more money, then I asked them to provide it, or be responsible to raise it. Occasionally a kicker would show up, usually claiming to speak for the majority. I was always glad when they came to my door, I could then deal with them. I did not accept private delegations nor petitions. They were advised to make their presentations through proper channels, namely their elected representatives, for whom the door was open at scheduled times.

The nearest we came to a group protest came in the early seventies when a number of students showed up one evening at the door of the Dean of Students asking—almost demanding—to be allowed to see a hockey game in Moose Jaw during student study hours. The counsellor held firm. He knew he had my backing. Later, rebuked by the student council, the students apologized.

From its outset the student body was well organized with an elected executive headed by a president and a larger council where each class was represented. A constitution setting out guidelines for student policies, responsibilities, activities, and elections was developed by the Dean of Students in cooperation with student leadership. The respective student committees attend to campus weekend activities. Sports are under the direction of a student committee led by our Director of Physical Education and his assistant. Classroom programs are organized by each class, assisted by a faculty advisor, and presented on Sunday nights. Student committees are also active for musical ministries, Christian Service, and off-campus ministries led by faculty department heads. Our students believe they have a fulfilling student activity program.

Students seem to have a sixth sense when it comes to electing their presidents. They make it a matter of prayer, and their constitution sets good guidelines, so that no novice qualifies for the office. Over all the years, we have had, as a whole, excellent student body presidents. They were especially strong and gave good leadership during the rebellious sixties. They allowed none of it and pinched it in the bud each time rebellion clamoured for hearing.

The student council is under the direction of our Dean of Students and his associates. Their relationship is excellent and contributes to the healthy atmosphere enjoyed by the student body on the campus from year to year.

Mr. Alvin Lewis assisted Mr. Walter Fender as our first high school counsellor. A former sergeant of the army, he enrolled in our Bible School. He graduated in '49 and continued his studies in Winnipeg. Alvin joined our staff as counsellor in the fall of '51. He married Miss Audrey Steven, our post-mistress. Mr. and Mrs. Lewis and family have served faithfully with us ever since.

When Alvin moved into leading the student-work program, Mr. and Mrs. Harvey Zink, graduates of BBC, joined our staff to assist Mr. Fender in the counselling department. When for health reasons Mr. Fender could not continue, Harvey Zink became our Dean of Students and has been leading this department for 15 years.

Mr. Zink is now assisted by five counsellors and a number of residence assistants. The counsellors are rendering a tremendous service to the students and contribute much to their development. To the counsellors and student leadership we say, Thank you.

The students come with their hopes and fears—so young, often so immature. To see them grow in grace is encouraging and rewarding. To see them respond, catch motivation, try their wings, then fly away with confidence to appointed missions at home and abroad is so exciting! I feel as keenly about that today as I did those first few years at Briercrest. The romance of their witness around the world is the story of the following chapter.

30

The Sun Never Sets on Briercrest Alumni

And he said unto them, Go ye into all the world, and preach the gospel to every creature. Mark 16:15

In her lecture to the Alumni Homecoming of 1980 Mrs. Myrtle Wipf, teacher of Missions at BBC, illustrated from the world map that our missionaries are located around the world, so that the sun never sets on Briercrest alumni. I have selected a few highlights of this fascinating story.

When one of our leading Christian businessmen spoke to BBC students, he mentioned how grateful he was that God had enabled him to develop companies that provided employment for 5,000 people. Later in our home he continued the discussion about serving our fellowman. Work for 5,000 is benefiting a lot of families and communities, I freely acknowledged. And then, half-teasingly, I mentioned that it may be of interest to him to know that BBC has over 6,000 alumni all over the world, preaching the Word of Life as they were taught at the college. He seemed surprised, then he acknowledged that this campus is but a center, a launching pad for world evangelism. The real work goes on in the far-flung mission fields of the world. He continued, "And what's more, I have to pay every person to keep them in my employment, while your students pay to get their training!"

We both laughed, and I trust that you are receiving it in the same spirit as we share it with you. The real ministry of BBC is extended to fields at home and unto remote mission fields of the world. Every week we have mission and church leaders on our campus seeking recruits. We are grateful that our students respond, and are serving Christ all over the world. Let me take you quickly for a day's journey with the sun around the world.

Our alumni are serving in increasing numbers throughout our provinces from east to west, including the Yukon and the Northwest Territories. They serve from the southern states north to Alaska. They minister in pastorates like the Carl Friedrichs in Bethel, Kingston, Ontario; to Don Josts an associate in People's Church, Toronto, Ontario. Our alumni serve with the different missions. The Walter Aikenheads work in the head office of the Canadian Sunday School Mission. The Vaughan Durstons lead the Child Evangelism Fellowship in our province. The Arthur Tarrys with the Collies founded the Northern Canada Evangelical Mission, and the Joe Jollys lead the beautiful work of the Native Evangelical Fellowship throughout Canada. This is to mention just a few of hundreds engaged in Christian work in our own lands.

From here we follow the sun across the Pacific and stop at the Hawaiian Islands where the Ron Dirks serve with the Pacific Area Mission.

On to Japan, where the Iwao Ikenouyes lead the Japanese Bible Institute under JEM/TEAM. Freda Rempel and Carol Gunzel labour in Taiwan. Tom and Pat Macleod served with Wycliffe Bible Translators, translating portions of the New Testament into the tongue of their tribal people of the Philippines. Although Tom is now in glory, Pat returned to the field of their labour of love.

The sun moves westward, and we mention a few of our alumni who serve with the Overseas Missionary Fellowship in East Asia. Gerald Dykema in Indonesia; Ann Burgess among the Yao Tribe in North Thailand, where she is translating the New Testament into Yao. Ednagrace Kellie ministers in the Christian hospital in Saiburi, South Thailand.

We follow the sun to India, the country of Ghandi, Nehru, Indira Ghandi and now Rajiv Ghandi with its millions. It is the scene of labour for Roy and Adelina Martens, Ed and Helen Schroeder, and Margaret Rodin, working with The Evangelical Alliance Mission. Bruce and Doris Sinclair and Bert and Helen Birch labour with the International Christians. We must pause to say hello to Peter and Pauline Hanks, who found entrance in Nepal under TEAM.

We would like to give time to so many more of our alumni in all of these countries, but you will have to forgive us. We can only visit a few. In Pakistan Marian Grant is reaching out to the children of that people under Child Evangelism Fellowship. Eunice Hill with TEAM ministers to the children of missionaries. Alan and Iola Isely serve with TEAM at the Oasis Hospital in the United Arab Emirates. Ken and Grace Betts are missionaries with the Worldwide Evangelization Crusade in Aman, Jordan. Wayne and Carol King minister with Child Evangelism in Nazareth, Israel.

Now let's drop down a bit and quickly call on a few of our many alumni missionaries to Africa. Tony and Rose Dickens are teaching at Rift Valley Academy, a large missionary school in Kijabe, Kenya. Although under the umbrella of the Africa Inland Mission, this academy serves many children of other faith missions. We view the work in Zimbabwe, for years the field of our first missionaries, Reginald and Kay Glen. Drop way down and you will find Don and Annette Douma, agriculturalists teaching crop production and with it, the production of the good seed of the Word.

Moving north again, we pause in the Cameroons where Carl and Winnie Grebe with Wycliffe Bible Translators are translating the New Testament into the native language. Then there are so many of our alumni with the Sudan Interior Mission in Nigeria. Allow me to mention David and Shirley Boyes. Carey and Shirley Lees also serve with this great mission in the Niger Republic. Jim and Leona Mason work in literature distribution in Ghana. Carol Priebe ministers in medical work with the Gospel Missionary Union in Mali, and Kenneth and Evelyn Geake serve with WEC in the Canary Islands.

Moving considerably north we observe the tremendous work done by BBC graduates at the Word of Life camps situated on Germany's summer resort sea at Starnberg. They are Chuck and Katie Kosman, Bob and Betty Parschauer, and Larry and Joy Locken. Larry and Joy are now leading the Word of Life Camps near Nairobi, Kenya, East Africa. This camp is an extension of the camps in Germany and supported by them.

Time does not permit me to describe the great thrust of evangelism in German-speaking Europe by the Janz Team. Only eternity will reveal what this has meant to those countries. In Italy, Bernie and Lynn Oxenham are leading the Institute Biblico Evangelico. In France Harvey and Anna Louise Schultz are field directors for the Bible Christian Union. Moreover, Abe and Joyce Wiebe are directing the North Africa Mission from their headquarters in France. A good witness is borne by our alumni in Spain, Holland, the British Isles and the Scandinavian countries.

We speed with the sun across the Atlantic to South America to just name a few of our grads. Bruce and Betty Cole (TEAM) lead the Las

Delicias Bible Institute in Venezuela. Eileen Adams serves in Brazil, Don and Janet Clements lead the work in Boliva. Henry and Pat Klassen carry on a fruitful ministry with the Quichuas high in the Andes of Ecuador, all with the G.M.U. Mabel Ayer and Jim and Marlene Hiebert serve in hospital work under HCJB, and Dave and Barbara Pasechnik work in the radio ministry of HCJB.

Ted and Gloria Engel serve with W.B.T. at the Wycliffe Research Centre in Dallas, Texas, as linguists, anthropologists, and missionaries. They formerly worked among the Pocomchi people of Guatemala translating the New Testament.

The Royce Barons (G.M.U.) and the Richie Andersons (W.B.T.) serve in Mexico. And so many, many more! We wish we could visit them all, but the day was too short as the sun made its circuit. We return to where it all began, Briercrest Bible College.

Many serve with distinction in professional and vocational areas. Again, let me select just a few. In education: Dr. and Mrs. Henry Budd, president of BBC; Dr. and Mrs. Neil Snider, president of Trinity Western, Canada's only Christian university. Dr. Dan Kelly serves as anthropologist and linguist at Ontario Theological Seminary. In the field of medicine BBC alumni include Dr. George Goertzen, Dr. Don Clunas, and Dr. Lorne Penner (BBC campus doctor). Serving in government are Allen Engel, M.L.A. and Gerald Muirhead, M.L.A. Jack Stenekas serves in the field of music.

Again, who can measure the loyal service rendered our churches and the business world who are looking for people of integrity?

The pastor was delighted with the Sunday evening service. The attendance was good, the singing lively and the presence of God evident. After a warm welcome, I ministered with freedom.

Since my flight was not due to leave until 11:00 a.m. Monday, the pastor invited me to his study for a visit earlier that morning. After the usual words of greeting, he assured me that he had appreciated my ministry but I was not to presume that his pulpit at Fundamental Baptist Church was open to interdenominational representatives.

I was taken back by the inference and asked why he found it necessary to say so. He proceeded, "Since coming to minister in this prairie city, I have become very disillusioned with the interdenominational work. Some of my young people have attended interdenominational Bible Schools and returned antidenominational altogether." I was disconcerted, hesitated at first, then asked, "Pastor, the young man who appeared to be the head usher, is he disloyal to you and your church?" "No," replied the pastor, "I can always count on him. He is a son of one of our fine church families." "What about the young lady that was playing the piano, can you count on her?" I asked. "Yes, she is always there when you need her. She makes a wonderful contribution to our services," he replied. "What about the two young ladies that ministered so sweetly in song," I continued. "They too are dependable" answered the pastor. He proceeded, "And why are you asking about these?" I named all of them and then said, "I'm so glad they serve you so loyally." He wondered how I knew them. I told him that they were students and grads of our school. The pastor was surprised but pleased. He conceded, "I'm afraid I'll have to change my view about your school.

The pastor drove me to the airport and we enjoyed good fellowship on the way. He assured me BBC was welcome in his church.

On another occasion the pastor of Grant Memorial Baptist Church in Winnipeg publicly expressed his appreciation of Briercrest as he welcomed me to his pulpit. Said he, "The chairman of our board, the Youth Director, Christian Ed Director, secretary, and a number of our Sunday school teachers are all alumni of BBC. We owe a great debt to you."

Our alumni are equally loyal to BBC as they are to their churches. They have been led over the years by faithful Alumni Executive Directors. Bert and Doris Hiebert visited some of the older leading Bible colleges and obtained information as to how they guided their alumni. Alumni directors from some of these schools visited our school and gladly offered help. With the material on hand, Mr. Hiebert organized the BBC Alumni with elected representatives to serve as the executive committee and with its elected president to sit on the official board of the college. Moreover, alumni chapters function in many areas of our home lands, and several chapters operate in foreign lands. The most recent one was formed in Pakistan.

Metro and Peggy Leskewich followed the Hieberts as alumni directors and gave a good deal of momentum to the organization. Metro's enthusiastic songleading fired up many an alumni chapter so that it was often referred to as "good old BBC singing," a reminder of chapel singing while at school.

After twenty years of leading this great organization, the Leskewiches surrendered leadership to Lloyd and Doreen Lees who direct this body today. Lloyd is giving a spiritual emphasis to its membership, having come through the revival sparked by the Sutera Twins. Lloyd stresses the need of prayer for each other as alumni, and, in turn, for their churches and BBC. God is answering their prayers, and we feel its impact.

Most of our 6,000 or so alumni are bearing a good confession within the church and secular world. Many of our grads have surpassed us and are doing greater works and are doing it better than we ever did. If there will be a reward for any of our labours in glory, it will be a bonus. We feel the ministry to the young people of our land is all so fulfilling. Their response and prayers more than compensate for whatever efforts we are privileged to invest in them.

It has been said, "If there is one thing more important than the sending of a missionary, it is the training of a missionary worth sending." I believe that BBC has been called to this exciting ministry of training young people. I believe it is the way of securing and perpetuating our trust.

The story is told of the little lad who wept as he saw his New Testament torn from him and cast into the fire. Tearfully and innocently he asked, "And what are you going to do with the twenty-four chapters that I have memorized?"

"We can silence you," answered the culprit.

The boy caught the point. Wisely he sought out ten other little boys his own age. Faithfully he repeated his twenty-four chapters to them until they knew them word perfect. He reasoned, that in the event he too was cast into the fire, ten other little fellows remained with the deposit of twenty-four chapters of the Bible in their hearts.

This is how we seek to discharge our trust, "And the things that thou hast heard of me among many witnesses, the same commit thou to faithful men, who shall be able to teach others also" (2 Timothy 2:2). Reproducing reproducers!

"And Jesus came and spake unto them, saying, All power is given unto me in heaven and in earth. Go ye therefore, and teach all nations . . . Teaching them to observe all things whatsoever I have commanded you: and, lo, I am with you alway, even unto the end of the world. Amen" (Matthew 28:18-20).

31

The Bible School Movement on the Prairies

So shall they fear the name of the Lord from the west, and his glory from the rising of the sun. When the enemy shall come in like a flood, the Spirit of the Lord shall lift up a standard against him.
Isaiah 59:19.

> The surge of evangelism that covered much of Alberta and Saskatchewan in the mid-thirties, at the height of drought and depression, and that threw up the remarkable phenomena of the Prairie Bible schools, best exemplified by those at Three Hills and Briercrest, sent hundreds and even thousands of young people to the mission field. These missionaries naturally carried the torch of evangelism with them. The prairie movement may yet be seen to be one of the most significant Canadian contributions to the world church.[1]

What caused the remarkable phenomena of the Prairie Bible schools? The depression and drought on the Prairies? They created an abnormal situation which stopped many a Westerner dead in his tracks and made him reconsider his ways. In some localities a number of vivacious Christian young people were in peculiar circumstances. They were eager to work but there was no work. There were no harvests and no grain. There was no livestock which had been disposed of due to the drought. They wanted to study the Bible but had no finances to go to far-away schools. Therefore, why not have pastor lead in Bible studies? So, many a young pastor found himself in an embarrassing, happy position. Young people were asking for more Bible classes.

In some instances this led to organized Bible courses, and some of these led to the establishing of a Bible school to serve chiefly the interest of local communities. The depression and drought of the Prairies created opportunities to study the Bible, but must we not look for the real answer elsewhere?

Others suggest the answer lies in the seasonal work of the farmer, which gives young people free time during the winter months. True, this condition contributed to the development of the Prairie Bible schools, but the secret goes still deeper, for several schools were founded before the great depression. Let us not forget that a heaven-born desire to study the Word of God is the work of the Holy Spirit within the soul, as Dr. Rennie points out. It was the surge of evangelism that threw up the remarkable phenomena of the Prairie Bible schools. The schools in turn preserved and fostered evangelism at home and abroad during very difficult times.

A much more difficult burden had settled upon our land than the great depression. On the Prairies, it stalked in the open in the twenties. The young collegians and seminarians that took up their summer pastorates were proud and aggressive about their new philosophies. Three mainline denominations had united. They were hopeful of drawing into their union the remaining churches and thereby consolidate their sweep of liberalism.

The liberalism that swept the field on the Prairies robbed us of most churches, hospitals, and schools, and then blamed the few evangelicals remaining for a lack of social concern! Although some denominations survived, they were reeling under the modernistic onslaught. Several ethnic denominations were not taken in, but it seems they are under considerable pressure today, and that from the same source.

Many of our Prairie Christians had their misgivings. They discerned that this new teaching with which the young seminarians were so enamoured was not the Word of God. After listening to one of these "high-philutin" lectures in a seminary chapel one day, a professor asked, "Hildebrand, what would your Saskatchewan farmers think of it?"

I replied, "Sir, our Christian farmers would be too honest to pretend to know what the lecturer was talking about. But one thing they would be very certain about, that fellow was not teaching the gospel."

"But you must admit that he has his finger on the pulse of modern theology," asserted the professor.

"I am not so sure," I replied. "It seems to me it's more like having his fingers in its trap!" In the twenties and early thirties, liberalism had free sway on the Prairies.

But God did not leave Himself without a witness. Truly, "when the enemy shall come in like a flood, the Spirit of the Lord shall lift up a standard against him." One of the standards raised by the Spirit of God on the Prairies was the Bible school movement. The birth of the earlier Bible schools on the Prairies took place in the 1920's.

Then came the great depression. Liberalism began to vacate many rural areas for lack of support. This gave the evangelicals an opportunity and foothold in the rural areas. Meanwhile, evangelical work got started in the cities. Though their churches were few and small, they formed a nucleus and were ready for the increase during and after World War II. With the trend toward moving into the cities after the war, the evangelical churches reaped the benefits from the rural evangelical work, so that today the larger, growing churches in Prairie cities are evangelical.

There was a genuine hunger for the Word of God. Since pastoral candidates from the universities and seminaries had become suspect, evangelical Christians believed that the only way to get Bible preaching ministers was to train them in a Bible school. Encouraged by the ministry and growth of the earlier Bible schools, the thirties saw the beginnings of many more such schools. However, with the exception of Prairie Bible Institute, which had a head-start in the twenties, these new schools remained small. Their facilities were so limited, so was the training of many of their teachers. We were a feeble lot, a byword in the academic world. But, "who hath despised the day of small things" (Zechariah 4:10)?

The liberals spoke of the Bible school movement as another depression plague. As soon as normalcy returned, this plague would end, just like a grasshopper plague ends when rain comes. But did normalcy ever return? The depression lasted until the beginning of World War II. The war tested these schools severely but did not stop them. Immediately after the war, the Bible School Movement took off.

Students enrolled in increasing numbers. Faculties were strengthened, courses were developed, and the academic level of entrance requirements for students rose considerably. Total enrollments rose from about 300 in the late twenties to about 6,000 in the seventies. Governments began to recognize these Bible schools and gave to some the authority to grant degrees. An Association of Canadian Bible Colleges was formed with over fifty schools joining. This does not count all the schools in Canada. A few of the Bible colleges applied, and upon meeting the requirements of the American Association of Bible Colleges, were accepted. Today the enrollments of some are among the highest in the Association, ranking among the first ten in faculty qualifications.

With the growth of the Bible College Movement, several evangelical seminaries have been founded, providing graduate training for Bible college graduates. These are providing excellent training for pastors, missionaries, and Bible college faculties.

Today, few pastors in our evangelical churches have not studied in a Bible college. Some of these evangelical pastors are ministering in the leading churches in our land. But one of the chief Bible college contributions was to supply missionaries for fields abroad. Dr. Kane, Missiologist from Trinity Evangelical Divinity School, estimates that of North American missionaries 75 percent or more received Bible college training.[2] The Bible schools of the Prairies have contributed a large share of this number.

Moreover, the workers of the evangelical-para-church movements are mostly Bible school trained. They are key leaders in these home missionary societies. Many are counsellors at their camps and teachers in Bible clubs and daily vacation Bible schools.

The Bible college movement has sent countless numbers into professions and vocations who, as Christian laymen, are having an impact for good in our society. In the face of idleness and theft, of strikes and strife, employers are turning more and more to Bible college young people. Add to this their influence in the local church at the side of the pastor, and you can understand the strength of evangelical Christianity in our land. Who of us could have thought fifty years ago that evangelicals could become so visible? While prominence exposes weaknesses and subjects us to criticism, it also gives us an opportunity to be heard.

There are areas of concern. We have been used of God so far to keep the dams from bursting, holding back the pressures of iniquity; but we have not yet turned back the moral decay of a permissive society. We need to get more influence for good into political life; likewise into our universities and mass media. There remains, oh, so much to be done!

The danger of being diverted from our main task as Bible colleges is always there. To gain credits and/or acceptance with the universities we are pressured to accommodate our courses to fit their system. The danger is ever present that we will yield even our core subjects. When the chapel, symbol of the spiritual thrust of a school, loses its primary place among the academic and counselling community of the college, the students soon sense this shift and plead that chapel attendance become voluntary. The result, those who need chapel most are absent.

The presidents and academic deans must constantly remind their associates of the main task to which their schools were born—teaching the Word of God. Only thus can they fulfill their mission.

To do so, the schools must be supported by the Christian public that they serve. They must join to bear the cost of such a ministry. Students and teachers alone cannot do it. We must join hands to make this great service rendered by the Bible College Movement not only possible, but more efficient. And so these schools will become more effective in their great work of preparing men and women to serve the present generations. Let us respond in gratitude to God, and it shall be said of the Bible College Movement what was said of Jacob, "What hath God wrought!"

32

Transition . . . Transfer of Leadership

As I was with Moses, so I will be with thee: I will not fail thee, nor forsake thee. Joshua 1:5.

"Transition in the work of God is not the cessation of a significant ministry but a forward step into a new dimension of service."[1] It was my finest hour. It was such a delight to hand over the leadership to a trusted colleague who had stood at my side for a number of years. We did not have to look elsewhere. Dr. Henry Budd took his grade XII in our high school. He graduated from our Bible school, took his graduate studies at Wheaton College, served two terms as a missionary in Africa, joined our faculty in '65, and completed his doctoral studies at the University of Oregon.

The inaugural service is described by John Ward in the Special Presidential Issue of *The Echo,* the school's paper.

> Two thousand people packed the newly renovated BBI gymnasium-Conference hall on Sunday afternoon, October 2 to witness the public transfer of the office of President from Dr. Henry Hildebrand to Rev. Henry H. Budd. With the inauguration of Mr. Budd as President, Dr. Hildebrand was installed as the first Chancellor of Briercrest Bible Institute in recognition of his 42 years of dedicated service.
>
> Both men knelt with their wives as Rev. O. Swenson, Principal of the Bible School, led the prayer of dedication for the laying on of hands.
>
> Mr. Ernest Enns, first Vice-Chairman of the Board of Directors, presided over the Inaugural Service in which Dr. Kenneth Hanna, President

of Winnipeg Bible College, brought greetings on behalf of the Christian colleges.

The Inauguration Service was the climax of a challenging and inspiring Bible and Missionary Conference. . . .[2]

In the message preceding the inauguration I said,

As we come to this moment of transition, we believe it is within God's plan. God selects His men and sets them apart. He gives the means and the time to accomplish their appointed work—and then He appoints a successor.

In case some of you feel there is a touch of sadness to see me withdraw from active leadership—let me point out that this is an occasion for rejoicing to see how God provides for our present need of transition. Moreover, Mrs. Hildebrand and I will remain with the School in a new and challenging position. . . .

It is with joy and confidence that I turn the leadership of BBI over to my associate, Rev. Henry Budd.

This choice is personally gratifying, as I have observed with admiration the progress of Henry and Evelyn as students and missionaries, and on our campus as they joined our BBI family—when Mr. Budd served as faculty member and as an administrator. He has served loyally at my side. I have confidence in God that he is God's chosen man in the succession of leadership.

Times of transition are sometimes cause for concern, but this transition is one about which we have prayed and planned for a long time—ever since our 25th anniversary seventeen years ago. I see it made with confidence and peace. BBI is now in good and trustworthy hands. In the appointment of Mr. Budd to the office of President, I encourage him with the word of the Lord to Joshua, "As I was with Moses, so I will be with thee; I will not fail nor forsake thee" (Joshua 1:5). BBI is a great work that will need constant vigilance and a strong, firm hand of love in its leadership.

To reach this point in pursuit of God's prize, BBI has required your support in prayer and gift, as well as the tremendous effort by faculty and staff. It is essential that your continued and increased support be given to meet the greater challenges of tomorrow.

For your undergirding and involvement in BBI in days past, I personally thank you. Your confidence and encouragement by prayer and gift to the ministry of BBI is very sincerely appreciated. As my responsibility now passes into the hands of Henry Budd, I plead for your intensified support of him and of all his associates who with him will carry the work forward in the days ahead.

By accepting the office of the Chancellor, I officially turn the Presidency over to Mr. Budd. And as I do, I encourage him with the Word of our Lord in Joshua 1:8, "This book of the law shall not depart out of thy mouth; but thou shalt meditate therein day and night, that thou mayest observe to do according to all that is written therein: for then thou shalt make thy way prosperous, and then thou shalt have good success." And 1 Timothy 6:13-15, "I give thee charge in the sight of God, who quickeneth all things, and before Christ Jesus, who before Pontius Pilate witnessed a good confession; that thou keep this commandment without spot, unrebukeable, until the appearing of our Lord Jesus Christ: which in his times he shall shew, who is the blessed and only Potentate, the King of kings, and Lord of lords. . . ."[3]

In his inaugural address, Dr. Budd replied with his appreciation of the past to build upon it, basing his address on Deuteronomy 8:2.

Remember how God led in the establishment of Briercrest Bible Institute. There are people here today who were part of that beginning. Dr. Hildebrand, of course. Mrs. Whittaker, who with Mrs. Hillson went to Mr. Hildebrand when the issue was in doubt, when the prospect of starting a Bible school seemed so preposterous, sharing with him their hearts' vision and pledging their support in the work. Odd Brygmann, who, when Mr. Hildebrand said, "If we start classes, will anyone come to study?" replied, "I will, and there are others too!" Who but God would begin a school in Briercrest?

Remember how God led to Caronport. Remember the vision of Mr. Whittaker. Imagine—purchasing this particular air base of the several available after World War II! Remember that it was years after the move that the Trans-Canada Gas Line and the Trans-Canada Highway were brought right across our property, locating us on the mainline of Canadian development, not isolated in some rural corner.

Remember how God led us by the provision of leaders—men of God who stayed with the work, nurtured it, and saw it grow to maturity. What a heritage of leadership we have at BBI; what commitment, devotion, practicality, humour, and drive! I take off my hat to Dr. Hildebrand, forty-two years President of this Institute; an entrepreneur, a forger of new things, who was also able by the grace of God to grow in his leadership with the growth of the work, and so bring to maturity the work which he began.[4]

President Budd pointed out how Moses reflected upon what God had done that they might learn the lessons of their history. But "Moses did not immerse himself in the past. The future was before him—the future was the challenge and the future was good! Deuteronomy 8:7-10.

We also can look toward the future with joyful anticipation. We are not confident of the future because of any feeling of our own adequacy. Even less is our confidence born of looking at the circumstances around us. Indeed, there is much in the world situation that could dampen enthusiasm and hope. We are hopeful regarding the future because of three things:

a) Because our God is good

God did not bring Israel to the verge of Canaan just to disappoint them. He led them to a good land—because He is good. He wants that which is good for His children. Our faith is in the goodness of God—in His good will toward us.

b) Because God has equipped us to do a job

"Give us the tools," cried Winston Churchill to America during the testing days of World War II; "and we will finish the job!"

In a remarkable way, over many years, God has been giving us the tools to do a job here at Caronport. God brought us to this air base—this campus, which gave us room to grow. In recent years God has been supplying the material resources needed for this ministry: fine classrooms, a beautiful library with growing holdings, equipment for instruction, for business operations, for maintenance of the physical plant. Surely God has equipped us for something!

But the chief instruments for God's work have always been people—people with a singleminded devotion to the work of God. God has given us the personnel. God has brought together on this campus, at this time, a remarkable group of men and women. I am proud of the faculty and staff at BBI. I am thrilled with their gifts and abilities, stirred by their enthusiasm, humbled by their commitment to Jesus Christ. They know themselves to be "workers together with God."

I spent last year at a great university. I may have found there more learned men and women; but I did not find better teachers. The president of that university would have given his arm to have what we have here—teachers and staff members who want to work with students, to love them, counsel them, care for them, share with them.

I fully believe that the men and women who serve today at BBI are as deeply committed to Jesus Christ, as much in love with this ministry, and as ready, if need be, to sacrifice for its continuance, as they have been at any stage of the School's history. I am proud to be a member of this team. Surely God has brought "this band of brothers" together at this time for a purpose.

c) Because there is a job to be done

Never in its 90-year history has the Bible school movement faced the challenge and the opportunity that it does in the late 1970's! That opportunity arises from the acknowledged moral bankruptcy of Western civilization and its educational system. Watergate and its many satellite events was not the tragic drama of one man; it was the indictment of a society. Watergate was an open window upon the soul of a civilization.

Education, particularly higher education, stood indicted. A generation of secularized, technically streamlined, heavily-financed education produced graduates with a reduced moral sensitivity. Higher education was grinding out scientific giants and moral dwarfs.

In the last few years there has been a great cry rising from the circle of higher education concerning the need for an education that will teach moral values. Men like Max Lerner in his book *Values in Education* stress that all education is, and must be, value education; that if positive values are not taught and learned, negative values will be imbued.

But a great barrier rises before the secular educator. How can we reach even a minimal consensus regarding values to be taught? Upon what basis can we establish, let alone teach, values? A recent class in a Saskatchewan college of education, faced with the proposition that they must teach moral values to children, refused point blank. All, apart from one or two in the class, felt that they had no sure moral principles which they could share with youngsters, and no basis for the formation of any. They could not teach values!

What a challenge for Bible school education! Our kind of school was established to give "instruction in righteousness." From the very beginning we have emphasized the Scriptures as the one and only basis for establishment of a moral system. We have been sharpening our intellects and our skills while holding fast to our spiritual purposes. "Who knows but that we are come to the kingdom for such a time as this?" We have the kind of education for which our society is dying.

Biblical, spiritual, life-training, practical, Christian education has never been more relevant, more needed. That is Bible school education! If we are sharp, prepared, aware, thorough, committed, solid in our knowledge and convictions, we stand in a position to give leadership in our generation such as we have never before been called on to give. We are called to a great work, and we must not fail our generation.[5]

Our President continued his address with a call to careful introspection, to examine ourselves and prepare ourselves for the tests that lie ahead and concluded:

This is for us a historic moment. We pause for this moment between the past and the future. We stand upon the Plains of Moab and look around us. It is a time to look.

Look back in retrospect, and thank God for His constant presence and His gracious care.

Look forward in prospect, and see a future bright with promise because the Lord our God is good.

Look inward in prayerful introspection, and ask if we have prepared ourselves and fortified ourselves in Christ for the tests which lie ahead.

Look up with faith into the face of Jesus, to be encouraged and armed for the challenge of our calling.[6]

Dr. Budd referred several times to the skills, commitment and love of the men and women of the college who serve "with a singleminded devotion to the work of God." Perhaps the greatest contribution that God enabled me to make to the cause of Christ was in the selection of the people who grew with the work and were ready to carry the responsibilities of this great ministry.

Let me refer to a few of the younger men that were ready when the President selected them as his immediate associates:

Dr. John Barkman, as Vice-President of Campus Ministries, is the President's right hand man. He has earned the respect and love of staff and students and has now served at the college for 19 years.

Dr. Carlin Weinhauer, our Vice-President of Public Ministries, served most acceptably in the extension ministries of the college for 15 years.

Dr. Paul Magnus, our Vice President of Education, is known for his hard work and efficiency in all his activities. He has served here for 15 years.

Mr. Harvey Zink, our Dean of Students, with his counselling staff set the guidelines of student life and serves them in their personal needs. How often has he taken the brunt and burden of student problems and helped them to carry them to Jesus.

Dr. David Hildebrand, as Associate Dean—Education, gives his talents in education, organization, and music to the task. He has served here 15 years. Together with his wife, Jean, and Dr. and Mrs. Lyman Reed, they serve the married students in a counselling ministry.

Mr. Ellery Pullman, as Associate Dean—Faculty, serves that department admirably. Mr. Allan Johnson, our qualified Librarian, serves the academic community with distinction.

Mr. Wilfred Gaertner is leading our Music Department and honours the Lord by leading staff and students in worship.

Dr. Donald Moore is Director of Graduate Education. His enthusiasm and leadership in this department is serving the graduate students well.

All of these were first graduates of our college before they proceeded with their graduate studies. They and their wives and families contribute so much to this work.

As for Mrs. Hildebrand and me, we gave our first two years after Dr. Budd's inauguration to a ministry out in the country to make sure that our supporting constituency transferred loyalty to our new President and his administrators. Now we are very happily engaged as good-will ambassadors of the school, teaching in the classroom of the college and its graduate school. We also serve in conference ministries and special weekend rallies.

It is with great delight that we can report as we had anticipated. The college is in excellent hands under the leadership of President Budd and his associates. The college is progressing steadily in every area of ministry. Its numerical growth during the last eight years is well known, so is its strength and spiritual devotion to God and His Word. Inger and I are encouraged to see BBC committed to the same goals for another generation. The command of 2 Timothy 2:2 is being continued, "And the things that thou hast heard of me among many witnesses, the same commit thou to faithful men,who shall be able to teach others also." Briercrest Bible College is continuing to "Reproduce Biblical Reproducers!"

33

The Golden Years

Hear counsel, and receive instruction, that thou mayest be wise in thy latter end. Proverbs 19:20

"Andrew, pray that both of us may wear well to the end." This prayer that Andrew Bonar's father requested of his son is our desire.

Before God, Inger and I had sought to prepare ourselves for the transition of leadership and the "Golden Years" to follow. God provides wonderful grace and marks the way so beautifully. President Budd and the college family made the transition much, much easier than we could have anticipated.

We were the same people the day after we handed over the leadership as before. Granted, adjustments had to be made in our relationships to the new leadership, associates, students and supporting constituency. But we did not find it difficult. We enjoyed leading this great work. We enjoy it even more in our present relationship. God in His grace has preserved us from the bitter cup of false friends. How grateful we are to Him!

Inger and I as a woman and a man, as persons, still have a service to render, even though our steps have to be measured. Henry W. Longfellow wrote so beautifully:

For age is opportunity no less
Than youth itself, though in another dress,
And as the evening twilight fades away
The sky is filled with stars, invisible by day.[1]

As long as God leaves us here upon earth, we are resolved to glorify Him and speak well of Him and His mightly acts to the younger generation. Did not David pray, "O God, you have helped me from my earliest childhood—and I have constantly testified to others of the wonderful things you do. And now that I'm old and gray, don't forsake me. Give me time to tell this new generation (and their children too) about all your mighty miracles" (Psalm 71:17-18, Living Bible)?

I say we had prepared our hearts and God wonderfully supplied the grace to enjoy the transition, to see BBC in good hands, and to enter our Golden Years with confidence. One thing, however, we were not prepared for, namely the honours and awards that have come with transition. So much has come that we are concerned that there will be nothing left to place at our Lord's feet in glory! We are committed to place honours as they come at Jesus' feet now. Instead of coasting into glory, we mean to continue to labour, though in another dress, to receive His "well done," without which nothing will count.

The greatest honour came from our own BBC family and friends of the school. While we had been alerted to the plans of the Testimonial Evening, we were completely surprised by the extent and the depth that President Budd and his associates had planned.

One evening Glen, our youngest, and his Mother and I were discussing the prospects of the Testimonial. His mother protested, "I don't see that if an evening for us has been planned, why we can't have it on the campus, sort of low-key. Why did it have to be in the Centre of the Arts in Regina? Who will want to go to Regina? I think it's going to be a big flop." Glen replied, "O Mother, you won't need to be worried about that. There will be a good attendance. What's more, they'll bowl you over with surprise."

Something clicked in my mind, what would bowl his mother over but that her relatives from Norway would show up? We had been in Norway that summer, and, when reference was made to the transition of leadership and a Testimonial, there had been silence. A bit unusual for the Soyland clan! But I let it go by. I thought, if I squeeze Glen about what I for the moment suspected, he would be forced to lie, or to let the secret out and spoil it. So I dropped it and forgot all about it, so completely that when it actually took place, I was as surprised as Inger!

The theme of the Testimonial event was "The Longer I Serve Him, the Sweeter He Grows." The evening has been described by Robert Adam, Jr. in the winter edition of the Alumni News, 1978. For the benefit of the whole constituency I have reprinted it here. Robert Adam, Jr. is now Director of Public Ministries.

About 860 guests, from as far as British Columbia, Ontario, New York State and even from Norway, gathered in Hanbidge Hall at the Centre of the Arts for the Testimonial Banquet. A further 750 visitors (making a total of over 1,600 people) later attended the public program in the main auditorium to hear the words of appreciation and tribute being paid to Dr. and Mrs. Hildebrand.

Excitement had been building for many weeks and reached a high pitch on 'Port in the final few days as the inevitable last-minute preparations were finalized. Finally the "big day" arrived and by 6 p.m. all was in readiness.

When all the guests had been seated, the Hildebrands were ushered in to the background music of "The Longer I Serve Him the Sweeter He Grows." An anticipatory hush fell over the audience as a taped message from Mr. Olav Soyland, Mrs. Hildebrand's brother, came over the P.A. system bringing greetings from her relatives in Norway. That hush was soon broken by gasps of disbelief from the Hildebrands as "the man behind the voice"—her brother Olav, along with six other relatives from Norway—entered the banquet hall! (The seven special guests were Mrs. Hildebrand's three brothers, Olav, Kjell, Toralf, their wives, and her aunt, Mrs. Anna Anderson.) It was worth the price of the ticket just to see the looks of disbelief, astonishment, and delight register on Mrs. Hildebrand's face! Then, speaking in English, with his beautiful Norwegian accent, Mr. Olav Soyland brought "first-hand" greetings and congratulations to the Hildebrands.

After the meal itself, Mr. Swenson, the Master of Ceremonies for the evening, read some of the many telegrams which came for the Hildebrands. We all shared in the excitement of hearing the congratulatory messages from many officials and political leaders, among them Governor General Leger, Lieutenant Governor of Saskatchewan George Porteous, Prime Minister Trudeau, former Prime Minister John Diefenbaker, Opposition Leader Joe Clark, and former Premier T. C. Douglas. There were also greetings from Rev. Simon Forsberg, former President of Winnipeg Bible College when the Hildebrands attended in the thirties, and from several other friends and alumni of BBC.

At the banquet, Mr. Colin Thatcher, MLA for the Thunder Creek riding, of which Caronport is a part, brought a welcome from the people of the Caron area and spoke of the relationship betwen BBC and the surrounding area. Mayor Henry Baker of Regina then brought a greeting from the people of Regina and made a presentation to the Hildebrands from the City of Regina.

The music for the banquet was beautifully provided by the upperclassman musical group, "A Joyful Song." Their ministry has been with great blessing in the last couple of years, and their songs—among them "Fairest

Lord Jesus" and the moving testimony song, "It's the Greatest, Greatest Story Ever Told"—were deeply appreciated by all.

The scene then changed to the main auditorium for the public service. Over 1,600 people were on hand to listen to the words of tribute and to share in giving honour to the Hildebrands. And what better way to begin than by hearing from Mrs. Whittaker. She charmed the audience with her lively wit and humour in recalling the days when Mr. Hildebrand "came as a young man to us." Her vivid recollections of the amusing and the touching incidents of those early days and of the Hildebrands' faithfulness in those years were most warmly received.

Rev. David Hildebrand then gave us a family perspective of his parents. His warm tribute to his mother compared her to the mother in Proverbs chapter 31. He mentioned his parents' qualities of generosity, firm discipline, their ability to listen, but most of all, their deep spiritual concern for each member of the family.

Leading the tributes paid by the civic leaders, Mayor Herb Taylor of Moose Jaw spoke of the rapport between BBC and Moose Jaw over the years. "You could be sure there would be someone from Caronport there to help if we were looking for a missing person or hit by a flood. This only comes about through good leadership."

Mr. Doug Neil, Member of Parliament for Moose Jaw, extended personal congratulations to Dr. Hildebrand and the school. "The contributions of Henry Hildebrand and his followers have created an atmosphere of oneness in the cultural mosaic of Western Canada. It is a oneness not seen anywhere else in Canada."

Premier Allan Blakeney gave tribute to the insight of the Hildebrands in the Depression years and the inspiring example set by BBC over the years. He stressed the need for humanitarian and spiritual leadership, and said that Dr. Hildebrand has provided just that. "Dr. Hildebrand," he said, "will continue to mold young lives through the many students he has trained over the years."

Those who were more directly connected with the ministry of BBC also paid tribute. Greg Dalman, Student Body President for 1977-78, led the student body in thanks to Dr. and Mrs. Hildebrand. Then Mr. H. Alvin Memory, Chairman of the Board of Directors, paid tribute to the characteristics and qualities of leadership displayed by the Hildebrands—in the areas of discipline, devotion, hospitality, and spiritual example. As Mr. Memory stated, "Like the apostle Paul said in 2nd Corinthians, 'they first gave themselves to the Lord in loving dedication and then to all of us.' "

The final tribute was paid by President Budd. Mr. Budd discussed the qualities of Christian leadership laid out in Scripture and as reflected in the life of Dr. Hildebrand. He particularly focused on the aspects of aspiration, and the quality of servanthood, both in caring and in service.

Not all the ministry was in spoken word. The musical ministry was rich and varied. Further music was provided by "A Joyful Song," along with the upperclassmen choir led by Mr. Wilfred Gaertner. Mrs. Paul (Corinne)

Hildebrand and Mrs. David (Jeannie) Hildebrand sang a beautiful duet "The Lord is My Shepherd," accompanied at the piano by David Hildebrand. Obviously these songs could not directly pay tribute to the Hildebrands, but certainly directed our praise and worship to our God for His goodness and blessing to all of us. A fascinating audio-visual presentation, "Yours in His Loving Service," narrated by Mrs. Myrtle Wipf and Mr. Metro Leskewich, gave a panoramic view of God's blessing upon the lives of Dr. and Mrs. Hildebrand over the years.

Beside tribute in word, there were also several tangible gifts of thanks and congratulations. Mr. Memory presented the Hildebrands with a love gift in the form of a cheque from the many friends who had sent in contributions, and with a book compiled by Mr. David Nadeau containing personal tributes and reminiscences from family, alumni and BBC friends over the 42 years. Mr. Ernie Enns, on behalf of the Board of Directors and the entire BBC family and alumni, presented the Hildebrands with a lovely stereo set. President Budd then presented Dr. Hildebrand with the third volume of the memoirs of the Right Honorable John G. Diefenbaker, personally autographed by the former Prime Minister, and, in a highlight of the evening, presented to Dr. Hildebrand the Queen's Silver Jubilee Medal. This medal commemorates the 25th anniversary of Her Majesty's ascension to the throne.

As we have come to expect and appreciate, Dr. Hildebrand would not accept any credit for the success of BBC. "I give all the honour and glory to God. Without Him, there would be nothing. And without His helpers here on earth, there would be nothing. I did not do this work alone. Tribute is due to my wife, to our supporting constituency, the staff and faculty at the school over the years, to the wisdom of the Board of Directors, to the students and thousands of alumni."

While reflecting on the past, Dr. Hildebrand closed on a note of faith in God and hope and vision for the future. "God has a greater ministry in store for BBC. Millions of people still need to hear the Word."

The theme of the Testimonial evening "The Longer I Serve Him the Sweeter He Grows" has been wonderfully demonstrated in the lives of Dr. and Mrs. Hildebrand. We join in expressing our gratitude to God for their lives.

More interesting to you may be the actual tributes that were made by the leaders of our Dominion of Canada and of my closest associates. It will give you an insight as to "What God Hath Wrought" through an immigrant boy who with his parents fled from a country where religious liberty was denied and came to a land of religious freedom that provided the climate where such a work of God was possible. It also expresses their appreciation of the nature of this ministry.

The tributes describe more the man of God I would love to have been. Having placed these at the feet of Jesus to Whom all the glory belongs, I share these with our readers. You will read with profit if you forget about the clay and focus your attention on the Potter.

Dear Henry and Inger,

Congratulations and God Bless You!

How we love to remember you as two dear, dedicated young people as you were with us at the Winnipeg Bible Institute, '31-'34—ever rejoicing in the Lord.

God's hand has been on you for good as you have diligently followed His leading, in spite of trials, and sacrifices, even misunderstandings sometimes. With great faith in God's promises, you have pressed ahead for the Glory of God.

Henry, like Barnabas of old, has been a, "Son of Consolation," encouraging and strengthening many believers. Inger, in her quiet way, has been a loyal helper to her husband and family, and a staunch supporter of B.B.I.

Yes, we are thankful upon every remembrance of you, Phil. 1:3, dear Henry and Inger, for your steadfast love and devotion to God and to His people. Our prayers follow you as you press onward to the "mark for the Prize of the High calling in Christ Jesus."

Rev. and Mrs. Simon E. Forsberg

Please convey the following message from Governor General to Dr. Henry Hildebrand on the occasion Testimonial dinner Nov. 10.

I am particularly pleased to join in the tribute being paid tonight to Dr. Henry Hildebrand. With all of you I would like to thank him for the eminent role he has played as President of the Briercrest Bible Institute. The development of this Institute over the past 42 years is a measure of the growing spiritual needs of our contemporary youth.

I am sure that Dr. Hildebrand will continue to be, for many years to come, a source of inspiration and hope for many young Canadians in their search of God.

Governor General Jules Leger

It gives me great pleasure to extend to you my sincere congratulations as you and Mrs. Hildebrand are honoured at a Testimonial Dinner. It is indeed fitting that your many friends should gather to pay homage to someone who has contributed such a great deal to his country. I know that you were instrumental in the founding of the Briercrest Bible Institute which has now become one of the largest theological training institutions in Canada. You have played an important role in guiding young people to spiritual fulfillment and to acquisition of the qualities of good citizenship that will stand them in good stead for the rest of their lives. As President of the Briercrest Bible Institute, you have proved yourself a great educator and minister of the gospel. I am confident that, as Chancellor, you will continue to have a very valuable influence on the lives of the young people with whom you come in contact. Please accept my very best wishes for the future.

The Right Honourable
Pierre Elliott Trudeau

It is an honour and privilege for me to participate in this testimonial and pay tribute to and recognize the years of faithful service and devotion of Dr. Hildebrand to the Briercrest Bible Institute.

As one of the staff members stated to me a short time ago:

"Today the sun never sets on Briercrest. In virtually every walk of life, hundreds of her alumni are scattered throughout the length and breadth of the globe, taking their rightful place in serving God and their fellow-men."

As Founder and President of the Institute, Dr. Hildebrand played a very significant role in building an Institute with an enrollment of 11 in the early Thirties to over 750 at the present time.

In these days of suspicion and doubt towards governmental and spiritual authority, it is refreshing and satisfying to see the progress the Institute has made over the years. It is a credit to you, Sir, and to other members of your staff who served with you during your term as President.

We in Western Canada are a mosaic made up of people of various ethnic backgrounds. It was into this mosaic that Dr. Hildebrand moved from Southern Russia with his parents in 1925 when he was 14 years of age. The contributions of Dr. Hildebrand and others like him, have, over the years, created an atmosphere of cooperation and oneness I would suggest, that is known nowhere else in this great country of Canada. We are greatly indebted to you for the part you have played in making this possible.

I was pleased to learn, Sir, of your appointment as first Chancellor of the Briercrest Bible Institute, effective September 1st of this year. As Chancellor I know you will continue to serve with the same spiritual devotion and dedication that has marked your service to God and to the Institute in the past.

In closing I would like to say again that I deem it a privilege and honour to take part in these proceedings and I would like to extend to you, Sir, and to your wife sincere best wishes for the future not only on my own behalf but on behalf of all the residents of the Moose Jaw Constituency.

May God bless both of you.

Mr. D. C. Neil
M. P. for Moose Jaw

Even more than in the days of the prophets, the worship of Mammon is evident in our society. The pursuit of material goals has contributed to making us greedy and unmindful of others.

The Christian Church has a mission and a message to teach our society about more lasting values.

It is through people that God works, and we are grateful to people like Dr. Henry Hildebrand, who, for 42 years, has given his life, living for this cause. We are all the richer for his leadership.

On behalf of the people of Saskatchewan, I express my thanks, and I know that his service to God and man will continue through all the young people whose lives he has influenced.

Lieutenant Governor George Porteous

Many inspiring stories have come out of the depression years on the prairies. Those were tough years, years when life here in Saskatchewan seemed so bleak that many people simply gave up hope. But those who survived often did so with a renewed faith in God and their fellow man. Like Job, the people of Saskatchewan found new strength in their adversity.

One of the most inspiring stories of that period is the story of Henry Hildebrand and the Briercrest Bible Institute. In the fall of 1935, at a time when most people were simply struggling to survive, Henry Hildebrand, his congregation and 11 devoted students started something which has had far-reaching consequences for Saskatchewan. Their project, the Briercrest Bible Institute, has been a beacon of faith and hope here on the prairies from that day to this.

I know that Dr. Hildebrand has faced much adversity in his life. But I know also that he and his wife have faced that adversity with courage and undiminished faith. They set an example for us all. Their memorial is not only in the flourishing institute at Caronport, but in the thousands of people, in every walk of life and throughout the world, who serve God and their fellow man with joy because they have been taught by Dr. and Mrs. Hildebrand. No one could ask for a greater reward on this earth.

My colleagues and I work to further the cause of free men governing themselves. We cannot long have a functioning democracy if the great mass of the people don't believe that the welfare of the community ought to take precedence over the welfare of any individual, or any group of individuals. That will only come about when we have men and women who have a sense of value, who believe in honesty and truth and loyalty, who have an appreciation of beauty, and who have a fundamental belief in the spiritual nature of the universe in which we live.

To this great task of shaping the lives of young people, Dr. Hildebrand and his wife have devoted their lives. On behalf of the Government of Saskatchewan I want to say "thank you." I feel sure that inspired by his example and nourished by his spirit those who carry the burden that he laid down will ensure that Briercrest Bible Institute will serve the cause of Jesus Christ for many years to come.

Premier Allan Blakeney

Greetings in the name of our Risen Lord.

I would like to thank you for seeing that Mrs. Anderson and I received tickets for the testimonial dinner in honour of Dr. and Mrs. Hildebrand.

I have known your President for a number of years and worked closely with him when the Saskatchewan Association of Private Schools first was organized and took as its primary aim improvement of relationships with the Provincial Government with the intent of receiving higher government grants. Dr. Hildebrand provided leadership and meaningful and fruitful input into our meetings and into our first brief to the Government. He and I were part of a committee of three who approached the Provincial authorities, including the Honourable Ross Thatcher, to convince them of the need to provide greater support.

I know Dr. Hildebrand to be a man of wise counsel, firm convictions and an unfailing love of His Lord and Saviour. I have met his wife on several occasions and have found her to be a warm and supportive person who has stood behind her husband during these many years.

Please be so kind as to bring them personal greetings from me and my wife and also fraternal greetings from the Luther College family.

Mr. Morris A. Anderson
President of Luther College
Regina

Shortly after I returned to Caronport to teach, our neighbor politely introduced my wife to some students, saying, "This is Mrs. Hildebrand, but not the real one!" Over the past 33 years it has been my privilege to know the real Mr. & Mrs. Hildebrand, and to know them *quite* well.

Mother is Dad's queen, and ours. Father was clearly the head of the home, but to a large extent Mother managed the house. She organized what had to be done, and she executed the organization. When Dad was away in the summers, the home switched into second gear smoothly and Mom carried on alone, including family devotions and spankings! She reminds me of another lady about whom I read that she manages the home, looking "well to the ways of her household." "Her husband is known in the gates, when he sitteth among the elders of the land." I am reading, of course, from Proverbs 31. The land knows her husband; we children know her, and tonight we "rise up and call her blessed."

Mom made home a special place for us. Marcia and Paul still drive miles to make it home for Sunday dinners. And often they leave with a bag of homemade buns under their arm. Mom is very generous to her family, both with her possessions and with her help. This same generosity is shown to the School. Often when things needed to be bought for a school function and there was a question whether or not to charge the things to the School's bill, we would hear Mom say, "Oh, it's for the work, I'll pay for it." She has shared with Dad a deep commitment to the work God has given them.

Mom did much to give us a sense of security, for when we would arrive home from school, we would automatically call our "Hello!" to be answered with the expected, though somewhat softer, "Hello." Sometimes we would bound into the kitchen, dinner was on the stove, but no "hello" responded. We would call again, and the hello would come back from up the hall in my Father's study, where Mom was finishing her quiet time with the Lord. When Mother and Dad wished you God's blessing, you could be sure there was a whole bundle of prayers, and maybe a tear, to back up their blessing. Such phrases were not thrown around as meaningless Christian jargon.

As for Dad, he exercised his leadership of the home in giving us spiritual leadership. This summer Glen was recalling bursting into Dad's study to find him on his knees. As a young boy, this seemed ordinary, but now the thought has come to him: It isn't every dad that is on his knees at the start of the day. Dad led the family altar when he was home.

And his firm hand supported Mom in the family disciplining. In fact, our most serious spankings were normally from Dad, as we recall! I remember dropping one of Mom's belts down the furnace register, but Dad's belt was more difficult to get rid of—he always wore it. Family discipline included an understanding that we should be in from our dates by midnight. So when parting was "such sweet sorrow," we could always put the blame on Mom and Dad. It worked well to help keep us out of mischief and to help keep us pure.

A strong characteristic, one that does not always accompany discipline, was the pleasure we had of talking to our folks. Our meal times at noon and supper facilitated this communication. And even if he was busy studying, Dad was interested to talk to us. How many times have I seen Mom and Dad in the study, Dad at his desk, and Paul Henry standing in the doorway solving all the issues in the world! As young teen-agers we would likely confide our heartaches to Mom, maybe as she was ironing away, but we soon learned we could confide in Dad too, and we did. They both had wise, practical Christian counsel. I recall shortly after marriage something which Dad wrote to us. Jeannie and I had competed for marks from grade XI all through Bible School. And so Dad wrote telling us to remember that *now* we were a duet, not a duel!

While we were never given the chance to take our parents' help for granted, Dad and Mom were all the same very generous in sharing with us what they got. In recent years, if the Lord blessed them materially, more than once some of the blessing was passed on to us, like maybe a Christmas check of $100 or more. And I well recall during my university days in Regina, shortly after I was married, I had to get some costly dental work done. Dad paid the bill, because, he said, they regretted not having had me visit the dentist more often during those earlier years when they just didn't have the money to send me.

Perhaps the characteristic that moves me most is Dad's very real spiritual concern for his family. When he thinks about how we're doing, his thoughts are really mostly about how each of us is doing spiritually. Often at mealtime you can see him listening intently, trying to discern from our comments our spiritual well-being. Tonight, Mom and Dad, the five of us—the nine of us want to say that your concern for our spiritual lives has become our concern too. We want to grow in the Lord. Besides pleasing Him, we know this would also be the best reward we could give to you.

David Hildebrand,
for the family

As a third year student I have appreciated the time and encouragement that Dr. Hildebrand has given me. Those times when he meets you on the street or in the hall, and takes the time to say "hi" and ask how you are doing. As well to see the individual concern that he has for the spiritual growth in the lives of students. As a music group his comments and life in the ministry have encouraged us to continue to serve the Lord with the abilities He has given us.

At this time I would like to have those present of this year's student body to please stand.

As a student body president, on behalf of the students, I would like to say "thank you for following the Lord's leading in establishing Briercrest Bible Institute, 42 years ago. For building it on the Word of God, resulting in a spiritual and moral growth in each of our lives which shall last throughout eternity."

Greg Dalman
Student Body President

The Man Hildebrand!

We have seen this man rise early in the morning to meet with his God and prepare for the day, when the strenuous activities of the previous day would shout "You have the right to rest this morning."

We have seen this man interrupt an already burdensome schedule to visit someone laid aside in the hospital.

We have seen this man take time to counsel an anxious student when a dozen pressing matters would have said "There is not time."

We have seen this man, when many miles from campus, decline an overnight invitation and fellowship with dear friends, because the call of duty said that the time could not be spared.

We have seen the home of the Hildebrands, and their hearts, opening in gracious hospitality during busy days when most of us would say "There is not time."

Dr. and Mrs. Hildebrand love people and wherever they go hearts are warmed whether they meet with a large crowd, a small group or an individual.

These are just a few of the things that come to me tonight as I let my mind go back over the 40 and more years that we have known the Hildebrands. This warmth, love and dedication found in their lives is what brings us all here tonight to give them the honour which is their due. I am sure that we are joined in spirit by countless others who could not be here, but whose lives have been equally blessed by their dedicated lives.

The lives of Dr. and Mrs. Hildebrand touched the lives of my dear wife and myself in the early years of our Christian life, and this had a great deal to do with the direction our lives took for God at that time.

God gave each of the Hildebrands the gifts they needed for the work, and, like the apostle Paul said of the Corinthians, they first gave themselves to the Lord in loving dedication and then to all of us.

Speaking on behalf of the board members of the present and the past I can say that it has been an enriching experience to have known you Dr. Hildebrand and to have served on the board during your presidency. Your able leadership, dedication to the task entrusted to you and example of hard work has been an inspiration to all of us. The Briercrest Bible Institute which you founded has reached people for God around the world and we consider it a great privilege and honour to have been associated with you in this work.

On behalf of all of us we say, "Thank you Dr. and Mrs. Hildebrand for giving yourselves unselfishly to God and all of us in 42 years of dedicated service. Our communities, Saskatchewan, Canada, the whole world is richer because of you. May God grant you many more happy years in His service!"

Mr. H. Alvin Memory
Chairman of the Board

I want to do something just a little different than what has gone before. I want to muse just a little about the quality of Christian leadership, the essence of Christian leadership. You know leadership is a very elusive and a very enigmatic quality. What is it that really makes a leader? What is leadership? I'm told that General James Wolfe whose troops stormed the Plains of Abraham in 1759 and changed the course of Canadian history, was the most unlikely kind of a leader. Wolfe we are told was very, very thin, red headed, boney, lankey, very ungainly. He was a man who had a most peculiar face. Can you imagine a man with a receding chin and receding forehead at the same time, whose whole face came to a point in his upturned nose. And yet, General Wolfe was a superb leader of men. Even the highlanders, who made up an important contingent of his troops, would follow him to their death although he was a Sassenach, a southerner.

What is it that makes a leader? What is a leader of men? And more particularly we might ask what is it that makes a Christian leader? On one occasion Jesus was speaking to His disciples. Two of them had aspired to leadership to places of prominence and afterwards the disicples hearing of it quarreled amongst themselves, and Jesus calling them to Himself said to them, "You know that those who are recognized as rulers of the Gentiles, lord it over them, and their great men exercise authority over them but it is not so among you. But whoever wishes to become great among you shall be the slave of all. For even the Son of man did not come to be served but to serve and to give His life a ransom for many."

What constitutes leadership? Jesus said concerning Christian leadership, that Christian leadership first of all meant aspiration. You notice here that Jesus said, "whosoever will be great, whosoever will be first." He didn't rebuke James and John because they aspired but simply because their aspiration took the wrong direction for Christian leadership. Leadership involves aspiration. The great Baptist missionary William Carey had as his motto of life, "Attempt great things for God, Expect great things from God." And when I think of those early days of Briercrest Bible Institute and of the early ministry of Henry Hildebrand, I'm sure that at that time Mr. Hildebrand never could have known what would have grown out of the ministry that was begun. And yet I know from knowing the man that in those days he had aspirations, he wanted his life to be at least within the sphere of his service, great in the service of God. He wanted to do something with his life that was significant for God. And when he had founded an institution into its growing, I know from working with him that he wanted it to have a standard of excellence and quality. He wanted to be involved in a great work. You see leadership means aspiration. And then secondly, you notice that Jesus stressed that leadership means servanthood. Jesus said to His disciples, "whoever will be great among you, shall be your servant and whoever will be the first, will be the slave of all." I believe that servanthood begins with caring about people. You can't serve people unless you see them. It's always amazing to me as I see students come and go at Briercrest Bible Institute. Do you realize that 43 classes of students have entered Briercrest Bible Institute from the beginning. And 41 classes have graduated. In the last few years those classes coming in have numbered somewhere around 240 in the Bible School, as many as 135 and 140 in the High School. And the graduating classes have been up to 140 in the Bible School and almost 100 in the High School. And I'm not beginning to say that Dr. Hildebrand remembers the names of all of those people that have passed through Briercrest, but I am constantly amazed at how many he does remember. And how many times after a student has departed for many years he will show up again and Dr. Hildebrand will greet him and maybe he'll stumble for just a moment but then he'll pin his name on him. Why is he able to do that? Because he has a tremendous capacity of caring about people, those students are not just another apple rolling up the conveyor belt. They're people in whom he has a personal interest.

I heard of an incident a few years ago when Dr. Hildebrand visited with a certain Christian businessman from Manitoba. And he met his wife and his family and visited in their home. It was somewhat near a year afterwards when the same man came to Caronport and in turn was visiting in the Hildebrand home. And as he was visiting there Mr. Hildebrand at first greeted him and then he said to him, "And how is so and so?" and he named his wife by her first name. And then he said, "How are the children?" The man was somewhat amazed at this time and so he said, "I bet you don't remember their names." And Mr. Hildebrand said, "I think I do." And he began to name them one, two, three, four. He not only named them by their first names but he named them in the order they came in. Then he said to the man, "You know that I wrote the names of you and your wife and family in a book and I have been remembering you in prayer." When I see this capacity in Dr. Hildebrand to care about people there are many times when I simply say, "O God, make me that kind of a leader."

Not only is it caring about people but servanthood is serving people and it has been mentioned here before, it means 42 years of a president's office that has been open to students, to staff members, to visiting friends, coming and going and receiving counsel, being encouraged and enthused in the work of God. And being given stimulation and discipline when it was needed, the service of people.

But most of all Christian leadership means Christ-likeness. When Jesus talked on the subject of what it meant to be a Christian leader He ended what He said by saying this. "For even the Son of man came not to be ministered unto, not to be served, but to serve and to give His life a ransom for many." Jesus included that because it was not incidental, it was not accidental. The very epitome, the very essence of Christian leadership is Christ likeness. And you see, that's not any kind of a cheap imitation; who can imitate the Christ? The life of Christ has to develop from within the life. We are told that when we receive Jesus Christ and come to know Him in that personal relationship, then as the Bible says, "I have been crucified with Christ, nevertheless I live, yet not I but Christ liveth in me. The life which I now live in the flesh I live by the faith of the Son of God Who loved me and gave Himself for me." Christ within the life. Christ radiating out of the life. The expression of Jesus Christ, that sacrificial life of Jesus Christ, who could say the Son of man came not to be served but to serve and to give His life a ransom for many. That sacrificial life being formed within and radiated without, that's what makes Christian leadership.

Let the beauty of Jesus be seen in me,
All His wonderful passion and purity.
Oh Thou Spirit divine, all my nature refine,
Till the beauty of Jesus be seen in me.

We have lived in the presence and worked in the presence of a great Christian leader and our lives have been marked indelibly by that encounter. It was Christ within, Christ that we give the glory. So, in the words of the book of Revelation we say, "And so to Him who sits upon the throne, and to the Lamb, be honour and glory, power and dominion, both now and forever. Amen."

Dr. Henry H. Budd
President of Briercrest Bible College

The alumni from almost every Mission Field as well as the homeland joined in appreciation of what God meant to them through these earthly vessels. Leaders of the Opposition in the government houses, and the former Premier of Saskatchewan, the Honourable T. C. Douglas, and former Prime Minister, the Honourable John G. Diefenbaker, added their words of recognition. So did pastors, fellow educators, and missionaries.

To the foregoing I responded in acknowledging first and foremost God's Grace, then my parents, my wife and family, and all my associates in the college, the students and the supporting constituency through whom God made the work possible.

I did appreciate, among many honours, inauguration into the Order of Canada—our nation's highest civilian honour—on October 24, 1979. The reason why I value most this honour—next to the Testimonial—is that I believe our government thereby honoured the entire evangelical constituency of our great country. As far as I know, this has so far been the only occasion when a person of the evangelical community has been so honoured.

When my name was called, I stood forth among the noble and government leaders of our land in Government House at Ottawa. The clerk's citation stated that the medal was presented for my contribution to the Christian education of our Canadian youth and, through them, to humanity at large.

As I stood there, I could hardly control my feelings as it suddenly came to me that the very faith for which I was being honoured in Canada had caused so much suffering for my parents in the old land. Canada may not be a perfect land, but it is a land of freedom. For this we must be grateful.

With the Golden Years and its honours come also grave dangers. The danger of pride where one is tempted to take more credit than is due. There's the temptation to think that we can coast along to glory before one gets there. How many of God's people in the Bible stumbled as they approached the finishing line! Our Lord taught us to pray, "and lead us not into temptation, but deliver us from evil, for Thine is the kingdom and the power and the glory for ever." Amen!

For whatever time God grants into the great future, I mean to be true to Him Who is our mighty protector and provider. "All day long I'll praise and honour you, O my God, for all that you have done for me" (Psalm 71:8, Living Bible).

34

Flashback

"A merry heart doeth good like a medicine . . . he that is of a merry heart hath a continual feast." Proverbs 17:22, 15:15.

"Humour keeps life from drying up, gives it freshness and flavour." Elizabeth Gray Vining

"The sense of humour is the oil of life's engine . . ." G. S. Merriam

"Imagination is given to a man to compensate him for what he is not, and a sense of humour was provided to console him for what he is." Thomas Carlyle

"When a thing is funny search it for a hidden truth." Bernard Shaw[1]

In view of the above I felt free to share with you a number of incidents that will mean most to the Briercrest Bible College family. I am seeking to relate them as accurately as I can recall them, or as they were related to me. You really have to know the people and circumstances involved to appreciate them fully.

We were approaching the Spring Conference when, as usual, a building program was to be presented to the guests. Conscious of her husband's continual appeals for support, Inger cautioned me, "Go easy on the audience. Don't pressure them. I'm sure that when you are gone, some donor—with a sigh of relief—will inscribe upon your tombstone, "And it came to pass that the beggar died."

"Don't worry Honey," I replied, "First he would have to donate the tombstone."

* * *

The quartet and I were ministering in the Cambridge area of Ontario. Our friends from Galt, as it was known then, had booked us very heavily that Sunday. We could hardly make it in time for the evening service with the Salvation Army at Hespeler. Captain *MacCorkodale* was waiting for us. We were rushed, so introductions were brief. Neither the captain nor I got each other's names properly. He hurriedly outlined the evening program and we stepped on to the platform. The opening hymn completed, the captain welcomed us graciously to his citadel and then introduced us saying, "We will now turn the evening service over to Rev. Henry *Heidelburg* and the quartet." The members of the quartet chuckled, and I stepped to the pulpit and thanked Captain *McCrocodile*—The boys exploded, and so did the captain and the audience. It took a little time for all of us to become serious enough to carry on with the meeting.

* * *

Dr. Pietsch of the radio program, "Songs in the Night," was our conference speaker one year. He was hosted in our home. In the relaxing home atmosphere between services we shared our early experiences as pioneer missionaries in the rural areas of our great countries. He recounted a story when he was invited by a bachelor to a meal. He described the shack and its condition. Fortunately, the untidy bachelor asked his guest what he would like to eat. Dr. Pietsch said that he liked boiled eggs. He commented, "In that setting, I figured that boiled eggs were the only sanitary food to be had."

To give Inger an opportunity to attend the Sunday services, I mentioned to our guest that we would have our noon meal at the school. After the morning service, however, I saw the long lines waiting for dinner, and, since I had preparations to make for the afternoon graduation service, I decided to go home to get a quick bite. No sooner had I started out than I heard a man puffing behind me, trying to catch up. I looked around. It was Dr. Pietsch. "Hildebrand where are you going?" he asked.

"The waiting line is too long," I replied, "so I decided to go home and have something to eat."

"May I go with you?" he wondered. "Sure," I said, "if you will be satisfied with what I can scrounge."

As we entered the kitchen, I began to look for goodies readily available. I asked if there was anything he liked we could fix in a hurry. "How about boiled eggs?" he asked. No sooner had he said it than he remembered our chit chat about our pioneer days! We looked at each other—then laughed.

* * *

Albert Staveness, a very sincere young man, enrolled in the fall of '39. He was placed with Henry Schumacher and Melville Kemp in the boys' dorm known as Walker House. Mr. Swenson was supervising that dorm. One evening, Albert came to me greatly disturbed. It was a beautiful evening so I suggested we take a walk and discuss his concern. He felt the place was not as spiritual as he had expected it to be. He was very disappointed and wished he had chosen another school. The atmosphere in the dorm wasn't good, he said.

I listened. All his complaints were generalizations. So I asked for specifics. Instead of praying during free time, the boys were rowdy. Some even fought with one another!

"You mean they came to blows?" I asked.

"No, surely not in a Bible School, no," he continued, "but pillow fights, etc. What's needed is to have the dorm set in order."

I asked for his assistance to "set the house in order." He readily agreed and assured me he would do all he could to help.

In the meanwhile, Mr. Swenson was concerned about the boys in Gilroy House, the dorm that Mr. Reginald Glen was supervising. He felt the boys in that dorm were getting away with murder, and that made it so much more difficult to supervise his dorm.

The following week I decided to visit the dorms during study hours. I entered the Gilroy House. You could hear boys talking in an undertone. Considering there were four boys in the one room, and several more in the other separated only by a curtain, I felt that was acceptable. I went upstairs. All was quiet. I saw Mr. Glen in his room and he assured me that it was a typical evening.

Then I proceeded to the Walker House. Before I opened the door I could hear it was rather lively. As I entered I saw a number of boys looking in on the larger room to the right to see what was going on. I wanted to see too. Nobody noticed me at first. I was just another boy trying my best, standing tip-toed, to see a pillow fight and a wrestling match. The actors were Albert Staveness and Henry Schumacher, going at it. Melville Kemp, their room-mate, spotted me. He rocked with laughter, and tried to inform the fellows of my presence. I went upstairs, wondering if Mr. Swenson were out of the dorm. I knocked at his door. Sure enough, he was in, buried in theology notes and books. He thought it was rather noisy downstairs, but he had to complete his lesson before he could investigate.

After a short visit, I went downstairs. The house had become quiet as a mouse. I knocked at the door of the room where all the excitement had taken place. Respectfully the boys welcomed me. Each now was at his table with Bible and notebooks open. I stood silent for a moment. Finally Henry Schumacher explained that it was all in innocent fun. Albert kept his nose in the books. So I addressed him. He looked up and blushed. I asked, "Isn't this a bit of a rough way to help us set this house in order?" It must have worked because I had no more complaints about dormitory discipline and spirituality that winter.

* * *

For a time Inger and I lived in a two-room suite in the old Yale Hotel in Briercrest. Next to our kitchen roomed two energetic, eager young fellows. Melvin Ralston was in his senior year. John Rodine was a freshman. Melvin was a firm believer in eternal security, while John, with his Arminian background, felt it was heresy. Both young men had strong convictions. You can imagine the heated discussions time and time again!

On one occasion I came home to a frightened spouse. Inger said, "I'm so glad you came home. You should go in and calm down those boys. Today it got so serious I'm afraid they will come to blows."

"I don't think I should," I replied, "the atmosphere in that room won't tolerate a third person." We listened for awhile. It had quieted down considerably, Inger thought. Had they heard my footsteps? Hardly, because they couldn't hear each other, though they shouted at the top of their voices.

I wasn't too disturbed. Frankly, I had more hopes for students who argued about their convictions than those to whom doctrinal issues didn't matter. Well, what became of those debaters? Both served well in Baptist pastorates for life. Melvin became moderator of the Baptist Union, and I understand John likewise became moderator of the General Baptist Conference for Western Canada.

* * *

When studies got a little heavy for me, I usually visited the boys dorm to add spice to my evening. I was seldom disappointed. One evening the excitement centered in the southwest barracks of the east wing of Dorm E. The doors were closed, and, I soon discovered, guarded as well. So I knocked—no answer. I knocked again, and a voice above the din shouted, "Stay out of here." I knocked again. This time I was seriously threatened. "If you show your face in here you'll get a bloody nose." I continued knocking, the door opened and a shocked Ronnie Wilson fell to his knees to apologize. Almost quicker than eye could scan, each student was at his desk, counting, it seemed, his beads of the rosary!

* * *

The hall lights were dim and the rooms reasonably quiet. As I was nearing the centre partition, a fellow swooped around, managed to avoid me, and disappeared. I quickly reasoned—if there is one fleeing, there is one pursuing. So I stood with my back against the wall to avoid being run down. Sure enough, the pursuer dashed around as quickly. Spotting me pressed against the wall, he assumed I was his victim. He grabbed me and shook me and wrestled me down, saying, "I dare you to tease me about Elsie again!"

"Elsie who?" I asked. We had three Elsies in school that year. As soon as he heard my voice, he hesitated, looked again and recognized me. He too sank to his knees, pleading forgiveness. I said, "John, stand up. I also am a man. You are forgiven."

* * *

On another occasion I entered the dorm. As I quiety moved along I heard three taps from room to room at a speed slightly ahead of my pace. Apparently that was the signal that the President was inside. The boys worked it smoothly and speedily, but the gathering in the washroom heard no tapping. They were entertained by Erwin Lutzer, grade 12 student, now senior pastor of Moody Memorial Church in Chicago. He was impersonating me. "Now students, we don't encou*rrr*age such a thing here—we don't need to . . ." Erwin had as hilarious a time as the dozens of fellows enjoying it. I showed up at the climactic moment. The fellows roared.

Erwin with his back toward me thought the boys were responding to his act, so he went at it with greater intensity. Then he turned sideways and saw me standing there enjoying it with the boys. So he stopped, flustered, looked out the window and stuttered, "I guess it's snowing out there." We all roared, because the moon was shining brightly.

* * *

Mr. Walter Fender, the dean of students, visited a room during study hours when students were not to visit another's room. He often called on his boys just to encourage them. So he knocked at one door. No answer, only a rustle inside. He knocked again. After a good while, one opened the door. With Bibles open, the boys explained they were having their evening devotion. Would he mind leading in prayer? In his prayer Mr. Fender prayed for the two boys and concluded, "And meet the need of the boy under the bed. He needs your help too." Upon this Mr. Fender left the room. The two boys sat staring at each other. How did the dean know there was a boy hiding under the bed?

This incident travelled through the dorm at breakneck speed. By evening prayer every boy in that dorm wondered about their dean's mystic knowledge. When I heard about it the following day, I asked Mr. Fender to explain. "As I entered the room, I saw under the bed a pair of shoes standing on their toes with their soles facing me. Since shoes don't stand on their toes by themselves, I figured there had to be feet in them." Sound reasoning, wouldn't you say?

* * *

The first year at Caronport the faculty took turns supervising the dorms during study periods to give the dean a break. It was Mr. Muirhead's turn. The High school boys had something exciting going on in one of their barracks that seemed not too conducive to study. Mr. Muirhead showed up to restore order. His voice could scarcely be heard above the din. One of the grade 12 boys, stronger than his fellows, said, "Mr. Muirhead, it's not safe for you in this barrack. I better take you out to safety." So he picked up Mr. Muirhead in his arms and carried him to the supervisor's room, advising him to keep the door closed and he would be safe for the evening.

* * *

During the early years we had cattle grazing on the campus. Mr. Whittaker felt it served a double purpose. They kept the lawn mowed as well. But one day the boys got an idea. They pushed a heifer into the girl's dorm. Imagine the combination of the girls' screams and an excited heifer in the same dorm! I understand it was Wes Edwards' idea. When our current president writes his memoirs, he may wish to tell us who all the boys were. In fact he can tell you much more about dormitory life—seeing he lived there for four years. He could also tell you about a collapsed chair, and how it flew through the window, and who carried Mr. Muirhead to his room.

* * *

Much more than these related incidents was involved in dormitory life. The total experience shaped the student's life, building relationships, developing study habits and a prayer life. Most students would not have chosen to go through Briercrest without the dormitory-campus life of the whole school family. We are all grateful to God for providing this training, a plus to student development.

The classroom ministry is well understood. That's why we have school. But classes too provided spice to break the monotony of routine.

I had related the story of a man who had been married for 40 years and had yet to remember his first misunderstanding with his wife. We had a few married couples in class. I turned to one and asked, "John what do you say to that?" John blushed and Millie beside him was fidgeting, hoping John wouldn't say too much. Finally John blurted out, "Mr. Hildebrand, I would like to know what you yourself say to it?"

"My married life has not been that dull," I answered.

Relieved, John responded, "That's what I say!" thumping his desk, "that's what I say." Millie felt relieved and the class enjoyed it. When I asked Mrs. Whittaker that question she replied with a twinkle in her eye, "Aye, Aye—I wonder what went wrong with that man's memory?"

* * *

We were in need of a registered nurse for the term about to begin in a few weeks. Unknown to me, Henry Hildebrandt, a student who was my name's sake, was just beginning to court Carol Glen, a nurse. Carol was working in the Moose Jaw Union Hospital. I phoned her at the hospital, a no-no during working hours, but I did not have her residence phone number, and I was in a hurry. They called Carol to the phone.

"This is Henry Hildebrand calling," I said.

"Oh hello Hank," she replied.

I hedged a bit and she caught on who was speaking hoping I had not heard her familiarity. David, my son, was attending school and assured me that things were developing nicely between Henry and Carol, so I felt it was safe to relate the incident in a class that both attended. Somehow it fitted a point, and the class enjoyed it. Henry blushed, but Carol said to herself, I'm sure, "Wait till I get even with you some day!" Both are my good friends to this day.

* * *

I like an informal, open atmosphere in the classroom so that students feel free to interact with their professor. But I don't allow conversation or whatever to be carried on independently of the classroom discussion. My lecture must have grown a bit dull. I noticed some special interest exciting the boys which seemed to have nothing to do with the subject under discussion. So I asked for the piece of paper that was being handed about. There was one of my talented students displaying his skill in art, plus his feeling toward whomever. I'll let you judge whom! The sketch showed a tall, handsome student with his hands on the throat of a short fellow behind a lectern.

* * *

Again, another lecture apparently grew dull. One fellow fell sound asleep. A guy poked Sam Beatty in the ribs saying, "Hildebrand is asking you to close in prayer." He got up and prayed. I discerned what had happened. The boys could not restrain their laughter, nor could I.

And so the incidents could be multiplied, but these will serve to show how "variety is the spice of life."

* * *

One Sunday after the communion service John Baptist knocked at our door. He was agitated. He had been unable to participate in the Lord's Supper, yet he observed that Earl Nefzger, with whom he was feuding, had participated. I was to stop such unrighteousness on our campus at once.

I was aware that Big John had threatened to finish off little Earl and wipe up the pavement with him in front of their suites. "But I understood you fellows got reconciled, is that correct?"

"Yes and no," replied John. "I called him into my suite. When he arrived I asked Millie to leave. Thereupon I asked him for forgiveness. But he stood by the door with his hand on the doorknob, in fact he had the door a bit open and sort of looked out of the corner of his eye, only saying 'yes' or just merely a grunt. Why would he do that? I really don't call that reconciliation. Why would he stand there like that? I had hoped after forgiving each other we'd have prayer together but . . ."

John was sincere, and I knew he meant well. I loved him. But I was a bit amused. I asked, "You wonder why he kept his hand on the door knob with the door a bit ajar? Has it not occurred to you that he tried to play it safe? If the forgiving did not proceed correctly, he wanted to make sure of his escape.

"Is that why!" mused John. "Maybe I should try to understand him in view of my threats."

On another occasion John mentioned that we shouldn't mind if students saw us frequently, "After all we are your bread and butter." So true, and much more than that—our love, our very life!

* * *

One evening after supper I had some things to do in the office. While there I noticed a colleague fussing about, and I wondered why. Soon I learned as I saw Elwood Sanderson taking my secretary out for a date. My colleague protested. "There ought to be a rule against such things."

About a week later, we saw my colleague taking a walk with my secretary, Clara Kvalness on a street in Moose Jaw that led to Crescent Park. I could not resist the temptation, so I opened the door of our car and called out, "Mr. Swenson, there ought to be a rule against such things!"

* * *

Remember the cows serving as lawnmowers on our campus? Mrs. Swenson came to the office counter and complained grievously to Mr. Brygmann that the cows had gotten into their garden. She pled that it was time that something was done about it. I could hear from my office, how *calmly* Mr. Brygmann explained that these things happened sometimes and that we should not get too excited about it. In time it would all work out.

Mrs. Swenson persisted, "What's more, Brygmann, they are in *your* corn now."

"What!" shouted Brygmann. "Those cows ought to be shot!" Quick as a flash Brygmann grabbed his hat and dashed out after the cows. Even Mrs. Swenson wondered what struck our calm and emotionally-controlled brother. The office staff enjoyed that immensely.

* * *

Ever heard of guys' hair standing up, literally? Those were the days when men groomed and greased their hair into submission. Our executive committee of the administration had serious financial decisions to make. Our treasurer, Mr. Brygmann, was occupying the chair. I sat at his side with a window opposite, on the other side of Brygmann. In the midst of the debate on money issues, Art Sundbo made a startling proposition and waited for our treasurer's reaction. He got it! Brygmann lifted his papers over his head, came down on the desk with a bang, and issued an emphatic, "Brother, No!" With that his hair popped straight up.

* * *

The choir was singing a lively hymn as I meditated on my message to follow on the broadcast. Across the room Mr. Whittaker crossed his legs and sort of beat time to the rhythm of the hymn. I noticed that his socks did not match! We were both due on the platform later in the morning, so after the broadcast I mentioned the mismatched socks to him. He lifted both trousers a bit, looked at his socks, and looked up and said, "It may be funny, but I have another pair just like these at home!"

* * *

Invariably Mr. Whittaker would answer the phone in the following manner, "This is Whittaker speaking." One evening the family sat down for their meal. They waited for Mr. Whittaker to say grace. As they bowed their heads, instead of hearing the grace, they heard the opening words, "This is Whittaker speaking." Absentmindedly he had spoken, introducing himself on Heaven's telephone.

* * *

Perhaps the strangest story unfolded in the late fall of 1951 at Davidson in Saskatchewan. A trio, accompanied by Claire Greiner with his accordion, and I were ministering at the church pastored by Rev. Dennis Brucks. Cecil Cowards invited us to their home in the country for the evening meal. Lillian Coward described an elderly couple—The Ole Ophaugs—living a few miles from them in abject poverty—the like of which she had never seen. The couple had no children and no relatives in Canada. We had an hour or more before supper, so Cecil proposed that we visit them with the team.

We found a barn that looked more like a tumbled down shack. The old house had not been painted for decades. A crowbar leaned against the outside door to keep it closed, giving the appearance that the people were not home. We knocked at the door, only to be answered by the barking of a dog inside.

As we turned to leave, I noticed smoke coming out of the chimney. I insisted that we go in and learn for certain whether the elderly couple were home.

"I'm afraid of the dog," said one of the trio.

"So am I," I replied, "but we'll take a chance." Entering into the porch, we could barely see to find the inside door. The dog was really furious, but he must have been tied. As we knocked at the inner door, we could hear a faint voice saying, "Who are you?" We entered and saw an elderly couple in their eighties wearing wadded clothes sitting up in bed with a horse blanket for cover. They looked frightened.

Mr. Coward reassured them and introduced us. Yes, they listened regularly to our broadcast. We sang familiar old hymns. They relaxed. I read Psalm 23 and explained the way of salvation. Fred Thiessen, a fine servant of God, had visited them a year earlier and they responded to believe in Jesus. After prayer they thanked us for the visit. We bade them goodbye and returned to the Cowards for the evening meal.

Lillian Coward asked if we had ever seen such poverty. "Not since we came to Canada," I answered. I asked how long they had farmed there. Cecil thought perhaps close to 40 years. But all the time they were so poor, they could not afford a car, not even machinery for their farming. They always had it custom farmed.

"It is obvious," I reasoned, "that these folks have not spent any money on luxury, not even what we would consider the necessities of life. They had no family expenses. My guess is that they are among the richest people of the community."

I can still hear Cecil laugh, "We always knew that if there is a dollar around Hildebrand would smell it, but this time I think he is only smelling old mouldy newspapers."

I pled for him to take me seriously. Although the Ophaugs were saved in their eighties, with all their years of savings, they could recover those years and invest their life's earnings in Christian work, and so receive a reward in heaven. "And since you, Cecil, have their confidence, you should counsel them accordingly."

Two weeks later, at the request of Mr. Ophaug, I preached his wife's funeral. He was not well either, and had been taken to the Davidson Hospital, so he had not attended the service. I visited after the funeral to share with him the message I had given. He reached into his drawer, picked up an old sock, and drew out a number of crisp 20 dollar bills for our work. I spoke to Mr. Coward again to counsel the elderly gentleman, who it seemed had not much longer to live.

Hardly a month later I was called upon to take Mr. Ophaug's funeral. But now the lawyer and the dignitaries of the community and a government representative were present. I knew why.

The story unfolded. While still in the hospital, Mr. Ophaug worried that someone might enter his house and rob him of his money. He confided in the Cowards his concern and asked them to search for his money in cans, amid newspapers, and in hidden corners. Thousands of dollars were found. One suggested that the total worth of the estate, with land and cash, came to around $200,000. And very little invested in eternity.

* * *

I have shared these experiences with you. Those who know the people involved will value them the most. But remember Bernard Shaw's axiom, "When a thing is funny, search it for a hidden truth."

35

Retrospect—Prospect

Look among the nations and watch—Be utterly astounded! For I will work a work in your days which you would not believe, though it were told you. Habakkuk 1:5 N.K.J.V.

Inscribed on the portico of the National Archives building in Washington, D.C. is the statement: "What is Past is Prologue." When Carl Sandberg, the poet, was asked about its meaning, he replied in rather unpoetic language, "It means, You ain't seen nothing yet."

To pause and rehearse what God hath wrought has both Old and New Testament precedent and can be very profitable. To help us remember, God has put sign posts into our calendar year; birthdays, anniversaries, and special occasions. "This do in remembrance of me." "Forgetful Green" was one of the most dangerous spots for Christian in his pilgrimage from the city of Destruction to the Celestial City.

A good memory lays hold of its history to learn lessons for the present and future. It has been said that a society that does not understand history has no destiny. History and destiny keep the "now" in proper perspective.

Churchill said, "If the present quarrels with the past, there is no future." But "an assessment of the present and past is only useful as it provides perspective on the future."[1]

If we are wise, we will stop long enough to remember and learn from the past, but not too long, lest we become petrified in our progress, like Lot's wife. We have looked back with gratitude to see the faithfulness of God. We seek to assess our goals. Did God indeed enable us to commit to faithful men the Word of God who in turn are teaching others also? We believe He did.* Due to our human limitations, we may have disappointed the expectations of some. But we also trust that, since God obviously used men and women with all their weaknesses, many more will take heart, believing that God will use them too in ways beyond their expectations.

In these memoirs I have tried to share with you how God began this work. I introduced you to people that He used—not perfect people, not great, but ordinary human clay, moulded by His hand. These were enabled by God's grace to do the job. I hope the story has brought encouragement to you.

If you looked for the ideal, I know I have disappointed you. If you wait until the ideal is reached before you venture into God's work, you will wait too long. God uses cleansed vessels who are committed, but vessels that need continual cleansing. Take heart believer, trust God. He will be gracious to you.

Now we look to the future. In view of God's faithfulness in the past, and in view of the ultimate hope of the people of God, we build with confidence, for the future belongs to the people of God. It would be very easy for me to sit down and plan the future of this work; easier, I say, than it was to write these memoirs! But I shall not step into that trap. That job belongs to the President, not the Chancellor. That's why God provided younger men and women whom He has selected to serve their generation. Younger men, although committed to the same Lord, the same Word and the same goals, bring a fresh outlook, vigour and vitality necessary for today.

I commend them to you, to your prayer and to your support. President Budd and his associates have established themselves well and earned your confidence. The record of the past eight years speaks for itself. Without a ripple, the college has moved forward in every area of its growth.

The future is one of hope for the college as for the people of God. It grieves me when I hear some servants of God whine a dirge of pessimism. I ask, "Where is their God?" We have confidence in the future because the God who was equal to our past needs is equal to our needs today. He will be more than equal to the needs of His

*A survey taken in 1985 reveals the following:
47% of BBC graduates have been and/or are in full-time Christian service.
94% are in regular church attendance
82% are involved in church work.

people and work in the future. We face the future with confidence because we believe God.

"The path of the just is the shining light, that shineth more and more unto the perfect day" (Proverbs 4:18). That is as true for the work of God as it is for the man of God. Inger and I are in our Golden Years—precious years of experiencing God's continuing goodness. Still, we must live with reality. We do not have many years left. But with sunrise in our hearts, we enter the sunset of our life upon earth. Once more we pause to praise God and express gratitude to all who have stood so faithfully at our side. We rest in confidence that God will enable our college to serve the future.

The work of God must go forward. We are aware of dangers ahead, battles to be fought, and the job to be done, but we believe God remains in control. The prophet Habakkuk saw a great work by God among the nations. True, the immediate setting predicted the Chaldean invasion of Judah, a type of the great tribulation. The tendency of some is to sit back and let the world move on to judgment, "why paint a sinking ship?"

Let us not forget that when Paul launched his great missionary career with the message at Pisidian Antioch, he quoted Habakkuk, applying the prophets words to the great work of evangelizing the nations (Acts 13:41). God has a prophetic word for us today.

> For God so loved the world, that He gave His only begotten Son, that whosoever believeth in Him should not perish, but have everlasting life.
>
> For God sent not his Son into the World to condemn the world; but that the world through Him might be saved.
>
> He that believeth on Him is not condemned: but He that believeth not is condemned already, because he hath not believed in the name of the only begotten Son of God (John 3:16-18).

We are in the age of grace. God's will is that none should perish. So, in the will of God, let the Church of God move forward to accomplish its task of world evangelism. Let our Bible college be one avenue in this great mission, fulfilling its mandate of training men and women for the great task of world evangelism.

I believe BBC is ready to contribute its share in this great mission. I have set before you my hopes and aspirations for the future in a general way. Some will say, "That's all fine, but you will be gone before too long." I know that. What about the present leadership, how does it view the future and Briercrest's place in it? The past eight years of President Budd's leadership attest to the increasing ministry of BBC. I know you will want to read his vision for the future and how the college will seek to serve God in it. He has consented to set forth his views in the closing chapter of these memoirs.

And now, dear readers, "I commend you to God, and to the word of His grace, which is able to build you up, and to give you an inheritance among them which are sanctified" (Acts 20:32).

AFTERWORD

by Henry H. Budd

REACHING FORWARD

I do not count myself to have apprehended; but one thing I do, forgetting those things which are behind and reaching forward to those things which are ahead, I press toward the goal for the prize of the upward call of God in Christ Jesus. (Philippians 2:13, 14—NKJ)

To those of us who have the privilege of knowing Dr. and Mrs. Henry Hildebrand well, reading his reflections upon their lives and service evokes two principle thoughts. The first is a sense of the great faithfulness of God. The Hildebrands would be the first to insist that "the miracle on the prairies" which is the Briercrest Bible College transcends any human vision or achievement. Like every great endeavor, it exacted its price in human commitment, determination, toil, sacrifice and tears, but it is not merely the product of them. It is above all a product of the sovereign will of God and of His enablement, provision, and grace. "Great is Thy faithfulness."

The second thought is of the tremendous impact of lives well lived for God. Confronted by the challenge; "The world has yet to see what God can do with a man who is totally yielded to him," D. L. Moody is reported to have responded; "By the grace of God, I will be that man!" I doubt that Moody ever claimed or thought that he had attained that level of 100 percent commitment. Neither would Henry Hildebrand claim that his life and ministry were unmixed in motivation and unwavering in dedication. Nevertheless, the Hildebrands displayed a commitment to Christ and Christian ministry, a sacrificial spirit, and a consistency of purpose which God chose to use in a remarkable way in the field of Christian education. They have left an indelible imprint on the lives of thousands of students, friends and colleagues associated with them in the Briercrest Bible College.

Fifty years in Christian ministry is admirable; fifty years in one ministry is remarkable. To live and work acceptably with people for that long is in itself commendable. To be instrumental in the founding of a Bible school, and to see it grow in those fifty years to enroll almost 800 students with another 300 in its affiliated high school is, from a human perspective, a tremendous achievement. Still, our interest is not primarily with the past but with the future. As I know them, Mr. and Mrs. Hildebrand are remarkably young in body, mind, and spirit. They have no inclination to live in the past. No more does Briercrest Bible College.

I believe there is at Briercrest a remarkable sensitivity to and appreciation of the college's heritage, as is evident in the celebration of the fiftieth anniversary. Nevertheless, the mood on campus is not to dwell in the past or to feel a false complacency, but to press on into a productive future in the will of God. Briercrest Bible College was not built to be a monument but a living testimony.

One of the key tests of a leader's qualities and effectiveness is what happens to the work after he leaves or retires. It is no commendation to a leader if the ministry falls apart after his departure; rather it raises the suspicion that he has built on the shifting sand of his own personality and prestige. Henry Hildebrand passed to other hands the administration of a vigorous organization with a fine depth of leadership and a committed faculty and staff. The grace and thoroughness with which he relinquished control, and the wholeheartedness with which he has served the Lord and Briercrest Bible College since, have made him nothing but a blessing to me and have provided Christian organizations with an example of how leadership can be transferred.

What of the future? Where, by the grace of God, is Briercrest going? First, let me be very clear that it is our intent to continue *to serve this and future generations within the Bible school model.* Some have suggested that a Bible college is just a Bible institute on its way to becoming a Christian liberal arts college. At Briercrest, at least, this is certainly not the case. I was recently queried rather closely by an alumnus of the college who wanted to know if that was the direction in which we were headed. I assured him that, while we respect other forms of Christian higher education, Briercrest has been from its foundation a part of the Bible school movement, a heritage we have no intention of abandoning. Out of this movement have come fully 75 percent of all evangelical missionaries serving today as well as thousands of pastors and other Christian workers, and there is no real indication that ministry for Bible college graduates is drying up. Even our new and successful graduate program has been structured so that it will not in any way impede our program of undergraduate Bible college education.

A Bible college has as its central purpose the training of men and women for Christian church-related ministries. This embraces the preparation of pastors, church staff members, missionaries, evangelists and workers in Christian organizations, but also includes training and motivating lay people for service in their local churches and communities. To accomplish this mission, a Bible college like Briercrest offers a variety of programs, all built around a core of theology and Bible, offering appropriate courses to build knowledge and skill for ministry, and a smaller or larger component of general studies sufficient to support the particular program and its educational and ministry objectives.

Several features have been characteristic of Bible school education, and these we want to maintain and strengthen at Briercrest. The first is *an emphasis on the cultivation of Christian life and commitment.* We are determined, to the best of our ability under God, to "present every man mature in Christ Jesus" (Colossians 1:28). Bible school training looks for personal application and life change. There should be no place to hide on our campus from the searching questions of the Christian life. Men and women will be constantly exhorted and instructed to yieldedness, fervency, the fulness of the Spirit, godly living, and commitment to the service of Christ.

Secondly, as a Bible school *we are committed to the centrality of the Scriptures in all our programs.* It is not only the chief textbook, but it is relevant to guide us in all the College's activities. Furthermore, it is characteristic of the Bible school *to teach the Bible directly and with personal application.* It is possible in educational institutions to study a great deal *about* the Bible while learning very little Bible. It is also possible to get bogged down in technical and controversial matters to the neglect of Bible content and doctrine. It is imperative in this day and age that students know something of these technical and historical matters, but we are determined to teach the Scriptures so that students know their contents and are able to make application to their own lives and to the lives of others.

Thirdly, we want *to intensify our commitment to world missions and evangelism.* For several years, over 40 Briercrest graduates per year have been entering missionary service. While we are gratified, we are not satisfied. With billions of people in our world yet unevangelized, why should we be satisfied? Missions and Bible schools have gone hand-in-hand throughout the past century and we will strive to maintain that alliance. To that end, it has been characteristic of Bible schools to provide *training in service.* At Briercrest, over 90 percent of the students are engaged each semester in Christian service or "field education" assignments which integrate with their program of study. We are constantly seeking new ways to make the students' experience in ministry more vital and more preparatory for future service for Christ.

Within this framework of Bible college education, it is the purpose at Briercrest *to be flexible and creative and to provide training relevant to the students' needs.* If a school is training people for ministries, then its programs must be changing, because ministries change. During the past ten years we have been constantly upgrading, changing, and varying programs to make them more suited to the students and their vocational aspirations. In the future we expect this to continue. Being discussed are such things as ministry to the elderly, a program of native studies, training for church support staff (secretaries, etc.), financial ministries, and the preparation of teachers for Christian schools. We are also concerned to provide better life-training for those who are university bound.

Briercrest will also be seeking to enhance its ministry to local churches and the Christian community as a whole. Any significant Christian institution of higher education has a ministry to the church, not only through training students, but directly through the service of administrators, faculty and students. We hope that we can continue to minister with blessing through seminars, conferences, preaching engagements and publications. It will be our goal to increase the quality of ministry so as to warm the hearts, stimulate the minds, and challenge the commitment of the people of God.

We would also like to speak with a firmer voice in matters of moral conscience. While not desiring to politicize our ministry, nor to drain away our energies from the work of education by engaging in endless controversy, we feel that we must speak out on important issues. With our nation reeling under the moral and social impact of such things as abortion, pornography, sexual promiscuity and prostitution, family breakdown, and divorce, it is sinful to be silent, and we will lend our support to those who oppose the true evils in our society.

In all our plans, there is *a commitment to quality.* After a recent meeting in Manitoba, someone commented to me on the ministry of the Briercrest team involved. "They never made a mistake," she marvelled: "They were so beautifully prepared! Of course, that's what we have come to expect from Briercrest." Working from the inside, I was, of course, only too well aware of the many mistakes we make and the frequent imperfections. Nevertheless, the lady did express the high expectations that many people have of Briercrest Bible College, and perhaps also the unfulfilled aspirations which we have for ourselves. We would like to do well whatever it is we do, to the very best of our ability. To do less than your best is not glorifying to God nor worthy of the Lord Jesus Christ. Educationally this applies equally to Caronport High School and Briercrest's Summer Graduate School. Whatever we do, we will strive to do well, seeking to offer to God, in the words of one of the great saints; "My human best filled with the Holy Spirit."

What about growth? We are frequently asked by friends, and the not-so-friendly; "How big are you going to get at Caronport?" Ultimately the answer to that is in divine hands. The future is with God. Certainly the growth of the college has been consistent and even spectacular in the past 12 years with enrollment doubling in that time. Growth in the coming decade will for practical reasons be at a slower pace, but we hope to grow and have predicted three percent annual enrollment increase for the next 10 years. If there are those who want a Briercrest education, we want to give them that opportunity. Every student is in training for the service of Jesus Christ in some form or other. If, through restrictive admissions policies or discouragement of applicants, we turn people from our doors, each person so denied is a man or woman of potential for Christ, somebody's son or daughter, perhaps the son or daughter of BBC alumni or longtime friends, for whom they have high aspirations. We don't want to do that, so we will recruit vigorously and look to God to provide the accommodation for those who wish to study at Briercrest, just as we have done throughout our history.

The secret to attracting students is to provide a spiritual and intellectual climate on campus that will assure them of a vibrant educational experience. In the words of Dr. Robert Baptista, former president of Taylor University, "When a Christian student understands the special mission of the college, when he experiences a first-rate educational program, when he has sound opportunities for spiritual growth and development, and when he is in contact with people on campus who consistently demonstrate Christian love and concern, it is then that a student can expect a satisfying experience." We might add that, when his experience is truly satisfying, he will surely tell his friends and family. As we press forward on these principles and with these aspirations, Briercrest Bible College will be building upon the heritage established and cultivated by Henry Hildebrand and his associates fifty years ago.

Notes

CHAPTER 11

1. John Bunyan, *Pilgrim's Progress,* p. 91.
2. Bernard and Marjorie Palmer, *Miracle on the Prairies,* (Caronport, Sask.: Briercrest Bible Institute, n.d.). pp. 97-98.

CHAPTER 14

1. Paul Cedar, *Leadership,* (Summer, 1984): 21.

CHAPTER 15

1. H. Alvin Memory, *Lecture to A.A.B.C.*
2. Ibid.
3. Ibid.
4. Ibid.
5. Chancellor H. Hildebrand, "Tribute to Mr. and Mrs. H. Alvin Memory" in *The Echo* (Fall, 1981): 4-5.

CHAPTER 16

1. O. Brygmann, *Article,* (November, 1984): 4.
2. Ted Bergren, *Article,* (November, 1984): 7-9.

CHAPTER 17

1. Edith Schaeffer, *Tapestry,* p. 58.

CHAPTER 18

1. *The Echo,* (Spring, 1981): 2-3.
2. Bernard and Marjorie Palmer, *Beacon on the Prairies,* (Minneapolis, MN: Bethany Fellowship, Inc., 1970), pp. 198-203.

CHAPTER 20

1. Abraham Penner, Dr. Penner's father's letter, Dec. 7, 1945.
2. Bernard and Marjorie Palmer, *Miracle on the Prairies,* (Caronport, Sask.: Briercrest Bible Institute, n.d.), pp. 142-143.
3. Homer Edwards, *Article,* December, 1984).

CHAPTER 22

1. *Daily Bread,* Friday, June 15, 1984.
2. Oswald Chambers, *My Utmost for His Highest.*

CHAPTER 24

1. J. Oswald Sanders, *Spiritual Leadership,* p. 109.

CHAPTER 25

1. Paul Cedar, *Leadership,* Vol. 3 (Summer, 1984), pp. 22-23.
2. J. Oswald Sanders, *Spiritual Leadership,* p. 9.
3. Ibid., p. 9.

CHAPTER 26

1. Richard E. Day, *Shadow of the Broad Brim,* p. 72.

CHAPTER 27

1. Richard E. Day, *Shadow of the Broad Brim,* p. 72.

CHAPTER 31

1. Ian Rennie, then pastor of Fairview Presbyterian Church, Vancouver, B.C.; now Dean of Ontario Theological Seminary in *Christianity Today*, (1976), p. 7.
2. David Rambo, President of Nyack College (A.A.B.C. Newsletter), p. 1.

CHAPTER 32

1. Dr. H. Hildebrand, "Transition . . . Transfer," *The Echo* (Fall, 1977): p. 13.
2. John Ward, "Fall Conference Report," *The Echo* (Fall, 1977): p. 15.
3. Dr. H. Hildebrand, "Transition . . . Transfer," *The Echo* (Fall, 1977): pp. 13-14.
4. President Henry Budd, "The View From the Plains of Moab." *The Echo*, (Fall, 1977): p. 14.
5. Ibid., pp. 5-7.
6. Ibid., p. 9.

CHAPTER 33

1. Sam C. Reeves, *The Bright Years*, p. 15.

CHAPTER 34

1. Jacob M. Braude, *Lifetime Speaker's Encyclopedia*, pp. 370, 885.

CHAPTER 35

1. Gross, During the inauguration service at Gordon College, 1976.